AMERICA IN THE
TWENTIETH CENTURY

AMERICA IN THE TWENTIETH CENTURY

A study of the United States since 1917

BY

D. K. ADAMS

Senior Lecturer in American Studies
University of Keele

CAMBRIDGE
AT THE UNIVERSITY PRESS
1967

Published by the Syndics of the Cambridge University Press
Bentley House, 200 Euston Road, London N.W. 1
American Branch: 32 East 57th Street, New York, N.Y. 10022

© Cambridge University Press 1967

Library of Congress Catalogue Card Number: 67-12844

Printed in Great Britain
at the University Printing House, Cambridge
(Brooke Crutchley, University Printer)

CONTENTS

Acknowledgements   *page* viii

I American Themes

Voyage west   1
The frontier   3
Expansion and imperial conflict   6
The revolutionary theme   9
Consolidation of the new nation   13
Nineteenth-century themes   15
Nationalism triumphant: the United States waves the
    'big stick'   28
Involvement in world war   30

2 Normalcy

The background to normalcy   33
The effects of war   34
The resurgence of partisan politics and disputes over the
    peace   37
Post-war tensions and the election of 1920   41
Politics in the era of Harding and Coolidge   46
Economic policy   50
American society in the 1920s   52

3 Internationalism *v.* Isolationism

European policy 1921–1929   61
The Washington treaties   65
Abandonment of 'the big stick' in Latin America   68
Manchuria   70
The chimera of disarmament and security   72
International economic problems   73
Roosevelt confronts the isolationists   77

4 Depression, New Deal and War Prosperity

Causes of the Great Crash   83
Hoover and the Great Depression   85
Election of Roosevelt and the character of the New Deal   90
The New Deal in action   93
Roosevelt breaks a political tradition   103
The economy at war   105
The Negro, civil liberties and the atom   109

5 Intervention, War and an Uneasy Peace 1939–1950
The road to war   *page* 113
War 1941–1945   121
Conference diplomacy   124
The United Nations, a revolution in American policy   126
1945–1947, the world divides   127
Containment and Cold War   129
Perils in the Far East, 1945–1950   132

6 The Burdens of World Leadership
Crisis in Korea   135
Republican foreign policy: the strategy of Eisenhower and
Dulles   140
Diplomatic failures in the Far East   144
European and Middle Eastern policy 1953–1959   148
Eisenhower diplomacy, 1959–1960   155

7 Domestic Affairs, 1945–1961
Truman accepts the challenge   160
1948, year of political confusion   164
The Fair Deal in operation   168
Loyalty, disloyalty, and Joseph McCarthy   170
The election of 1952   173
Eisenhower Republicanism   174
The affluent society and its tensions   180
The election of 1960   185

8 New Frontiers
Civil rights and the Negro   193
Kennedy and the New Frontier   196
Assassination   206
The New Frontier—second phase   208
Lyndon Johnson and the Great Society   209

Epilogue   215

Appendix 1 The Constitution of the United States of
America   220

Appendix 2 Statistical information   238

Table 1 Population of the continental United States
Table 2 Non-white population of the continental United
States
Table 3 Gross national product 1919–1964
Table 4 Unemployment in the United States 1918–1964

Contents

Maps Section

  1 The United States of America   *page* 241
  2 The territorial expansion of the United States, 1776–1867   242
  3 The United States in 1861.   243
  4 The confrontation of the North American continent and the U.S.S.R.   244
  5–10 State voting patterns in presidential elections:

      1920, 1924   245
      1928, 1932   246
      1936, 1940   247
      1944, 1948   248
      1952, 1956   249
      1960, 1964   250

Guide to Further Reading   251

Index   255

ACKNOWLEDGEMENTS

Thanks are due to the following for permission to quote extracts: Random House Inc. for the quotation from Archibald MacLeish's *Voyage West*; Houghton Mifflin Co. for the quotation from Archibald Mac-Leish's *American Letter*; Thames and Hudson Ltd. for the quotation from Bryan Robertson's *Jackson Pollock* and New Directions Publishing Corporation for the quotation from Lawrence Ferlinghetti's *A Coney Island of the Mind*.

1

AMERICAN THEMES

It is a strange thing—to be an American...
...Neither a place it is nor a blood name.
America is West and the wind blowing.
America is a great word and the snow.
A way, a white bird, the rain falling,
A shining thing in the mind and the gull's call.
America is neither a land nor a people,
A word's shape it is, a wind's sweep—
(ARCHIBALD MACLEISH, *American Letter*)

America is both the land and the people upon the land. The great land received the people and the people, separated from their history, created a new life and a new nation in the loneliness of the land. As they slowly conquered the environment their habits, thoughts and institutions were moulded into new forms which finally resulted in a distinctive American society.

The question 'what is an American?' was first posed by Hector St John Crèvecœur in 1785 and the task of trying to define this 'new man' was thenceforth to be a leading preoccupation of both American and European commentators. The answers given were many and varied but each stressed certain common themes in the development of the American identity, themes which were inherent in the European impact on North America from the earliest years of discovery and settlement. The qualities which came to be regarded as characteristically American were individualism, egalitarianism, self-confidence, ingenuity and a belief in divine providence. These were products of the dominant themes of the American experience.

VOYAGE WEST

Norsemen had sailed to the northern latitudes of America in the tenth century, but throughout the Middle Ages Europe's only legacy of these explorations were seaport rumours generally discounted by practical men. The rediscovery of America came about not by design, but by grandiose accident. Christopher Columbus stumbled across the islands of the Caribbean whilst trying to find a western route to the Indies in 1492, and on later voyages struck the mainland itself. In the same decade Englishmen from Bristol sailed across the North Atlantic to reach Newfoundland and Labrador:

> There was a time for discoveries—
> For the headlands looming above in the
> First light and the surf and the
> Crying of gulls: for the curve of the
> Coast north into secrecy.
>
> (ARCHIBALD MACLEISH, *Voyage West*)

Discovery was followed by settlement and the motives for settlement provide, together with the land itself, the first themes.

Men emigrated for a number of reasons. When Sir Walter Raleigh tried in 1585 to plant a colony on Roanoke Island in Pamlico Sound he was partly influenced by the Utopian ideals of Sir Thomas More, but in the seventeenth century Englishmen went to the New World in pursuit of more immediate self-interest. The first settlers carried with them either a well-developed expectation of profit or the hope of religious freedom. The early colonies were tangible expressions of these desires. However in their view of America they were perhaps not so very different from the Utopians. Even before the land received its people Europe possessed an image of the New World as the land of opportunity, an image which, despite many blemishes, is still retained.

The first permanent English colony was that founded at Jamestown in Virginia in 1607. It was a commercial venture: Michael Drayton commemorated the sailing of the *Sarah Constant* and her sister ships from London in December 1606 with an *Ode to the Virginia Voyage* which emphasised the promoters' hopes of finding 'pearle and gold'. In this they were disappointed, but riches of another kind were exploited when tobacco was introduced from the Indians; financial success led to the proliferation of settlements until by the end of the century the English were firmly entrenched along the coastal strip to the south and north of the original enterprise. Other and more famous emigrants were those upon a single ship, *Mayflower*, who on 9 November 1620 sighted the sandy beaches of Cape Cod, a low promontory jutting like a fish hook from the American coast far to the north of the Virginia colony. After narrowly escaping shipwreck on the shoals off Monomoy Point they established a temporary base at what is now Provincetown and then, as winter approached, moved across the bay to a more protected anchorage and landed at a spot they named Plymouth after their English port of departure. This was the group that came to be known as the Pilgrim Fathers. They were religious nonconformists who rejected the episcopal church established by the Elizabethan settlement and wanted to lead their chosen religious life free from restriction and interference by the state. They too were followed by many of their brethren.

These religious migrants to the northern provinces, or New England, were to make a particular contribution to the civilisation of the New World. William Bradford, governor of the Plymouth colony for most of the period from 1621 until his death in 1657, wrote a history of the plantation which concluded with the words: 'Thus out of small beginnings greater things have been produced by his hand that made all things of nothing, and gives being to all things that are; and as one small candle may light a thousand; so the light here kindled hath shone unto many, yea, in some sorte, to our whole nation.' Many of the later immigrants, like the Puritans who founded the Massachusetts Bay Colony, were themselves intolerant of diversity and sought to establish a theocratic commonwealth in the New World. As their influence spread, a strong New England tradition was established, based upon religious conviction, an emphasis upon the dignity of the individual within the body of the church, a belief in thrift, and an insistence upon conformity to the God-given order. This tradition was to dominate much of the intellectual life of the new nation.

THE FRONTIER

All of these transplanted peoples shared one experience in common: they occupied the first frontier of the new land. They were pioneers in the wilderness and in carving out their new life had to battle with the immense extent and physical extremes of the continent. Six hundred miles separated the Pilgrims from the Virginia settlements and each group was faced with geographical conditions very different from those to which they were accustomed. New England is a rocky mass cut by infrequent rivers running roughly north–south. The tidewater plain is narrow, like the river valleys themselves, and forests covered the upland and the mountains. Away from the coast snow falls heavily in winter, and the climate is harsh; even in Boston itself temperatures ranging from 104° to −18 °F have been recorded. In this barren land agriculture could be developed only on a small scale, with fields painfully cleared from the forest and the rock. The life of the inhabitants naturally gravitated towards the sea which, more than the land itself, provided their livelihood: the forest gave them timber for shipping; the indented coastline offered shelter and harbourage; the ocean provided fish. The hardy maritime race which Sarah Orne Jewett commemorated two centuries later in *The Country of the Pointed Firs* emerged early as a distinctive group.

The evolution of the southern colonies was also conditioned by environment. The hot humid climate and rich soils of the wide lowlands were ideally suited to the cultivation of cash crops such as tobacco, cotton, and in some places rice; and as these were most profitably grown on large production units extensive plantations became the characteristic feature of the economy of Virginia and the Carolinas. These plantations also had a social function and great houses like the Byrds' home at Westover in Virginia became centres of colonial life. Labour shortage and a growing belief that the white man was unsuited to field work on the plantations led to the introduction of Negro slaves in 1619, and increasing numbers of Negroes were imported from Africa to meet the demands of the expanding economy. The addition of this coloured population and its slave status laid the seeds of future racial tensions in the American south.

The frontier both developed individual qualities in the settlers and stimulated community feelings. When men lived by their own resourcefulness they valued their personal and corporate relationships; and family and community groups drew together in their mutual struggle against the wilderness. This frontier process was quickened by the lack of easy communication between communities; in the north there were few trails across the hills and traffic relied heavily upon coastal shipping; in the south the swampy forest-covered alluvial land between rivers also made travelling difficult and dictated reliance upon water-borne transport.

In New England the double thread of individualism and corporate fellowship was strengthened by the vitality of the Puritan creed which, although it stressed the individual communion of man with his creator, also emphasised the Church, the congregation of people under a minister which gathered together in the service of God. The Puritan system of church government helped to dictate settlement patterns. Entire congregations often migrated with their ministers and established themselves beyond the line of immediate settlement in the way that the Pilgrim Fathers had originally travelled from Europe to America. Sometimes congregations departed because of religious disagreements; sometimes they were merely seeking better conditions and new land away from the existing townships. Their religious beliefs and organisation also had political implications. Before landing at Plymouth the Mayflower congregation had signed a compact establishing a 'civil body politic' which embraced the egalitarian concepts of the separatist religion, and in the practice of the later colonies democracy of church membership produced a democracy of political government. This was by no means an absolute democracy; only church members enjoyed the full privileges of religious and civil society and these did not constitute the whole population. Through the town meeting each full citizen had the right to participate in government at the local level, as he also came to have the right to elect representatives to the colonial legislature.

In the southern colonies there was also a wide measure of democracy. In part this was a transplanting of English parliamentarianism, for the ties of the colonies with England were close and the growth of colonial institutions was considerably influenced by developments at home. However, in America the authority of the crown, to which Englishmen in the New World as in the Old were subject, was diminished by distance and they were allowed a greater latitude than they might otherwise have enjoyed in the establishment of representative government. Although the suffrage was not universal it came to include most property-owning adult white males. Individualism and local loyalties were strongly felt along the whole colonial frontier and from the beginning the settlers were impatient of outside authority. Although they grudgingly accepted the subordination of their elected assemblies to governors and councils appointed by the king, political and class barriers were less meaningful in primitive conditions which stimulated belief in the equality of men.

In addition to these characteristics the early colonies displayed another common tendency: the impulse towards expansion. They reached out to the westward, first to the foothills of the Appalachian chain, then to the mountains themselves, and eventually to the lands beyond. Common curiosity about the hinterland was stimulated by necessity. Land hunger grew as the lowland settlements became more densely populated through immigration and natural increase; and as repeated cropping depleted the soils of the original farms and plantations, the virgin land to the west became a constant magnet to the more adventurous or desperate of the colonial peoples.

EXPANSION AND IMPERIAL CONFLICT

This vigorous expansionist instinct resulted in an imperial conflict for control of North America because in his invasion of the New World the Englishman was not alone. Spaniards in the wake of Columbus not only occupied the islands of the Caribbean but made deep journeys into the hinterland. Their mercenary and missionary zeal in the pursuit of gold and converts took them far into North and South America and in the process they carved out an empire which ranged from the Andean mountains to the Florida peninsula and the desert uplands of Mexico. To the north of the English colonies were the French. In the 1530s they had penetrated the valley of the St Lawrence and a permanent settlement at Quebec was founded in 1608. From this base they moved down the St Lawrence and fanned westwards to the Great Lakes. A scattered web of fur trappers worked the Ontario peninsula, extended their operations across the prairie to the headwaters of the Mississippi, moved downstream to the delta which they reached in 1682, and in 1718 established the port of New Orleans. A fourth European power made a brief entrance on the American scene in the early seventeenth century. In 1609 Henry Hudson, an English navigator in the employment of the Dutch, discovered the river which bears his name and by 1626 the Dutch settlement of New Amsterdam had been consolidated by the purchase of Manhattan Island at the mouth of the river from the Indian tribes. As a trading post it was of considerable importance, but the Dutch interest in commerce was fostered at the expense of settlement backed up by productive agriculture and in the Anglo-Dutch wars of the 1660s New Amsterdam fell as a rich prize into the hands of a British fleet commanded by the Duke of York, after whom the new possession was renamed. The Swedes also made small settlements, but they never developed sufficient strength to challenge the major colonial powers and were rapidly absorbed.

Apart from the struggle with the environment the history of North America from the mid seventeenth century to the mid eighteenth century is the history of a clash of empires. The contending powers, after the expulsion of the Dutch, were the British, the French, the Spaniards and the native population. These were called 'Indians' because of Columbus's original mistaken belief that he had reached the Indies of the east. The immigrants were severally trying to expand their footholds and capture a continent; the Indians were fighting to preserve their homeland from expropriation by the aliens from beyond the sea. The British colonies were hemmed in on three sides by the possessions of the other colonial powers: the Spanish held Florida and checked their advance to the south; the arc of French territory in Canada and the Mississippi valley contained them to the north and west. If their expansionist desires were to be fulfilled they had to break through these barriers by directly challenging the power of France and Spain.

This imperial theme in American history was intimately related to the balance of power in Europe. Just as the European system was affected by the inter-play of overseas forces so was the struggle for empire influenced by events in Europe. However, as important as these external factors in determining the final result in North America were the 'national' characteristics displayed by the settlers themselves. Sociologists have recently abandoned the old concept of national character, and have substituted explanations based upon the varied social, religious, and economic experiences of individual societies. These are merely new phrasings of the old device, and in the colonial period of American history the different European colonists exhibited widely different motives and aspirations which in their turn produced significant variations in the colonial patterns.

The Spaniards in the south and the remote south-west were not primarily agriculturists, and in general did not see themselves individually as permanent settlers in the New World. Apart from the clergy, their role was one of quick exploitation and return to Spain. Like the Spanish empire French Canada was also sparsely populated. The ties of the land of France itself were too strong for Frenchmen to uproot themselves easily to settle in a new country. New France was rigidly controlled from Paris, and these controls, together with the colony's limited function as a producer of pelts and timber products did not encourage individual enterprise. The stronghold of the Catholic church prevented it from becoming a refuge for French protestants. Only the English displayed during the colonial period the qualities that were necessary to conquer the land. This was not the result of particular virtue but a consequence of their own historical experiences, and they were impelled by varying motives. Of these the Puritan desire to found their kingdom of God in the wilderness was perhaps dominant, but there were many other factors which drove Englishmen in steady numbers to the American colonies. Overpopulation in rural England following the enclosure movement and political unrest stemming from the conflict between Crown and Parliament were major stimulants to the flow of migrants. These migrants saw themselves as permanent residents in the New World.

In the seventeenth century the chief point of friction between the empires lay in northern New England, but in the eighteenth century the immediate challenge to British interests lay in French occupation of the Mississippi valley. As the British colonists moved steadily westwards across the mountains and into the valley the territorial insulation which had kept the empires apart rapidly dissolved and a clash became inevitable. War broke out between the two nations in North America in 1754 and this became the Seven Years' War of 1756–63 when to the tensions in the trans-Appalachian West were added rivalries in India and a diplomatic revolution in Europe which realigned the alliance system. It was, however, primarily a war for the domination of a continent, and neither side looked for compromise. In the end the different natures of the British and the French colonies and the superiority of British sea power gave victory to Britain. The treaty of Paris of 1763 marked the end of a long era in the history of North America: France transferred the whole of French Canada to the British Crown together with the vast expanse of territory between the Appalachian Mountains and the Mississippi river; New Orleans and the delta country were transferred to Spain, a change acceptable to Britain as Spain no longer ranked as a major European power and the existence of a weak neighbour to the south presented no substantial threat to British interests.

British power was supreme in 1763. But the peace did not inaugurate a long period of prosperous consolidation of the North American empire. The removal of the French threat in fact marked the beginning of a phase in which old grievances between mother country and colonies came to the surface and, being fused with new and specific complaints, culminated in the revolution of 1776.

THE REVOLUTIONARY THEME

Under the old colonial system the mercantilist policies of the Crown regarded the colonies as subordinate but complementary and integrated parts of a vast economic system. Under this system Britain manufactured, and the colonies supplied the raw materials for industry; the colonial market absorbed manufactured products, and was closed to competition from foreign rivals. Restrictions on trade were an essential part of mercantilism and although the fact that they belonged to an integrated Atlantic common market gave substantial advantages to the North American colonists these restrictions also slowed down the pace of colonial economic development, and from the colonial viewpoint the system came to be regarded as a tyrannous imposition. Latent in the empire therefore was a desire for greater economic independence. This was paralleled in the political sphere by an increasing restlessness. Royal appointment of colonial governors and formal control by Westminster was generally palatable during the lax years down to 1763, but positive interference by the Crown in Parliament after 1763 led to rapidly vociferous colonial protest.

Before the Treaty of Paris the imperatives of defence were perhaps the major inhibition on colonial dissent. Despite their great achievement in the capture of the fortress of Louisbourg on Cape Breton Island during the earlier troubles with the French in the 1740s the colonies depended on the British army and on British sea power for their survival. They were unable to defend themselves against the French without assistance, and the army of red-coats and the British fleet were the barriers behind which they could expand without too much danger of external attack. The Indian menace, which was a recurrent fear if not a continuous threat during the seventeenth and early eighteenth centuries, also underlined the necessity of the protective shield of British power and acted as a deterrent to any move towards independence from parliamentary control. However, as the Indian was thrust westwards before the advance of settlement, and as the colonial militia developed the particular skills needed for Indian warfare, the traditional tactics of the regular army became an increasing liability rather than a positive help and colonial feelings of self-confidence grew stronger. The removal of the French by the provisions of the treaty of 1763 allowed the colonists the luxury of believing that their survival no longer depended upon the military strength of the British. This mood moreover developed at a time when the British government began to tighten the mercantile system in an attempt to make it more efficient.

The first act of the new policy sought to resolve the problem of the western lands. By proclamation in 1763 the British government temporarily restricted expansion to the line of the Appalachians. Its motives were twofold: to provide for orderly development by avoiding the over extension of the seaboard colonies; and to give time for a peaceful solution of the Indian problem to be worked out. On both counts the government was sincere, but particularly in its desire to find an answer to the Indian question other than extermination of the tribes. On both counts the colonials rejected British policy. They asserted their inherent right to expand into the new lands beyond the mountains, and realising that humane solution of the Indian problem would conflict with their own territorial ambitions they were almost unanimous in their conviction that the only good Indian was a dead Indian. The outbreak of war in 1763 with an Indian confederation led by Pontiac, chief of the Ottawa, did nothing to change this view. The proclamation of 1763 seemed not only a challenge to their independence of action but also a threat to the survival of their frontier outposts.

The proclamation of 1763 was obnoxious enough, but it was quickly followed by even more inflammatory measures. Britain's national debt had risen from £70,000,000 to £130,000,000 during the Seven Years' War, and the annual cost of maintaining the civil and military establishment in America had risen by an even greater proportion, from £70,000 in 1748 to over £350,000 in 1764. In the post-war climate of opinion it seemed to the British government only fair that some of these expenses should be borne by those on whose behalf they had been incurred.

Taxation for the restraint and regulation of trade had been an accepted part of colonial status under the pre-war imperial system, but in its new mood the British government decided to impose taxes for the admitted purpose of raising revenue. The preamble to the Sugar Act of 1764, and the Stamp Act of 1765, made this quite clear and marked a significant innovation in colonial policy which the colonists almost unanimously resisted. Revenue duties were also imposed on other enumerated products which formed a significant percentage of colonial trade. At the same time additional Admiralty courts were set up to discourage smuggling and the use of writs of assistance, or general search warrants, was extended. The colonials realised that not only was the empire to be made efficient in the eyes of Parliament; it was also to help pay by direct taxes the cost of its own administration. Resentment increased since expenses of government seemed to be more than adequately covered by trade duties and by hidden taxes paid in the form of high prices for imported goods.

Following colonial protest the Stamp Act and most of the revenue duties were lifted, but the continued existence of the Admiralty courts and the retention by Parliament of the right in principle to levy taxes for revenue purposes fanned colonial irritation. The period from 1764 was one of increasing tension between the thirteen colonies and the Crown in Parliament. The cry of 'no taxation without representation' was raised, and invocations of the rights of the Englishmen were heard. They did not seriously want representation in the Westminster Parliament but the cry gave them a slogan whilst underlining the lack of real revolutionary feeling; they wanted to remain loyal to the Crown, provided that they were left free from parliamentary interference. What was later called dominion status would probably have satisfied them, but this was not a concept which had general currency in the mid eighteenth century, and it was certainly not held by George III himself, for it depended on the king being above politics.

Each year from 1770 incidents occurred in North America which the king's ministers, in the prevailing climate of opinion, could not ignore. A clash between British troops and citizens of Boston in the winter of 1770 resulted in an exchange of shots and the loss of one 'patriot' life. Two years after the 'Boston massacre' a revenue cutter, the *Gaspee*, was burnt, and in 1773 a band of citizens disguised as Indians threw a cargo of tea into Boston harbour in protest against the direct sale of tea in North America by the East India Company, so by-passing colonial merchants. Such overt challenges to British rule were met in 1774 by a series of Coercive Acts which included the closing of the port of Boston and the quartering of troops within the town. In the same year the Quebec Act, providing for the incorporation of the lands north of the Ohio into Quebec province, revived western territorial opposition to Britain and helped to unite the separate rebellious movements which were developing throughout the thirteen colonies. In September 1774 delegates from the colonies assembled in a continental congress at Philadelphia to co-ordinate resistance to British policy.

The proceedings of the congress illustrated the ideological limitations of the colonial position, and the extent to which they were as yet unwilling to cast themselves as whole-hearted revolutionaries. In 1774 they did not reject the authority of the crown, nor the right of Parliament to regulate trade. In a resolution drafted by John Adams and adopted on 14 October they asserted their fundamental right to participate in the governmental process by representation in parliament, but recognised that circumstances did not make representation at Westminster practicable. They therefore claimed full autonomy, subject only to the will of the sovereign, in all local affairs but their traditionalism found expression in specific acceptance of the parliamentary right to regulate trade and to impose duties for that purpose. The American revolution was latent and germinating, but whether the seed would flower was still conditional upon events. When the congress adjourned it stood upon the position stated by Adams, and made provision for a second congress to meet in 1775.

From this point the tempo quickened. On 19 April 1775 an armed clash occurred between British troops and a small group of colonial minutemen at Lexington and Concord, small towns some twenty miles from Boston. When the second continental congress met in May it found the Massachusetts militia besieging the British within the town of Boston and a state of war in being. In these circumstances, and in the light of what had gone before, the congress voted to raise an army and appointed George Washington commander-in-chief. Although the battle of Bunker's Hill on 17 June kept feelings high, and made it almost impossible for the disputes to be resolved by negotiation, they sent the Olive Branch Petition of 8 July 1775 to George III in a last attempt at peace whilst at the same time preparing for full-scale war. Two days after its arrival in London, however, the king issued a proclamation of rebellion, and later in the year a non-intercourse act was passed which rendered all American shipping liable to seizure on the high seas. In North America the first real call for complete independence of the British Crown came in January 1776 with the publication of *Common Sense* by a recent immigrant Thomas Paine. Paine's pamphlet rang like a clarion call throughout the colonies. It clarified the rebellion, and on 4 July 1776 the Philadelphia congress adopted the Declaration of Independence.

There are many conflicting interpretations of the causes of the American Revolution. Stress is laid on the supposed iniquities of George III, on the genuine aspirations towards freedom of the Americans, on economic and social tensions, and on the political motives of various colonial groups. The conflict of interpretations is unlikely to be completely resolved, but what is clear from the pattern of events is that the colonials came only slowly to repudiate the authority of the Crown: they stumbled almost by accident into a revolutionary situation. The forces that drove them were a combination of their own historical experience and the traditions of British imperial policy. Each side seems to have had little real choice in the attitudes it adopted and the paths it took. The significant result was that having claimed independence the colonials consolidated this claim by the successful prosecution of war, their victories culminating in the surrender of the British commander Lord Cornwallis at Yorktown in 1781. In this defeat of the British forces the French alliance of 1778 was of considerable importance for it placed the sea power of one of the major European powers at the disposal of the revolutionaries.

CONSOLIDATION OF THE NEW NATION

The Americans won their independence, but they won it as thirteen separate states, united until 1781 only by the Continental Army under the command of George Washington and by the unenforceable decisions of the continental congress. Local feelings were strong, and these local loyalties acted as a great divisive force. There was little sense of national identity or of national unity although citizens of the several states were fighting in a common cause and possessed, as Crèvecœur noted, certain characteristics in common. Even when the first constitution of the United States, the Articles of Confederation, was adopted in 1781 it established what was in fact as well as in name a confederation or league of states, not a unified national government. When the treaty of Paris was ratified in 1783 the future of the country remained in doubt. It was not clear whether the lands over which British rule had been repudiated would continue in unison or fragment into a number of separate regional states. An English observer, Dean Tucker, saw no possible future in the union and forecast inevitable fracture for the differences between the states were legion. They differed in climate, in religion, in their economies and in their social institutions. Slavery, for example, which had existed throughout the colonies was on the way to extinction in the north, although in the south it remained the foundation of the labour system.

Acting against these differences, however, were the unifying forces. Their British inheritance had given the states a common tongue and common attitudes and traditions of representative government; the physical environment had imposed on them qualities of courage and resourcefulness; they had been united in battle against a common foe. During the period from 1783 to 1787 the interplay of these often conflicting conditions forced them to realise that the Articles of Confederation did not provide a national government strong enough to resolve the myriad problems which confronted them. When a convention was called to consider revision of the Articles this was in itself evidence that the cohesive tendencies were stronger than the diversifying factors, and that a sense of common nationality existed and was growing. Upon the shoulders of the Founding Fathers who met in Philadelphia throughout the summer of 1787 rested the burden of giving shape and focus to the new nation.

The constitution which finally emerged from the Philadelphia convention was a compromise delicately balancing the divergent views to be found among the delegates, views which were to some extent reflections of increasingly different sectional interests. As Madison was later to write in its defence, the new system of government was to be partly federal and partly national. In place of the old confederation was to be substituted a federal government consisting of three parts, an executive branch, a legislature, and a judiciary, each having specific defined powers together with a degree of general authority which only practice and interpretation could make clear. Powers not delegated to the federal government were reserved to the states or the people. At no time was the question of sovereignty in doubt; everyone accepted that it resided in the people themselves and not in the institutions of government, and provision was made for amendment to the constitution so that the will of the sovereign people could at all times find expression. The balance of authority between the federal government and the separate states was echoed within the federal government by the balance of its three parts. The constitution of 1787 was a mixed constitution, embodying both the principle of the separation of powers and that of checks and balances. No one part had absolute authority, being limited by the other branches, by the constitution itself, and finally by the will of the people. The other vital principle contained in the constitution was that of compromise. This was also to be a source of strength for recognition of different views and interests was thereafter to guide the development of national political life and the evolution of constitutional doctrines. The occasions in the future when the stability of the union was to be seriously threatened were few, and they came at times when the fundamental principle of the necessity and virtue of compromise was abandoned.

The constitution came into effect in 1789 following ratification by the requisite majority of the states. It is still in force, although twenty-four amendments have throughout the years expanded and modified some of the clauses of the original document, and its relatively unchanged nature is in itself a tribute to the ingenuity and political skill of the Founding Fathers. Continued re-interpretation has enabled the Americans to match social and economic change by changes of emphasis in constitutional practice, and danger of the stultification of government in conditions radically different from those which prevailed at the time of the Philadelphia convention has been avoided. From the date of its adoption the constitution provided a focus for the growth of national feeling.

NINETEENTH-CENTURY THEMES

During the nineteenth century the character of American life was transformed by the interaction of a number of developments whose collective effect was to change the United States of 1800, agrarian, basically Anglo-Saxon and confined to the area east of the Mississippi, into an ethnically mixed, industrialised nation spanning the continent from coast to coast. Many of these developments echoed themes of the colonial period, but their form and expression changed with new circumstances and they created a new American who, although he continued to display recognisable European characteristics, reflected a wider spectrum of European society and embodied increasingly distinctive American cultural traits. The decisive elements in this metamorphosis were the westward movement, immigration, the urban and industrial revolutions, and ingrained moral and democratic ideals which played a significant part in moulding the character of twentieth-century America. It was accompanied by the growth of a strong sense of national identity which enabled the nation to survive the agony of civil war which it suffered between 1861 and 1865.

The westward movement

The factors which had stimulated movement into the trans-Appalachian west during the colonial period continued after the revolution to lure Americans across the continent, but out of the fervent nationalism of the new nation came a new justification for expansion.

The concept of 'manifest destiny', which meant a destiny to rule the continent from ocean to ocean, also implied the duty of the American to carry democracy and his own particular type of economic, social, political and religious freedom into the 'desert'. It was an imperial idea: just as the British settlements in North America had been originally outposts of empire so did the American people after independence enlarge the imperial theme by seizing for themselves vast lands outside the confines of their original jurisdiction. Sometimes skilful diplomacy served their ends, as when in 1803 agents of President Jefferson succeeded in purchasing the extensive lands between the Mississippi river and the Rocky Mountains from France. Sometimes war was the chosen instrument, and by this means California and the south-west were won from Mexico between 1846 and 1848. Always the rivalries and preoccupations of the great powers in other parts of the world gave the Americans opportunities which they were not slow to exploit. In the process the Indian was decimated, expropriated and thrust back, until finally the small numbers that remained were enclosed on federal reservations.

Apart from the call of 'manifest destiny' economic factors provided the main reasons for expansion. Agricultural opportunity played its part, settling the old north-west in the half century before the Civil War and enticing men across the Mississippi to the virgin cotton lands of the Red River valley in the south-west and to farm lands of the Willamette in Oregon on the Pacific coast. The Conestoga wagon in which many of the pioneers travelled across the continent along the Oregon Trial, through South Pass to the Snake River and the Columbia, became a symbol of their odyssey. Thousands died on the journey through hardship and Indian attack but many more survived. In the 1860s and 1870s the open range of the high plains and prairies made possible the establishment of large scale cattle ranching which wrote a separate chapter in the history of the West. In the wake of the rancher, the farmer invaded the prairie and the plain and farmers' fences destroyed the range. A few trappers went to the Rocky Mountains in search of pelts and these isolated mountain men were followed by hordes of miners and camp followers of all kinds when gold was found in California in 1848. The gold rush of 1849 revolutionised the history of the Far West and the 'mining frontier' was consolidated by later discovery of extensive silver, lead and copper deposits. In the conquest of the west, however, one other distinct movement deserves particular mention for it directly echoed one of the earliest colonial themes, that of the religious exodus. The Church of Christ of the Latter Day Saints, or the Mormons, finding themselves persecuted in the east moved steadily westward until in the 1840s they made their great migration to the Rocky Mountains and established Deseret, later to be called Utah. Otherwise economic factors, human necessities and greed drove men to the west and in the process they created stereotypes of folk heroes: the pioneer, the scout, the cowboy and the squatter, the marshall and the badman.

The immediate result of nineteenth-century continental expansion was a vast increase in the size of the national domain and incalculable additions to the national wealth, but there were other and more subtle consequences. As provision had been made in 1787 for the creation of new states out of the unorganised territories, states which were to be of equal status in the union with the original members, the imperial process resulted not in the acquisition of a colonial empire but in the expansion of the federal union itself. The political implications of such growth were profound.

The Founding Fathers had not envisaged the development of political parties, which were equated with factions and believed to be positively detrimental to the harmonious functioning of orderly government. However, during the administration of the first president, George Washington, such factions did develop and out of them emerged the first tentative party organisations. Each tended to appeal to different economic interests, or coalitions of such interests, and the natural division of the country into geographical regions, or sections, helped to define the nature of the new party groups. The Federalists gathered most of their support from the mercantile, banking and rising industrial interests whilst their opponents, the Jeffersonian Republicans, appealed to the agrarians. Differences of constitutional interpretation also influenced party development. Whilst Thomas Jefferson's followers believed that the powers of the federal government should in general be confined to those explicitly given by the constitution, and that the rights of the states should be defended against encroachment, the Federalists accepted a 'loose' interpretation of the constitution which gave 'implied' powers to the federal government and resulted in the diminution of state authority. Their view received endorsement by the Supreme Court of the United States under the leadership of its great chief justice, John Marshall, between 1801 and 1835, but the opposing theory also had its defenders, notably John C. Calhoun of South Carolina. Side by side with the nationalism of the early federal period, strengthened by the war with Britain of 1812 and the harmony of the 'Era of Good Feelings' which followed, germinated the seeds of disunion.

As the westward movement brought new states into the union, the south, believing that the agrarian sections had common interests which were opposed to those of the more industrialised and commercialised north-east, tried to forge a political alliance of south and west. However, although the Democratic party of President Andrew Jackson (1829–37) had a genuine national appeal, inherited much of the Jeffersonian tradition, and represented the re-invigoration of basic democratic ideals together with a new emphasis upon the rights of 'the common man,' it later became increasingly identified with the interests of the south alone. In the 1850s the political portrait of the country was simplified by the issue of slavery, for like the northern states, although for somewhat different reasons, the west was also opposed to the extension of slavery into those federal territories which were as yet unorganised as states. The Republican party, which was founded in the 1850s, had a strong appeal in the west and in the presidential election of 1860 western votes were decisive in securing the victory of its candidate Abraham Lincoln of Illinois. Southern threats of secession had been heard before the election and when Lincoln refused to deny the platform upon which he had been elected and rejected all proposals for compromise upon the question of slavery extension into the territories, South Carolina withdrew from the union. There had been crises about slavery before, notably in 1820, 1850 and 1854, but upon each occasion a compromise had been finally worked out which, although it did not fully satisfy either section, kept the union intact. This time Lincoln stood firm and the union was dissolved. By the late spring of 1861 seven southern states had left the Union and when troops of the southern Confederacy fired upon a federal garrison in Fort Sumter in Charleston harbour, civil war began. Lincoln denied the constitutional possibility of secession and believed that it was his duty to restore the union; the Confederacy interpreted the constitution differently and held that a state which had freely ratified the constitution could just as freely reverse its decision. The bitter war raged for four years until General Robert E. Lee surrendered to the union forces of Ulysses S. Grant at Appomattox in Virginia (April 1865).

The American Civil War, and the assassination of Lincoln shortly after peace was restored, had an indelible impact upon the history of the nation and upon the emotions of its people. Its memory still disturbs relations between north and south and affects the attitudes of the southern wing of the Democratic party. In the events leading up to the war the profound economic and political differences between the sections created a situation in which strife was possible; the continued existence of slavery in the south and the strength of northern abolitionism may have made it inevitable, but the occasion was determined by the territorial question and this was a direct result of the westward movement.

In the years after the Civil War the west continued to exercise an important influence over national politics, particularly in defence of the traditions of rural America against the progress of the industrial revolution; it played a significant role in reform movements in the twentieth century and its economic importance was unquestioned. The westward movement continued, but never again was it to be an instrument of fate threatening the existence of the federal union and the common nationality of the American people.

Immigration

Immigration, the second great theme of nineteenth-century America, played its part in the western movement. The steady trickle of immigrants in the early federal period became a flood as famine in Ireland, revolutions in Europe, rural depopulation, and the squalor of European industrial cities helped to increase the totals of disaffected, hungry, ambitious, and politically frustrated emigrants. The New World became once again a promised land offering political and religious freedom, social equality, and economic opportunity. The westward movement offered the prospect of free or at worst cheap land and a society open to all talents. Between 1820 and 1920 over 35,500,000 immigrants entered the United States. Of these almost four million came from Great Britain; over four million were Irish; two million were Scandinavians and five and a half million were Germans. The flood lost its predominately North European character in the last decade of the century as millions of Italians and South Slavs joined the great migration. Many of the immigrants, like those Willa Cather described in her novels *O Pioneers* and *My Antonia*, went themselves into the western states; but others, the poor, the sick, and the less sturdy, stayed in the ports of the eastern seaboard and in the nearby industrial towns. Here they indirectly contributed to the westward movement by encouraging many of the older inhabitants to undertake the journey to more open country, and to the less congested living and greater opportunity which were thought to lie beyond the mountains.

The immigrants also affected the patterns of political development. Political machines became dominant in the ports where they landed. Bosses welcomed them at the pier, fed them, clothed them, and found them jobs in return for their votes. The Republican party which had been in office during the Civil War remained in power during the post-war period of reconstruction. It became identified, however, not only with the union cause and with moral right in the controversy over slavery but with rapacious big business, insatiable banking and industrial interests, and political subservience to wealth. The city machines, representing the dispossessed, supported the Democratic party, and the character of that party changed as the influence of the agrarian south became balanced by that of the underprivileged urban immigrant masses of the New England and Middle Atlantic ports.

The general character of the United States changed too with the coming of new languages, new religions and new social customs. It ceased to be a country that was basically Anglo-Saxon in its heritage and became instead a complex microcosm of Europe, in which all the hyphenate groups, German-Americans, Italian-Americans, Polish-Americans, etc., made their individual contributions to society and filed their individual claims upon the state.

One of their major contributions was to supply a vast labour force which, in the second half of the nineteenth century, made possible a rapid industrial and urban revolution that irrevocably transformed the American scene and engulfed rural America in its wake.

The industrial and urban revolution

In 1800 well over 90 per cent of the American people lived in rural communities and even at the end of the Civil War 84 per cent of the population was classified as rural. However, by 1900 this figure had fallen to 60 per cent and by 1920 it was only 48 per cent The rise of the city was to a considerable extent the result of massive industrialisation.

When British restraints on American industry were finally removed at the time of the American revolution domestic manufacturing quickly developed; the factories at Lowell and Manchester in the Merrimack Valley of Massachusetts were noted by all European visitors, and they were duplicated elsewhere in New England and in the states immediately to the south. Industry flourished, but it was in the main small-scale industry. Not until the coming of the railroad in the 1830s was there a great demand for iron. Then the exploitation of the Pennsylvania coal field, of scattered iron ore deposits, and in the decades following the Civil War of the vast petroleum reserves of the Appalachian and associated fields, stimulated large-scale industrial expansion. All the factors necessary for growth were present: natural resources, transport routes, growing technological skills, foreign and domestic capital for investment, an expanding consumer market, and an abundant supply of labour in which the immigrants played a decisive role. They came in hundreds and thousands and manned the factories and the mines. Such industrial expansion and the rise of new industries based largely on iron and later steel affected the patterns of urban development. Before the Civil War most of the cities of over 100,000 inhabitants were eastern ports such as New York, Philadelphia, Baltimore and Boston; the one great exception was Cincinnati, a transit town on the Ohio where a number of the routes to the west converged. Although these cities continued to grow in the post-war decades new cities grew up on the coalfields, became centres of heavy manufacturing industry and reflected the new focus of urban expansion. Pittsburgh whose population rose from 49,221 in 1860 to 321,616 in 1900 is the prototype of this new urban development.

The industrial revolution was also stimulated by a revolution in agricultural production. Despite the increasing opportunities for advancement in the city the land retained its attraction. At a time when town population was beginning to outpace rural population more new farms were opened up than ever before: between 1860 and 1910 farm acreage trebled. However, the old prairie states had long since been settled, and the new farms were on the western lands, the high plains, in states like the Dakotas, western Kansas, eastern Wyoming and Nebraska. In these areas the land was poor and the climate fickle. The average size of farms tended to be larger than in the eastern Mid-West for more land was necessary for the individual farmer to make a living. In much of this region there were no trees for fencing, water supplies were poor, and the farmer relied more and more on industrial products in order to be able to exploit his environment. Farming also became more complicated and expensive as machinery was applied to traditional farm work. Mechanisation had begun before the Civil War, with the invention of the threshing machine and reaper, but the use of these devices was stimulated by the labour shortage of the war years and in the 1860s and 1870s twine binders, mowing machines, corn huskers and shellers, manure spreaders, four-plough cultivators and innumerable other machines transformed farm life. An industry centred on Chicago, the traditional marketing centre of the farm belt, developed to supply the farmer with his needs. A further stimulation of industrial development from the farming sector came with increased reliance upon rail transport. The farmer in the western states, which had few navigable rivers, needed the railroad to take his products to market, and by the end of the nineteenth century the whole of the farm belt was served by a network of railroads which exploited this dependence. They in turn increased demand for iron and steel products, not just for the rails themselves but for locomotives, trucks and terminal facilities. By the end of the century specialised wagons for particular products had been developed, including hopper cars for grain and refrigerated cars for meat. In many ways, therefore, expansion in the agricultural industry was accompanied by an expansion of heavy and service industries in the urban centres. Expansion in both sectors was helped by the availability of immigrant labour.

The reform impulse

Large-scale industry created massive social, economic and political problems. The historical experiences of the American people had been those of an agrarian society for which their institutions had been devised. The new society represented a fundamental challenge to established attitudes, and the endemic reform impulse sought to harmonise ideals with reality.

Despite its obvious inequalities, American society had always invoked democracy. At the time of the revolution this was not a completely egalitarian concept but was, in eighteenth-century fashion, limited to the 'better sort of folk'. However, the democratic idea, fused with the religious inheritance of many of the former colonies and with the experience of the frontier, encouraged belief in the inalienable right of 'the common man' to 'life, liberty and the pursuit of happiness'.

After the revolution the franchise became increasingly democratic as property qualifications and other restrictive tests gave way to general adult manhood suffrage, and by the 1830s De Tocqueville was able to detect a widespread egalitarian belief and practice in American society. This was, however, largely white suffrage only. In most states the Negro was not enfranchised; in one section, the south, he was still a slave. In the years after 1830 anti-slavery and abolition societies gained strength and the Negro problem came to dominate national politics and served as a focus for sectional jealousies. The south was driven to the defence of its 'peculiar institution' as a positive good, and the moral issue of slavery became entangled with the question of who should gain political and economic control of the territories. Opposition from the north and west to the theoretical expansion of slavery and the growing feeling within the south that it was a beleaguered minority section was the fundamental reason for the secession of the southern states in the winter of 1860–1, but although the south sought to gain its independence because it feared for the future of its domestic institution, the Civil War was not fought to free the slaves. Ostensibly the north went to war to preserve the Union, which Lincoln thought to be perpetual and indissoluble. However, abolition sentiments grew as the war progressed and one of the consequences of northern victory was emancipation of the slaves by the proclamation of 1863 and by the thirteenth amendment to the constitution which was ratified in 1865. The fourteenth and fifteenth amendments which followed sought to establish the Negro's citizenship and voting rights, but the history of the second half of the nineteenth century showed that legal freedom did not necessarily mean social, economic and political freedom. The effectiveness of the reform impulse when translated into political action had been demonstrated, but the success of white southerners in removing the Negro's civil rights whilst leaving his technical freedom intact illustrated the necessary dependence of reform movements upon genuine and widespread popular support.

In the post Civil War period preoccupation with problems of the franchise and civil rights continued, but attention also focused on the abuses produced by industrialisation and urbanisation and by the dominant philosophy of Social Darwinism. Application of Darwin's biological theories to society, as expounded in England by Herbert Spencer and in America by William Graham Sumner, produced a new justification of *laissez faire*. The axiom of the survival of the fittest was thought to sanction the practices of the new business and industrial entrepreneurs; their enormous wealth came to be regarded as tangible evidence of superior virtue and Rockefeller, Carnegie and other less worthy 'robber barons' of the Gilded Age expounded Social Darwinism in an attempt to establish their moral position within society. At the same time, however, there existed reform groups which rejected the prevailing sociology, denied the equation of material success with moral worth and dared to oppose the corporation, the trust and the baron. Their motives were partly selfish, for they represented those who had failed to secure what they considered to be their fair share of American abundance, but they included many who believed that in the new society Social Darwinism, although merely a psuedo scientific formulation of the traditional faith in freedom of opportunity, was incompatible with the American dream of an open society, and that the concentration of great economic, social and political power in the hands of a few necessarily deprived the many of full enjoyment of their rights.

The first opposition came from rural America. The long-standing antagonism of the farmer towards the east became increasingly acute as agriculture became mechanised and he fell deeper in debt to urban banking and financial interests. His absolute dependence on the railroad for the marketing of his crops focused his hostility, and the Patrons of Husbandry, or the

Grange, founded in 1867 as a cultural organisation to relieve the drabness of farm life, moved into politics primarily because of the abuses perpetuated by the railroads and grain elevator companies in fixing excessive rates and charges. The Grange was succeeded by the Farmers' Alliance and, in 1890, by a direct political party representing a mass coalition of agrarian protest groups. The platform of this Populist Party was a portfolio seeking to attract wide support, but two main features stand out: the desire to 'democratise' government, and the demand for governmental regulation of monopolistic industry and commerce. Opposition to the rise of the city was explicit in the party's attitudes, and it sought to redress the balance of national life in favour of the farm:

The great cities rest upon our broad and fertile prairies. Burn down your cities and leave our farms intact, and your cities will spring up again as if by magic; but destroy our farms and the grass will grow in the streets of every city in the country. (WILLIAM JENNINGS BRYAN, 1896)

Despite the deep emotional appeal of Bryan's 'Cross of Gold' speech of 1896 Populism, as a third party, failed to establish itself in national elections: southern agrarians preferred, for racial reasons, to stay with the Democratic Party and western dissenters were re-absorbed when the Democrats took over many of the Populists' planks. General economic conditions improved around the turn of the century, the farmer attained a new level of prosperity, and Populism disappeared as a coherent political movement. Rural America's protest against the new order was to take new forms in the twentieth century but for the moment it had failed.

However, with its decline a new reform movement prospered, solidly based in the new industrial order and in the city. In the absence of labour regulation, welfare legislation, and civic controls urban America was a jungle in which the palaces of the millionaires along Fifth Avenue in New York City rested cheek by jowl against malodorous slums. The proximity of wealth and stark poverty, of lighted streets and unpaved dark alleys, of grace and ugliness, which are moving features of Edith Wharton's novels of New York society could be paralleled in all major urban centres at the end of the nineteenth century. These conditions came under large-scale attack and informed criticism in the 1890s with the rise of a school of journalism that Theodore Roosevelt later christened the 'muckrakers'. Prominent among them was Lincoln Steffens, a reporter for *McClure's Magazine*, who published in 1904 a collected series of articles under the title *The Shame of the Cities*. Jacob Riis had already told of the slums of New York City in *How the Other Half Lives* (1890) and Henry Demarest Lloyd's *Wealth against Commonwealth* of 1894, an attack on Standard Oil, had set the pattern for muckraking exposures. Fiction such as Stephen Crane's *Maggie, a Girl of the Streets* (1893), and Upton Sinclair's *The Jungle* (1906) helped to arouse public indignation and to create a broad base of support for political action.

At state and local levels these progressives achieved a significant measure of success, and the elevation of Vice-President Theodore Roosevelt following the assassination of President McKinley in 1901 ensured powerful support at national level. Although no radical Roosevelt had a background of reform activities, particularly in connection with the civil service and the New York police commission, and genuinely felt that the social evils and political corruption which he saw about him were incompatible with the American dream of equal opportunity and individual liberty in a society geared to the pursuit of happiness. In legislation such as the Elkins, Hepburn, and Pure Food and Drug Acts Roosevelt's Square Deal marked the beginnings of extensive federal regulation of industry in the national interest. The Square Deal also sought to improve the position of labour. In the 1880s and 1890s bitter conflict between capital and labour had often resulted in strikes and armed battles between workers and employers. These reached their emotional peak in the Homestead strike of 1892 and the Pullman strike of 1894. The American Federation of Labour, organised in 1886, was an association of craft unions unable to cope with the problems of labour in the big heavy industries where the workers themselves were bedevilled by racial antagonisms and lack of cohesion. Roosevelt sought to improve the bargaining power of the unions, encouraged the establishment of arbitration commissions, and increased the status of the federal Bureau of Labor.

Another feature of the industrial scene during the post Civil War decades was the emergence of the trust as a form of business organisation which helped to create a monopolistic situation in some basic industries. The establishment of the Inter-State Commerce Commission in 1887 and passage of the Sherman

Anti-Trust Act three years later were attempts to regulate the size of industries and the growth of restrictive trading practices, but effective operation of the act was limited by the unwillingness of the courts to enforce its provisions against big business. By 1900 large sectors of American industry were dominated by a handful of massive corporations. Control of the trusts was an essential ingredient of progressive philosophy and Roosevelt supported the principle of regulation, but he was opposed to indiscriminate attack and sought to distinguish between good and bad trusts, believing that those which operated to the general benefit of the community should be left undisturbed. When he left the presidency there were more trusts in existence than when he entered the White House, but against the 'malefactors of great wealth' who flagrantly abused their economic power he had effectively asserted the power of the federal government and established significant precedents for later federal intervention in the economic life of the nation. His passionate interest in the conservation of natural resources also helped the progressive cause; millions of acres of timber and mineral bearing land were placed under government reserve and saved from private exploitation and waste, and many water-power sites were kept for development by the federal government. Although Theodore Roosevelt was, in the eyes of enthusiasts, only a moderate progressive his policies represented the most serious challenge yet made to the Social Darwinism of the industrial age.

Under his chosen successor, William Howard Taft, more conservative policies prevailed and a disillusioned Roosevelt broke away from the Republicans in 1912 to form an independent Progressive party which failed to win majority support. The Democratic presidential candidate, Woodrow Wilson, had himself acquired considerable reputation as a reform governor of New Jersey. The Progressive party, by splitting the Republican vote, ensured Democratic victory; but although the Progressive party had failed, progressivism was in the ascendant. Wilson's New Freedom programme went beyond Roosevelt's Square Deal and between 1913 and intervention in the world war an impressive body of legislation was placed upon the statute books, legislation characterised by an expansion of federal controls over the economy and an eroding of *laissez faire* in the attempt to create a more equitable society. Among Wilson's achievements were the creation of the Federal Reserve System to supervise the banking structure, establishment of a Federal Trade Commission, passage of the Clayton Anti-Trust Act strengthening the Sherman Act and specifically exempting the trade unions from anti-trust suits, the lowering of tariffs by the Underwood Act, and an extension of federal regulation of the railroads. When war came the reform programme necessarily lost much of its momentum, but reorganisation of the economy on a defence basis stimulated the trend towards stronger federal controls.

NATIONALISM TRIUMPHANT: THE UNITED STATES WAVES THE 'BIG STICK'

The new America that was emerging from the turmoil of rapid industrialisation, urbanisation, and social change at the end of the nineteenth century burst onto the world stage with the outbreak of war with Spain in 1898. The causes of war are usually complex, and those of the war of 1898 are no exception, but the interpretations given by historians of the events leading up to the Spanish-American war stem from an implicit if not explicit recognition of the changed nature of the United States. One interpretation puts forward the frontier theory in new form. The decennial census of 1890 had revealed that the line of continuous settlement had spread over the whole of the United States and that the frontier was therefore closed. With this report one of the dramatic themes of American history, the conquest of a continent by an expanding people, had ended. There was no longer a geographical and social frontier to which people might migrate. This did not mean decreased mobility on the part of the population, it did not remove the frontier of opportunity, but it has been argued with some force that having exploited the virgin continent the expansionist tendencies of the American people began to look for outlets overseas. There were precedents in earlier decades, when eyes were cast upon the Hawaiian Islands, but it may be significant that shortly after the 1890 report the Spanish-American war took the United States into the Caribbean and into the western Pacific.

It is also perhaps significant that during the decade of the 1890s the United States emerged without rival as the major industrial power in the world. In the production of coal, iron, steel and petroleum the United States far outpaced its competitors in Europe and consciousness of this industrial strength may also have made the nation more determined in its foreign policy. The effect of technology upon the art and the tools of war also helped to determine American action. The idea of a canal across central America to link the Caribbean with the Pacific had long been mooted. Construction of such a canal became more possible in the machine age and became more desirable as coal firing replaced sail as the motive power of ships of war; although rounding the Horn was a dangerous venture for sailing ships it was a very expensive one for steamers. Under the schooling of thinkers like Alfred Thayer Mahan the strategy of an isthmian canal came to include control of its approaches. Across the approaches lay the Spanish island of Cuba.

Moral and democratic impulses in the American people also played their part in the drift towards war, for Cuba, which provided the *casus belli*, was a Spanish colonial possession. Recent rebellions in the colony had been repressed with considerable ferocity by the military authorities in the island, and the construction of concentration camps led Americans to the belief that a freedom-loving people was being repressed by military authoritarianism and a dictatorial monarchy and that basic individual human rights were being denied. In the development of this feeling another feature of urban America played its part. Individual newspapers, particularly in New York City, stressed atrocity tales in order to increase their circulations and in the vicious battles for sales stories and news pictures were fabricated in order to attract readers. Such newspapers had considerable effect on educated opinion as well as on the emotions of the masses and the media of mass communication stimulated the pressures for war that from 1896 were being exercised upon the McKinley administration.

The president resisted such pressures until 1898, finally bowing to them after the blowing up of the American battleship *Maine* in unexplained circumstances in Havana harbour in February, and by the newspaper publication of personal attacks upon his own integrity written by an indiscreet Spanish diplomat. In the course of the war which was then officially declared the Americans 'liberated' Cuba, took possession of Puerto Rico, seized the Philippine Islands off the mainland of Asia, and took the occasion to annex Hawaii. The American empire now extended beyond the continent into the Caribbean, and across the Pacific ocean to the markets of the Far East. The United States, created out of a colonial rebellion, had now itself become a colonial power; its development as a major nation state, in nineteenth-century fashion, was complete.

The new-found power of the United States was truculently displayed during Theodore Roosevelt's presidency. He encouraged rebellion in the Panamanian provinces of the state of Colombia in order to secure American control over the projected canal. He extended Monroe's doctrine of 1823, which had declared that Latin America should not be a future area of European colonization and that existing colonies should not be transferred to new owners, by claiming the right of the United States to intervene in the domestic affairs of states south of the border. He mediated in the Russo-Japanese war of 1904 and offered his services in the Moroccan crisis of 1905. He sent 'the great white fleet' to show the flag round the world from 1907-9. He invoked the African proverb of talking softly whilst wielding a big stick, had a well-defined concept of the national interest and acted accordingly. It seemed that almost overnight the United States had enlarged its role from that of a hemispheric to that of a world power with a sense of world mission. It remained to be seen how the United States would use its strength in future years.

INVOLVEMENT IN WORLD WAR

During President Taft's administration the United States took little part in political affairs outside the western hemisphere but confined its energies to furthering American commercial interests overseas. Woodrow Wilson entered the White House in 1913. The following year war broke out in Europe and although Wilson had hoped to be able to concentrate on his domestic reform programme the existence of a state of war in Europe had to be faced. The president, and the people as a whole, decided on neutrality, believing that the country should set an example to the rest of the world, particularly as the war was not one in which the immediate and vital interests of the United States were seen to be involved. In such a situation neutrality was the traditional policy. For a few months in 1794, and during Jefferson's embargo policy of 1807-9 during the Napoleonic Wars, the country had abandoned neutrality in favour of a policy of complete economic isolation from war, but otherwise throughout the history of the union successive administrations had been content, in disputes where immediate national interests were not involved, to rest upon the wise advice of Washington's Farewell Address and keep aloof from other people's quarrels.

The years from 1914 to 1917 showed, however, that the original analysis of the position of the United States with relation to the war was faulty. Great Britain, at war with a continental enemy, employed her traditional weapon of blockade and this was met by a counter blockade. Wilson soon recognised that the neutrality of the United States was gravely threatened by both sides, as it had been in the years before the outbreak of war with Britain in 1812. Furthermore, use of new weapons such as the submarine posed more firmly than in the past the question of whether a neutral nation would, in the last resort, be prepared to defend its neutrality. In addition there was no longer the same separation of interests between the United States and Europe. The 'detached and distant situation' that Washington had recognised no longer existed: twentieth-century America was bound by extensive ties of trade and commerce to the non-American world. Events outside the western hemisphere now had a profound effect on American national life.

However, both sides infringed the rights of neutral America, and the issue of war or peace was not decided solely in terms of legal rights or material interests. The still dominant Anglo-Saxon tradition among many of the influential classes of society, and the effectiveness of Allied propaganda in creating an image of the heathen Hun, were perhaps as important in conditioning policy as the economic stake in an Allied victory given by the great volume of British war orders which stimulated American economic growth. Wilson's original neutrality 'in thought as well as in deed' was soon transmuted into a strong inclination towards the Allied powers. German submarine sinkings of American ships took American lives as well as interfered with the normal processes of trade; and in the last resort lives were more valuable than property. For Wilson and many of his people the war slowly became a struggle between democracy and authoritarianism, between right and wrong. Revelation of a German plot to rouse Mexico against the United States finally convinced the president of German iniquity, and in April 1917 he asked congress for a declaration of war against the Central Powers.

The short-term national interest of the United States might have been better served in 1917 by continued non-belligerency in the hope that a stalemate in Europe would provide the occasion for arbitration; but Americans did not consider their national interest purely in materialistic terms. Their religious and democratic heritage and their continental success had stimulated belief in the concept of manifest destiny. Their great industrial power had given them the means to extend their mission, which was partly selfish and partly altruistic, on to the wider world stage and they saw themselves engaged in a crusade for freedom and democracy. Intervention in the war in 1917 was more than a rational policy decision; it was also an emotional culmination of historical experience and a revelation of basic faith. In the post-war world both their hard headed materialism and their open handed faith were to have important consequences for the rest of mankind.

2

NORMALCY

Intervention in the Great War changed the fabric of national life profoundly. It stimulated government intervention in the economy and in society as a whole whilst at the same time reinforcing the fundamental belief in *laissez faire*. It clarified many of the deep-seated aspirations of the American people and at the same time strengthened many of their basic prejudices. The essential paradox of a peace-loving people fighting in a 'foreign' war for the preservation of democracy in Europe was echoed in the domestic sphere by the profound contradictions between ideals and reality, between expressed hopes and necessary actions which confused contemporary Americans. The fruit of these confusions was 'normalcy'. As a descriptive term it is completely inappropriate for the society which it enveloped, but it aptly symbolises the intentions of government policy. The Republican party which dominated the post-war decade seemed to be out of touch with the realities of the present and of the immediate past. It attempted to govern in terms of the old ideals of *laissez faire* and social Darwinism of the Gilded Age of the 1880s. Its standards of normality were anachronistic.

The United States was not as it had been in 1914 for the war and its consequences transformed the entire world and the western hemisphere did not remain untouched. Economic and political relationships, customs and manners and ways of thought had all been redirected, sometimes subtly, sometimes hesitantly, sometimes brutally. The America of the 1920s, of Scott Fitzgerald and John Dos Passos, was not the country of William Dean Howells and Henry James. The same points of reference were there still, but they were now blurred; stability had given place to flux, order to chaos. In his autobiography which was privately printed in 1907 Henry Adams had expressed unease about the nature of American development. Mechanical America, symbolised by the dynamo, was contrasted with an idealised portrait of the Middle Ages, symbolised by the Virgin. Adams was perhaps a pessimist, certainly a snob, and he failed to appreciate the extent to which the United States, in harnessing the industrial revolution, had continued to respond to the ideology of primitive America; but the 'degredation' which he sought to analyse was not entirely fanciful. The new immigration of the late nineteenth century was the catalyst that conclusively changed the character of American life from its earlier Anglo-Saxon protestant predominance, substituting for it a Latin, Catholic, urban aspect which not only upset the old political and economic order but completely overturned many of the traditional social values. In Jack London's novel, *The Valley of the Moon*, published in 1911, the old myths remain intact. The hero Billy Phillips and his wife Saxon represent the old ethnic strain, and although they confront the problems of urban America, engage in nascent union activity and indulge in strike action, finally seek their personal salvation on the land. Filled with the myth of the happy farmer, they walk away from Oakland California in search of free government land, and finally reach their Utopia in the Valley of the Moon. Nineteenth-century America still exists. In the literature of the 1920s on the other hand the urban hero seeks his salvation in the city, for him there is no flight. He meets his destiny among the tenements and on the pavements, not in the woods, hills and furrows. The dynamo had really come into its own, and the changes wrought by the Great War heralded this triumph.

THE EFFECTS OF WAR

The first impact of war was felt in the economic sphere. The naval blockades of the belligerent European powers seriously disrupted the patterns of American overseas trade, and the increase of trade with the Allied powers which resulted gave to American industry a new role, comparable to that which it undertook in 1940. As in the later period it became the 'arsenal of democracy'. But industrial expansion and the creation of war industries during the period from 1914 to 1917 was largely unco-ordinated. In 1916 during the 'preparedness' phase the President had, with congressional approval, appointed a Council of National Defence composed of Cabinet ministers, with an associated Advisory Commission constituted of leaders from industry, business and labour. These committees discussed the problems of economic and military mobilisation, and early in 1917 a Munitions Standards Board was established to supervise purchasing arrangements but this, like the other committees, had only advisory functions and its effectiveness was limited. After the declaration of war in April a stronger War Industries Board was set up but this also remained weak until Bernard Baruch was appointed chairman in March 1918. It was then given wide powers to co-ordinate industrial effort and under Baruch's leadership established priorities in the allocation of raw materials and helped to stimulate production. A Fuel Administration guaranteed minimum coal prices and this brought marginal mines into production so increasing essential supplies. The demands of war also dictated expansion in agriculture. Wilson's Food Administration of 1916 received congressional approval the following year and under its administrator Herbert Hoover wheat was supported at $2·20 a bushel and acreage jumped from 45 to 75 million between 1918 and 1919. Hog production also doubled.

Such production increases were, however, only valuable to the extent that the transportation system could cope with the increased volume of internal traffic, and in December 1917 Wilson placed the railroads under the control of a Railroad Administration, headed by the former secretary of the Treasury William Gibbs McAdoo, which ran them as an integrated system. The overseas shipping problem was met by the creation of the Emergency Fleet Corporation and the Shipping Board. These agencies did their best to counteract the effects of British losses resulting from the German submarine campaign, which amounted in 1917 to 25 per cent of the total British merchant fleet, by co-ordinated planning in the use of existing vessels and by the construction of new tonnage. 2,700 new ships were planned, and although the first of these did not come off the slipways until after the armistice had been signed in November 1918 they would have been of the utmost importance had the war continued. State control extended to the labour movement as well as to producers and employers. A National War Labor Board was set up to arbitrate disputes and later assumed wide powers over the labour force as a whole. In other areas of economic activity the War Finance Corporation served as a credit agency for industries engaged in the war effort, and a Capital Loans Committee regulated security issues and controlled the investment market.

Mobilisation of the economy behind the war effort resulted in what may validly be called a second industrial and agricultural revolution. The average value of farmland rose from $39.59 per acre in 1910 to $69.37 in 1920. The book value capital investment in manufacturing industries rose from $20.7 billion in

1914 to $40.2 billion in 1919. The social, economic and political consequences of this transformation were to affect the history of the 1920s.

Government regulation of the economy substantially modified the *laissez faire* system and mobilisation involved restrictions upon individual enterprise that extended to the ultimate control that government can exercise over the citizen in time of war, conscription. A Selective Service Act was passed by Congress on 18 May 1917, one month after the United States entered the war, which enabled an expeditionary force of 300,000 men to be mounted by March 1918. This rose to one million by July 1918 and was then augmented by an average of 200,000 men a month until the armistice was signed in November. These forces, under the command of General Pershing, helped to stabilise the western front at Chateau Thierry and Bellau Wood in the early summer of 1918 and to blunt the German offensive against Paris. In August they moved along the line of the Meuse and took part in the counter-offensive which culminated in the battle of St Mihiel in September. Their value was unquestioned and they were made possible by the draft, which even in its early months met with surprisingly little opposition and was generally met with enthusiasm. Not until the end of the war did widespread reaction against regimentation arise, but when it did it strengthened the desire to revert to 'normalcy'.

However, the emotional fervour aroused by the war and stimulated by the draft also helped to generate a war hysteria in which many of the more fundamental freedoms of the American democratic system were temporarily lost from sight. At first this took the form of congressional legislation which, although justified in intent, was excessive in its scope and operation. The Espionage Act of 1917 provided massive penalties not only for formal espionage but also for any activities designed to obstruct the war effort, and the Postmaster General was authorised to ban from the mails anything which was in his opinion seditious. The Trading With The Enemy Act censored overseas communications and the domestic foreign language press. The Sabotage and Sedition Acts of 1918 were invoked against pacifists. But apart from legal sanctions against domestic disloyalty there was a more ominous social reaction born out of fear and uncertainty. Although there were millions of citizens of German ancestry, language and customs, everything German was regarded with suspicion: teaching of the language was banned in many schools and German books were removed from public libraries; Bruno Walter, conductor of the Chicago Symphony Orchestra, was suspended from duty, and in some cases the playing of Beethoven was prohibited; sauerkraut and frankfurters were rechristened liberty cabbage and liberty sausage. These examples of prejudice, although often slight in themselves, were symptomatic of dangerous undercurrents coming to the surface of American life.

THE RESURGENCE OF PARTISAN POLITICS AND DISPUTES OVER THE PEACE

One of the consequences of the social and economic ferment of the immediate pre- and post-intervention periods was a general rise in prices. The presidential boards and commissions were more interested in increasing production than in keeping prices stable, except in certain basic industries like steel. In the boom war industries wages kept pace with prices, but the salaries of white collar workers tended to fall behind, and people living on retirement incomes felt the pinch of inflation. Farmers benefited from the relatively high guaranteed prices, but they resented the Food Administration's controls which denied them the chance of even greater profits as the level of world prices for primary products steadily rose. They also resented the high prices of industrial consumer goods. All sections of the population underwent the burden of high war taxation.

These sometimes real but more often imaginary financial hardships helped to strengthen the already considerable political opposition to the Wilson administration. The Republican party had only narrowly suffered defeat in the presidential election of 1916 and inflation strengthened its support among the electorate. War hysteria and the continued governmental invocation of patriotic virtues and national unity heightened the appeal of the party still identified with Abraham Lincoln, who had reunited the Union by victory in the Civil War. Hyphenate Americans of German ancestry, whilst not opposing the war, were at the same time less sympathetic towards the Democrats under whose leadership their new country had been brought into conflict with their former homeland. Many northerners reacted against the flow of Negroes from the south and their entry into previously all-white areas to work in new industrial plants. Finally, the natural swing of the political pendulum might, even without these other factors, have led to a decline in the fortunes of the party in power in the congressional elections of 1918.

However, the sudden political ineptness of President Wilson shortly before polling day turned the possibility of Republican victory into a probability. Wilson called for all who approved his leadership and wanted him to continue as the 'unembarrassed spokesman' of the United States at home and abroad to vote for the Democratic party. In so departing from his previously reiterated cry that politics were adjourned for the duration of the war the president seemed to be impugning the loyalty of the Republican opposition. This undoubtedly contributed to the Democratic party's loss of control in both the House of Representatives and the Senate as a result of the November elections.

This defeat, together with Wilson's display of partisanship, did not augur well for the fortunes of his projected peace settlement when it should come before the Senate. In a Message to Congress of 8 January 1918 he had already indicated the Fourteen Points which he hoped would be the basis for the peace. These Fourteen Points, which were developed in later speeches, advocated a peace without victory on the basis of open diplomacy; territorial and national self-determination; and the establishment of 'an association of nations...affording mutual guarantees of political independence and territorial integrity to great and small states alike'. It was not that Wilson had been blinded by his own propaganda and did not appreciate the nationalistic aims of the European belligerants, but rather that, understanding the difficulties before him, he hoped to mobilise general opinion shocked by the horrors of trench and submarine warfare into an irresistible force that statesmen would have to take into account in making the peace. He hoped thereby to be able to translate nationalistic ambitions into a genuine recognition of the necessity and desirability of international co-operation in the arbitration of disputes without resort to war.

However, the extent to which his aims conflicted with the realities of the European situation became evident in the summer of 1918 whilst the war was still in progress. The Allied powers made it clear that they could not accept the Fourteen Points as they stood and asked that some of them be interpreted to safeguard their own specific national interests. Such an 'Interpretation' was produced, largely by Colonel Edward M. House, the president's adviser on foreign affairs, and this was accepted by the Allied leaders and by President Wilson himself. When the German authorities sued for peace on the basis of the Fourteen Points the commentary was not submitted to them, except for the sections reserving free discussion of Article II, which related to the Freedom of the Seas, and those defining reparations broadly to meet the French insistence on indemnity for damage done to the civilian population of Northern France. The existence of the commentary, and the fact that it was not submitted in full to the German government, compromised Wilson's position before the armistice was signed and his power at the conference tables was significantly weakened.

On 4 December 1918 Wilson sailed for Europe, and in January found himself face to face with Clemenceau, 'the tiger of France', Lloyd George the British prime minister, characterised later by Lord Keynes as 'the Welsh witch,' and Orlando of Italy. The defeated powers were not represented at the peace conference. Each of the European leaders had well-defined aims: Clemenceau wanted to remove the possibility of Germany ever again being in a position to attack France; Lloyd George wanted to detach the German empire in order to maintain British imperial authority and naval supremacy; Orlando wanted to safeguard the northern frontiers of Italy by securing the line of the Brenner. These major issues were complicated by the demands of the former subject peoples of the Austro-Hungarian empire for territorial and national sovereignty, by the ambitions of the Japanese in China, and by innumerable other political, economic and financial questions. Dominating discussion of the European settlement was British unwillingness to satisfy the French desire for security by the conclusion of a continental alliance, a fear of continental European entanglement that was later to affect the history of the League of Nations.

In the negotiations Wilson, who relied heavily upon his personal popularity among the people of Europe, found himself outmanoeuvred on all points except the establishment of a League. The Treaty of Versailles which finally emerged contained the covenant of the League of Nations and this was, at Wilson's insistence, bound into the treaty so that ratification of the treaty meant acceptance of the League. In this way the president persuaded himself that the concessions he had made at Paris would eventually be put right by the harmonious functioning of a genuinely impartial international assembly. On all other points the treaty bore little relation to the spirit of the Fourteen Points. It was then imposed on the German government, which had no opportunity for negotiation and was in no position to reject it out of hand. 'Peace without victory' had been translated into more traditional forms. Too many men had died at Verdun and on the Somme for trans-Atlantic idealism to find much response in battered Europe.

When Wilson carried the treaty back to the United States in the spring of 1919 to present it for ratification by the Senate he could expect opposition over both the issues on which he had failed in Paris and over the League of Nations on which he had succeeded. Furthermore, the normal problems inherent in the process of ratification were enhanced by the fact that the president had already alienated sections of the Senate. The ineptness he had shown at the time of the 1918 elections had been followed by a series of tactical mistakes. The first was in going himself to Paris to negotiate with the Allies, an unprecedented step which to many Americans seemed to diminish the dignity of the presidency as well as reduce his effective bargaining power. Secondly, he took no Republican of note in his entourage and although there were no precedents for such action this irritated the party. Thirdly, despite the role of the Senate in the process of ratification he took no senator with him, nor did he inform the Senate of the course of the discussions in Paris. Before Wilson submitted the treaty to the Senate a draft published in the Paris press had already reached Washington. Senate dignity was affronted. Looking back on the summer of 1919 it is clear that the Senate were stung by these presumed slights, and would offer at least token amendments to the treaty in order to assert its power. This uneasy situation developed into a direct confrontation when the president made it known that he expected the treaty to be accepted without modification. Rigid and self-righteous, he regarded it as his treaty, whatever its faults, and he was unwilling to see it amended. It was perhaps his awareness of the ways in which he had been forced to compromise at the peace conference that made him now resist any changes in the already imperfect document. The arrogant traits of his personality asserted themselves, and he seemed to be left without political instinct.

The Senate was split into three main groups. There were those, largely Democrats, who were prepared to follow Wilson and accept the treaty as it stood. There were those, largely Republicans, who wanted 'mild' reservations attached. Lastly, there were the 'irreconcilables', largely Republicans, who were opposed to the treaty tooth and nail because they believed that membership of the League would represent a dangerous departure from the traditional policy of avoiding 'entangling alliances'. At first the irreconcilables were in a very small minority, and the original reservations offered did not significantly affect the substance of the treaty. However, Wilson instructed his followers to vote them down. His uncompromising attitudes hardened the views of the moderates and the next series of reservations were more severe. Again they were defeated by a coalition of irreconcilables and Wilsonian Democrats. As the president remained in a state of petrified irritation and unyieldingness his support dwindled to a hard core of loyal senators. The prospects of securing ratification with or without amendment retreated.

In the autumn of 1919 Wilson went on a speaking tour in an attempt to rally popular support behind the treaty, and at Pueblo Colorado suffered a stroke and partial paralysis. For the remaining eighteen months of his term he was kept in almost complete seclusion and with the removal of his dominating personality half of his remaining supporters deserted him. In March 1920 the treaty with amendments again failed to secure the necessary two-thirds majority for ratification, and it was not again voted on. Wilson had asked for all, had got nothing, and as a result of his failure the United States remained outside the League of Nations.

POST-WAR TENSIONS AND THE ELECTION OF 1920

The president's incapacity came, moreover, at a time when pressing domestic problems demanded solution and the absence of strong executive leadership was to be sorely felt. With the ending of the war in Europe most of the 4,800,000 men under arms wanted immediate demobilisation and a return to their homes and families. It was generally expected that the stopping of war production and the sudden expansion of the civilian labour force would result in widespread unemployment. However, although unemployment figures rose in 1919, this only represented an increase from 1·4 to 2·3 per cent of the civilian labour force. Instead of the expected slump there was a boom of considerable magnitude. It was caused by a complex of factors, including the continuation of heavy governmental expenditure, the release of discretionary income into consumer spending, the renewal of capital investment in new plant and facilities, and by a buoyant export trade. Demand was such that a new danger presented itself, that of violent inflation: prices, and hence the cost of living, rose at an increasingly alarming rate throughout 1919. The groups most seriously affected by this inflation were white collar workers, people living off fixed incomes and pensions, and public employees; but although industrial wages increased during the period they were outpaced by the rise in prices and 1919 was characterised by a wave of strikes throughout major industries. Beginning in the textile industry it spread to telegraph operators, longshoremen, printers, steel workers, railroad employees and mine workers. In Boston, Massachusetts, even the police force struck. Inflation and industrial instability helped to reveal fundamental weaknesses in the economy and in 1920 a recession set in, stimulated by the collapse of farm prices.

The causes of economic dislocation are rarely fully understood, and for the ordinary citizen they are often totally beyond comprehension. Fear bred of economic ignorance often results in the growth of intolerance, the persecution of alien minorities, and a search for foreign 'devils'. Such developments occurred in the United States in the immediate post-war years. They were not new to the American experience and they were to reappear later, but in 1919 and 1920 intolerance was particularly dangerous because it received the active support of responsible government officials.

The ground had been laid during the war in the persecution of German-Americans and the repudiation of German culture. Nationalism and the conscious cultivation of 'American-ness' formed a part of the general climate of opinion in which in 1915 William J. Simmons revived the Ku Klux Klan, a post-Civil War southern nativist and terrorist organisation, as a white protestant American crusade for the maintenance of traditional American virtues against the dangers of foreign and coloured infiltration. The sudden success of the prohibition movement can also be seen as a result of similar pressures towards conformity to ancient myths. As early as 1851 Maine had gone 'dry', banning the manufacture and sale of intoxicating liquors, but not until the end of the nineteenth century did the prohibition movement and its ginger group, the Anti-Saloon League, gain significant support.

By 1914 still only nine states were legally 'dry', but in 1915 and 1916 they were joined by another ten states which gave sufficient support for the successful introduction of a constitutional amendment to impose nation-wide prohibition. This eighteenth amendment was passed by Congress in December 1917, was ratified by the states by January 1919, and came into effect in January 1920. The Conscription Act of 1917 which banned the sale of alcoholic beverages on or near military installations, and the Lever Act prohibiting the use of grain for distilling, had already significantly reduced the consumption of liquor, and the appeal to patriotism which had been used to secure passage of this legislation was adopted by the prohibition movement as a whole. Like the Ku Klux Klan, it appealed to fundamentalist agrarian virtues against the wickedness of the city, the home of rum and romanism. Both movements found their centres of support among the white Anglo-Saxon Protestants of the country districts.

In 1919 these nativist anti-foreign prejudices became focused on radicalism, on the supposed 'red menace'. The Russian revolution of 1917 had been originally welcomed in the United States as a democratic rejection of Tsarist autocracy, but the intolerant nature of the Bolshevik régime and its commitment to world proletarian revolution alienated American feeling and aroused widespread fear of Bolshevik conspiracy. This became fused with the war hysteria, and produced equally unfortunate results.

American radicalism, represented by the American Socialist party, founded in 1901, and by the Industrial Workers of the World (1905), had already aroused considerable opposition and anxiety because of its complete rejection of traditional *laissez faire* capitalism. The I.W.W., which began as a union of western miners and lumbermen but then extended its appeal to un-organised industrial labourers in both east and west, had from its foundation advocated direct action through strikes and acts of sabotage in its battle with the employers. Its violence alienated the propertied classes and worried many others. The frequent strikes which paralysed many sectors of industry in 1919 led to a reaction against labour in general, against the I.W.W. in particular, and aroused fears that communists were attempting to take over the United States. These were enhanced when, following internal quarrels within the Socialist party, the Communist Labor party was founded on 31 August 1919 and the Communist party of America was organised the next day, developments which seemed at the time to be outward signs of an imminent communist coup. The fears were groundless, and might have been quietened had not Wilson's attorney-general, A. Mitchell Palmer, played upon them by ordering the Federal Bureau of Investigation to investigate all suspected radicals and urging Congress to pass a sedition bill which went far beyond even the wartime measure. In defence of Palmer it must be said that there had been a series of bomb outrages in the spring of 1919, and that a number of plots aimed at blowing up wealthy private citizens and prominent governmental officials, including Palmer himself, had been uncovered. However, it seems that he was more concerned with capitalising on public fears to build up his own reputation with a view to becoming the next Democratic presidential candidate than with serious investigation of the violations of public order.

Congress refused to pass the attorney-general's sedition bill and he acted unilaterally. On New Year's Day 1920 communist offices throughout the country were raided and six thousand people, many of whom were not members of the party, were arrested. Two thousand of these were eventually freed for lack of evidence, but of those tried over five hundred communist aliens were deported. Other members of the administration, particularly William Wilson, the secretary of Labor, opposed Palmer's actions, and no more raids were held, but persecution of radicals and suspected anarchists and communists was taken up at the state level. The case of Nicola Sacco and Bartolomeo Vanzetti, who were arrested and sentenced to death for the alleged murder of a pay clerk in South Braintree Massachusetts, was to become a *cause celebre* of the 1920s. One of the last of the bombings was also the most serious; thirty-eight people were killed when a cart loaded with explosives blew up outside the Wall Street offices of J. P. Morgan on 16 September 1920. After this incident, however, such anarchistic action became rare, and what seemed to be an endemic strain of violence in American life found new expression in the gang wars associated with prohibition and in hatred directed against the Negro.

It was against this background that the party conventions met in the summer of 1920 for the selection of candidates to run in the presidential election. The Democrats nominated the governor of Ohio, James M. Cox, with the young assistant secretary of the

Navy, Franklin D. Roosevelt, as his vice-presidential running mate. Cox won only after a deadlock had developed between two of Wilson's associates, the former secretary of the Treasury, William Gibbs McAdoo, and Attorney-General Palmer. The Republican convention in Chicago was similarly torn between General Leonard Wood and Frank O. Lowden of Illinois, and after a meeting of party managers in the famous 'smoke filled room' at the Blackstone Hotel, Warren G. Harding of Ohio emerged as the party's choice. Lacking any personal qualifications for the office Harding had a least the visual appearance of a president; he was a tall, stalwart, handsome man; and it was thought that he would be amenable to the wishes of the party bosses. The vice-presidential candidate was Calvin Coolidge, a quiet, laconic Yankee who had risen to prominence as governor of Massachusetts during the 1919 strike of the Boston police force. Although he had shown incompetence and lack of vigour in his handling of the dispute he had acquired a national reputation for strength by issuing a public statement, after the crisis had passed its peak, saying 'there is no right to strike against the public safety, anywhere, anytime'. On the crest of this undeserved reputation he rode to the vice-presidential nomination.

The Harding–Coolidge campaign became known as the campaign for 'normalcy'. In a speech earlier that summer he had stated that 'America's present need is not heroics, but healing; not nostrums, but normalcy; not revolution, but restoration; not agitation, but adjustment; not surgery, but serenity; not the dramatic, but the dispassionate; not experiment, but equipoise; not submergence in internationality, but sustainment in triumphant nationality'. Such phrases had an emotional appeal for a nation wearied by recent upheavals and anxious about its future, and part of the strength of normalcy as an electoral slogan was that it was undefined. On all issues it was uncertain where Harding stood. This was as true of the League question as of all others; sometimes Harding seemed to favour an association of nations; at others he vigourously opposed American entry in the League.

Although nothing is ever certain in politics it probably did not matter who the candidates were in 1920, for prospects favoured a Republican victory. The political pendulum was swinging away from the Democratic party. It had been in power for eight years; these eight years had coincided with the war, and the war had been followed by the dislocations of the peace. Woodrow Wilson had aroused serious resentments not only in the Congress but also in the country at large by his apparently rigid partisanship, by his conduct over the peace negotiations, and by his aloofness from the ordinary citizen. Furthermore he was, in 1920, a sick man and seemingly incapable of exercising the powers of his office. His heirs on the Democratic ticket faced an almost impossible task from the start.

However they did their best to rally the electorate, criss-crossing the country on extended speaking tours in an attempt to reach as many voters as possible. Harding on the other hand conducted what came to be known as a 'front porch' campaign, receiving delegations and crowds of the curious at his home in Marion, Ohio, but exposing himself as little as possible to the rough and tumble of the stump. The strategy was successful. He won by a landslide and carried with him substantial Republican majorities in both the Senate and the House of Representatives. The policy of normalcy went to Washington the following March when Harding was inaugurated, and in the years that followed received a definition that unintentionally made it one of the most inept and misnamed political slogans in the entire course of American history.

POLITICS IN THE ERA OF HARDING AND COOLIDGE

From the time he entered politics in the state of Ohio, Harding's career had been managed by a small town lawyer called Harry Daugherty, Daugherty was a man of great political ambition but with no personal political assets. He determined that if he could not be a king he would be a king maker, and ran Harding success-fully for two terms in the state senate and for one term as lieutenant governor. Although he failed to secure his candidate's election to the governorship in 1910 he got him into the United States Senate in 1914. Harding enjoyed the Senate, which has been called 'the most exclusive club in the world,' and although completely undistinguished as a legislator he built up a reputation for flamboyant oratory and always 'looked like a President ought to look'. He was also a devoted poker player and a reliable Republi-can, and these small assets, combined with Daugherty's political skill, were sufficient to give him the nomination in 1920.

When he entered the White House in 1921 his friends, the

'Ohio gang', reaped the rewards of their long loyalty. Daugherty became attorney-general of the United States; Albert B. Fall, an old senate crony, became secretary of the Interior; Daniel R. Crissinger, a lawyer from Harding's home town, became Controller of the Currency; his friend Charles B. Forbes, was made head of the Veterans Bureau. The later scandals have, however, perhaps given undue prominence to these names among the list of Harding's appointments. It should not be forgotten that the major cabinet posts went to distinguished and able men. The eminent jurist and former Republican presidential candidate Charles Evans Hughes was appointed secretary of State; Andrew Mellon, the Pittsburgh banker and industrialist, was put in charge of the Treasury; Henry Wallace of Iowa was made secretary of Agriculture; and Herbert Hoover, former mining engineer and wartime administrator of the Belgium Relief Programme, became secretary of Commerce. These were talented men, who, within the framework of Republican political philosophy, did their best to cope with the tremendous problems confronting the administration.

For Harding, however, the office of president was beyond his capacity. He himself is recorded as saying on one occasion: 'I am just a man of limited talents from a small town. I don't seem to grasp that I am president.' He had no coherent policy, and his remark about the federal tax structure is perhaps devastatingly representative of his reaction to most issues of high policy: 'I can't make a damn thing out of this tax problem...I know somewhere there is a book that will give me the truth; but hell! I couldn't read the book.' Such completely honest self-exposure, however admirable in a private citizen, is not a particularly inspiring quality in a president.

Although he did not personally indulge in corrupt practice the president, having naïve faith in their ability and integrity, kept no check on the friends whom he had elevated to high office and a series of scandals culminated in the Teapot Dome Affair. In 1921 the secretary of the Interior, Albert Fall, persuaded the president to transfer control of the oil reserves in the Teapot Dome field in Wyoming, so called because of the curious shape of the land, together with those at Elk Hills, California, from the Navy Department which had previously administered them to the Interior Department. Fall then secretly leased the areas to two private oil magnates, Harry Sinclair and Henry L. Doheny. His sudden affluence aroused suspicion, and a senate investigating committee finally revealed that Fall had been given $223,000 in government bonds, $85,000 in cash and a herd of pedigree cattle for his part in the transaction. The investigations continued throughout the next administration; Fall was eventually sent to jail, and the concessions cancelled. There was, however, a more immediate consequence of the scandal. Although weak and idle, President Harding had not participated in the public malpractice of his friends, the revelations gravely shocked him, and to rest his mind he went on a trip to the west, uncertain how to tackle his troubles. In California he suffered what is thought to have been a heart attack and died some days later.

He was succeeded by his vice-president Calvin Coolidge. Just as in 1920 Harding had seemed to represent the qualities needed by the country to restore domestic order and tranquillity, so in the changed circumstances of 1923 Coolidge appeared to be the embodiment of integrity. He was a good Vermont Yankee, reared according to the old fundamental agrarian virtues, and seemed eminently suited to bring morality back into the White House. He was called by William Allen White, the famous newspaper editor of Emporia, Kansas, 'a puritan in Babylon' and 'the moral symbol the times seemed to demand'. However, although a moral man Coolidge did not possess presidential quality. His concept of the role of the executive branch of the federal government was that, generally speaking, it should be passive, letting the sound common sense of the people and of the legislature guide the destinies of the nation. His refusal to act at the time of the Boston strike was characteristic of his policy in the White House. When Will Rogers the humourist asked him how he managed to stay fit in a job that had destroyed the health of Woodrow Wilson he replied that he avoided the big problems. Almost all that he did of a constructive nature was quiet political activity to secure his nomination in 1924. Coolidge's silence was not insignificant in terms of the party which he represented; the Republicans still clung to the traditions of *laissez faire*, and although society was in a state of rapid change they did not accept that the federal government had any great responsibility for control and regulation.

Nor did the Democratic party offer a coherent alternative choice to the electorate. After its defeat in 1920 tensions between the urban and agrarian wings of the party heightened, and the two opposing groups coalesced around McAdoo, representative of the 'dry' traditionalists, and Alfred E. Smith, reform governor of New York and hero of the 'wet' heterogeneous urban masses. Deadlock at the 1924 Democratic party national convention in Madison Square Garden led finally to the nomination of John W. Davis, a conservative New York lawyer whom it was hopefully felt would appeal to both sections of the party. This weak compromise choice contributed to Coolidge's victory in the presidential election and he won majorities almost as great as those of Harding's landslide success in 1920.

It was left to a new political movement to bring into the arena of political debate the fundamental political and social issues ignored by the major parties. A conference for Progressive Political Action had been formed in 1922. Supported by the Socialist party, which had run Eugene Debs as its presidential candidate in 1920, by the Farmer-Labor party, a mid-western agrarian protest group which had grown out of the Non-Partisan League of 1915, by the American Federation of Labor, and by liberal intellectuals who normally found their forum in the *New Republic* and in the *Nation*, the new progressive party nominated a slate of candidates under Senator Robert M. LaFollette of Wisconsin, a former Roosevelt Republican. The platform advocated public ownership of railroads, water power, and important natural resources of all types; freedom for collective bargaining in labour disputes; prohibition of child labour, and many other 'radical' measures. It denounced corruption in government and severely criticised the administration's financial policy. Whereas Debs had received less than a million votes in 1920 the LaFollette coalition polled more than 4,800,000 votes in 1924. In the mid-twenties, as the Democratic party came increasingly under the control of Smith's urban supporters, the lessons of 1924 were learned, and the more moderate Progressive planks were incorporated in the Democratic platform in 1928. The function of third parties in the United States is usually to act as a catalyst on the two dominant parties. In the long view this is the real importance of the LaFollette movement; it helped to take the Democratic party back to the traditions of Wilson's New Freedom and to move it forward into the direction which it followed in the 1930s under Franklin D. Roosevelt. Slowly in the 1920s the images of the two great traditional parties were becoming clarified. The Republicans continued to represent small government and strong private initiative; the Democrats came increasingly to favour a larger role for government so that in a complex society the rights of all groups could be protected and all individuals have the opportunity for self-fulfilment under the law.

ECONOMIC POLICY

After the depression of 1920–1 the United States entered into a period of boom and prosperity which lasted until 1929 and became known as 'the new economic era'. The policies of successive Republican administrations generally favoured the growth of large business units, and the social and technological revolution of the decade which was symbolised by mass-production of automobiles, increased use of aviation, spread of radio and the development of the motion picture industry was accompanied by an increasing trend towards oligopoly. Big corporations tended to get bigger and controlled an ever increasing proportion of total corporate wealth. Trade associations fixed price levels and the area of competition was reduced to that of product improvement and advertising. With the expansion of economic growth these practices did not mean the disappearance of the small manufacturer; in fact his numbers increased for he was protected through the associations from destructive price wars.

These associations were themselves encouraged by the Harding and Coolidge administrations through the policies of the secretary of Commerce, Herbert Hoover. Although from 1921 to 1925 the Federal Trade Commission, supported by the federal courts, campaigned against restrictive business practices as harmful to the interests of the consumer, with the appointment of a new chairman to the commission in 1925 the associations were thenceforth left free to maintain price levels. Progressives protested that government was becoming subservient to big business, but it is probable that without such self-imposed industrial regulation there would have developed a trend not towards oligopoly but in favour of monopoly.

The taxation policies of Andrew Mellon the secretary of the Treasury were more open to attack. Through tax cuts and refunds which largely favoured the wealthier classes of society Mellon sought to put into practice the Republican belief that tax relief in the higher brackets would provide the best stimulant to business activity by making more money available for investment purposes. He believed that such relief would provide a necessary incentive for business and industrial expansion, the beneficial effects of which would percolate down through the whole economic structure: employment would rise as more jobs became available and the cycle would be complete when the increase in consumer spending power itself began to have effect in a greater volume of production.

Republican tariff policies also provided ammunition for critics who charged the administration with conservative policies biased towards capital. The Fordney–McCumber Act of 1922 provided protection for domestic manufactures by raising duties to cover the difference between domestic and foreign production costs. For some products the new duties were prohibitive, and the virtual cessation of these imports was followed by a rise in the domestic price level. The act also sought to aid American agriculture, but as the farm belt's problem was over production and export difficulties because of high costs, rather than internal competition from overseas sources, the farmer realised little direct benefit from the new tariffs. Indeed as the domestic price of some consumer goods steadily rose, and as foreign countries also raised tariffs to protect their own agriculture, his relative position declined. However, as a piece of economic nationalism the Fordney–McCumber tariff was both a reflection of contemporary nativism and a precedent for further increases should the apparent prosperity of the 'new economic era' begin to collapse.

At first there were few outward signs of economic strain. The average American enjoyed a much higher standard of living than ever before. He possessed a motor car, radio, and innumerable household gadgets. He was better dressed, better fed, had more recreational facilities and travelled widely. The popularity of silk instead of cotton for women's clothing symbolised the greater affluence of the time. Unemployment declined from 11·9 per cent of the total labour force in 1921 to 3·2 per cent in 1929, the index of manufacturing production rose 28 points and the national income grew from $64,000 million to $87,800 million. However, the statistics also reveal less encouraging trends. Net farm incomes declined during the period and although the average earnings of industrial workers rose by 30 per cent they were still in 1929 $300 less than the annual $1,800 estimated to be the minimum wage necessary for a family to maintain a decent standard of living. Furthermore, over 60 per cent of all personal savings were made by the small proportion of families with incomes of over $10,000 a year, and the Republican administrations made no attempt to bring about a redistribution of incomes on a more equitable basis. Since industrial production was still rapidly increasing these factors went generally unnoticed. Despite widespread hardship among specific groups the people as a whole shared in the optimism of the administration, and were convinced that the good time for some would soon become better times for all.

AMERICAN SOCIETY IN THE 1920s

The inauguration in 1920 of prohibition, which Herbert Hoover called an 'experiment noble in motive and far-reaching in purpose', represented a victory for rural America, but the moment of victory marked the beginning of defeat. The city, instead of capitulating before the threat, immediately organised for battle, and even in rural America itself the long tradition of home distilling proved to be stronger than the impulse towards godliness; the expectation of increased profit outweighed the hope of salvation. It was clear from the beginning that the nation enjoyed a profound and general thirst which could not be slaked by water alone.

Laws which deny individual freedoms and conflict with the wishes of a significantly large minority of the population are usually only obeyed in proportion to the effectiveness of their enforcement. The Volstead Act, providing for enforcement of the eighteenth amendment, was no exception. The number of agents employed by the prohibition bureau varied between 1,500 and 2,300 men whose normal rate of pay was from $1,200 to $2,300 a year; their task was to prevent a population of 106,000,000 in 1920, and 123,000,000 in 1930, from drinking alcoholic beverages. As their numbers and rewards were meagre many succumbed to bribery, but the extent of their success in the enforcement of the law is surprising. The number of convictions for liquor offences rose to a height of 61,383 in 1932, of whom 44,678 received jail sentences; millions of gallons of wines, spirits and beer were seized each year, and thousands of illicit stills were destroyed. But it was like trying to sweep back the tide with a broom. Liquor was smuggled in from Canada at a rate conservatively estimated at forty million dollars worth a year; each year between fifty and sixty million gallons of industrial alcohol were diverted to bootleggers: illegal stills manufactured millions of gallons of moonshine and home brewing and the distillation of bath-tub gin became normal family occupations. Bootleggers supplied individual consumers, restaurants and hotels but found their chief market in the speakeasy, a substitute for the old fashioned saloon which rapidly became one of the most distinctive social institutions within the United States. In 1929 thirty-two thousand of them existed in New York City alone, more than double the number of saloons in 'the bad old days'.

Legal prohibition was clearly not effective. The law was flagrantly disregarded and the bootlegger became an open and almost respectable member of society. His indispensibility gave rise to a new class of millionaire gangster. Gangs had existed before prohibition, but the enormous profits from the trade gave them the means to control by bribery whole communities, including city governments, and to enforce compliance with their demands by terror and physical violence. Mobsters like Frank Costello and Dutch Schultz of New York, Chester LaMare of Detroit who is supposed to have grossed $215 million in 1928, and the legendary Al Capone of Chicago who ran a private army of between 700 and 1,000 gangsters and made between $60 and $100 million a year from sales of beer alone, not only presented a picture of an anarchistic society but contributed new anti-heroes to the mythology of American life. Profits were such that gang wars became a commonplace, and the St Valentine's Day Massacre in Chicago in 1929 when seven gangsters were machine-gunned to death by a rival organisation became as famous in its own context as the gunfight at the O.K. Corral in Tombstone Arizona in 1881.

The evils stemming from prohibition flourished in a society which was radically different from that which had existed before the war. One of the greatest changes was in the position of women. They had abandoned long skirts and donned overalls to work in war industries, and in the post-war years the rise of skirts to the knee seemed to symbolise their new freedom and social equality. Political equality was gained in 1920 when ratification of the nineteenth amendment gave women the vote. Moral standards had already become more permissive as a result of war conditions, and in the 1920s the flapper emerged as the characteristic type of young womanhood, given to 'petting', which often took place in the automobile, that 'house of prostitution on wheels'. Painted with cosmetics, her hair shingled, she smoked cigarettes, performed the shimmy, Charleston and black bottom, as well as more sedate steps, at the newly instituted tea dances; frequented the other new social invention the cocktail party; went freely to speakeasies and, when other sources of supply were unavailable, used the hip flask carried by her escort with a notable absence of restraint. Scott Fitzgerald delineated some of the customs of east coast urban America in his short stories and in the novels *This Side of Paradise* (1920). *The Beautiful and the Damned* (1922) and *The Great Gatsby* (1925). This sexual emancipation was exploited by the motion picture industry: Clara Bow the voluptuous 'It' girl became the idol of the crowds, and popular film successes carried such titles as *Married Flirts, Women Who Give,* and *The Queen of Sin.* The suggestive songs of the new popular culture reached an ever-widening audience through the radio, which from humble beginnings in 1920 had blanketed much of America by the middle of the decade.

These changes in the American way of life represented the triumph of the city and of the machine but rural America, although thrust on the defensive, still exerted tremendous influence and was determined not to be overwhelmed without a fight. The fundamentalist approach, with its simple solutions of complex human problems and its naïve self-righteousness was not content to rest upon the laurels of unenforceable prohibition. One of its most notorious counter-attacks on the new society was the anti-evolution movement. Believing that the teaching of biological evolution in schools and colleges would undermine the Christian basis of American democracy its leaders, among them the folk hero of rural America William Jennings Bryan, launched their crusade in 1921 and gained considerable support in the southern Bible Belt states and particularly in Tennessee. Academic freedom at the University of Tennessee was severely curtailed when six professors were dismissed for teaching the principles of scientific evolution, and in 1925 the state legislature passed a law banning the teaching in state schools and colleges of anything other than the Biblical account of creation. The law was challenged by a young high school biology teacher, John Scopes, and his case became one of the most celebrated trials in recent American history. Counsel for the state, representing tradition and prejudice, was William Jennings Bryan himself. The defence was supported, ironically enough, by Clarence Darrow, the famous criminal lawyer from Chicago. Darrow had, in the previous year, defended Leopold and Loeb when they were tried for the murder of Bobby Franks, a murder done out of curiosity to test the hypothesis of the perfect crime. The new America confronted the old. Scopes was found guilty and a fresh incentive was given to the anti-evolution movement. The spectacle of Bryan asserting, under pressure from Darrow, that the world was created in 4004 B.C. was so ridiculous though that liberal forces were strengthened at the moment of defeat. Groups such as the Bible Crusaders had some temporary successes in adjoining states but following the Scopes trial the traditionalists generally lost support throughout the south and the movement went into decline.

The year 1925 also marked the height of the influence of the Ku Klux Klan. This nativist, white, Protestant organisation grew rapidly in strength during the early 1920s; in 1925 it had an estimated membership of over five million and dominated the legislatures in at least five states. Part of its appeal was certainly its secret rites, hooded cowls and absurd mumbo jumbo. It met in Klonklaves at meeting places called Klaverns. Officers of the local dens were called Klaliffs, Klokards, Kludds, Kligrapps and Klabees; the national leader was dubbed the Imperial Wizard. The greeting Kigy demanded the reply Itsub, and flaming crosses were burned in the night. This native fascist movement relied on terror and violence to spread its influence throughout many parts of rural America, particularly the south but also in the mid-western and west coast states. Public reaction against the Klan was slow to mobilise but it began to be effective after the Grand Dragon of Indiana was indicted and convicted of murder in 1925. However, the bigoted racialism of the Klan was paralleled in the writings of Madison Grant and Lothrop Stoddard, who propounded theories of the superiority of the Nordic race, and in the uncritical nationalism of many patriotic organisations of the time. In the troubled post-war decade pressures towards what was called 'one hundred percent Americanism' came from many quarters as the Americans sought a satisfying national identity at a time of great cultural change.

New immigration restriction laws underlined the strength of the new pressure towards conformity. Despite the inscription on the base of the Statue of Liberty immigration had been regulated since the late eighteenth century when states on the eastern seaboard used their police power to exclude paupers, criminals and persons suffering from disease. Chinese labourers were denied entry by a federal act of 1882 and in 1907 President Roosevelt made a 'gentleman's agreement' with the Japanese government to discourage emigration from Japan. California and other western states attempted more positive discouragement with the passage of laws restricting ownership of property. The Immigration Act of 1917 established a literacy test for most immigrants whilst completely excluding those from Asia. A new act in 1921 imposed a quota on immigrants from permitted areas of 3 per cent of the number of each nationality residing in the United States in 1910. Designed particularly to restrict the new immigration from southern and south-eastern Europe the act failed to satisfy its critics and a final act in 1924 reduced the quota to 2 per cent and took as its base the census of 1890, thus deliberately favouring the nordic countries of Europe.

In this context the case of Sacco and Vanzetti assumed great significance. Originally tried and convicted in 1920 they were not executed until 1927. Liberal opinion at home and abroad rallied to their support in the belief that the trial had been prejudiced by dislike of their anarchistic political views and immigrant origins. Rigorous review of the verdict did not quieten these widespread doubts, and Vanzetti's last statement in which he nobly asserted his innocence helped to confirm the belief that they had been tried by bigots in a court of prejudice.

Fears that the United States had departed from its historic tradition of tolerance were associated in the minds of many liberals and intellectuals with the conviction that it had become a gross, business dominated society in which immediate material gain was cultivated to the exclusion of other and finer assets. In the preface to his trilogy *U.S.A.* (1937) a fictional account of America since the war, John Dos Passos wrote that:

U.S.A. is the slice of a continent. U.S.A. is a group of holding companies, some aggregations of trade unions, a set of laws bound in calf, a radio network, a chain of moving picture theatres, a column of stock quotations rubbed out and written in by a Western Union boy on a blackboard, a public library full of old newspapers and dogeared history books with protests scrawled on the margin in pencil. U.S.A. is the world's greatest rivervalley fringed with mountains and hills, U.S.A. is a lot of men buried in their uniforms in Arlington Cemetery. U.S.A. is the letters at the end of an address when you are away from home. But mostly U.S.A. is the speech of the people.

This contrasted sadly with the idealism of earlier years. Sinclair Lewis wrote ironically at the beginning of *Main Street* (1920):

This is America...Main Street is the climax of civilisation. That this Ford car might stand in front of the Bon Ton Store, Hannibal invaded Rome and Erasmus wrote in Oxford cloisters. What Ole Jensen the grocer says to Ezra Stowbody the banker is the new law for London, Prague, and the unprofitable isles of the sea; whatsoever Ezra does not know and sanction, that thing is heresy, worthless for knowing and wicked to consider.

Lewis satirised what H. L. Mencken, who together with George Jean Nathan founded the *America Mercury* in 1924, called the 'Boobus Americanus': the conformist, middle-class, anti-intellectual average citizen of the age of 'normalcy'. Disillusionment with society drove many writers, 'the lost generation' Gertrude Stein called them, into temporary self-imposed exile in Europe. They floated from country to country following the fluctuations of international exchange in order to gain the greatest benefit from their often meagre dollar resources, but always returned to Paris where they built a community life of their own on the left bank, centred around Sylvia Beach's bookshop '*Shakespeare and Company*' in the Rue de l'Odeon. There they perfected their craft and in novels like Hemingway's *The Sun also Rises* (1926) wistfully portrayed their search for personal identity and for a code of values independent of those which they believed pervaded their native land.

What they in fact rejected in their indulgent enjoyment of living was the Puritan ethic. The Puritan emphasis on thrift, acquisition and conformity which Hamlin Garland, Sherwood Anderson, Lewis, and countless others saw as the stultifying characteristic of rural America had been projected into the business-dominated urban society of the twentieth century. The same superficial morality and public orthodoxy prevailed in the new order as in the old. *The Seven Arts*, a review which had a short but significant life from 1916 to 1917, analysed the discontent of writers and intellectuals in the United States in terms of the prevalence of restrictive social, moral and artistic customs arising from the predominance of the business ethic; and the business ethic was blamed on the Puritan tradition. The theme was not new, and it was frequently reiterated during the post-war years. Socially the reaction of the lost generation to contemporary America was not so very different from that of the average citizen who adorned the speakeasies. Each was protesting against traditional social norms, but the expatriate writer persuaded himself that his own indulgence in Europe was somehow more elevated because it took place in a cultural context thought to be superior to that of New York, despite the existence of Greenwich Village, and infinitely more civilised than that which existed elsewhere in America. In part this represented a continuation of the mystique felt by Henry James a generation earlier that in some way Europe had reached a cultural level unattainable in the United States. Shadows were often confused with substance, but belief that in fact the business of America was business, and rejection of the values of the business community, dominated the intellectual life of the decade.

3

INTERNATIONALISM *V.* ISOLATIONISM

Wilson's crusade in Europe finally came to an end when the United States senate failed to ratify the Treaty of Versailles. As the covenant of the League of Nations was incorporated in the treaty rejection of the treaty meant rejection of the League. This has given rise to a belief that when confronted with a choice between internationalism and isolationism the country chose the latter policy; but the choice was not as simple as this, nor were the alternatives so clear. Issues of foreign policy in the 1920s and 1930s were mixed with emotional and political questions just as much as they had been during the debates over the Versailles Treaty, When considering the -isms, the conflicting schools of interpretation of American diplomacy, the problem for the student is largely one of definition.

Internationalism can best be defined as belief that the national interest can realistically be served only by a policy of active international co-operation, involving if necessary the joining of multilateral pacts and alliances. One of the internationalist's basic tenets in the 1920s was American membership of the League. In the 1930s the League was not a real issue, except among an extremist fringe, and internationalists came to focus their attention more particularly upon security through individual association with other democratic nations. Continuity within the period lies in the general conviction that the United States could not maintain its security in isolation from that of other states. Isolationism, however, is a more difficult term. It has been identified with opposition to League membership, and then projected forward to embrace all anti-internationalists of the inter-war period. Although some consistent attitudes can be observed, a complete continuity has here been falsely assumed. The 'isolationists' of the 1920s were traditionalists who wished to maintain the historic American policy of non-involvement in political affairs outside the western hemisphere, and who feared the dangers of entangling alliances. The true isolationists are those people in the 1930s who were prepared to *abandon* major parts of America's traditional foreign policy in order to insulate the country from foreign war, which was believed to be the ultimate and untouchable evil. They wished to cut off all contact with belligerent states, even at the expense of traditional neutral rights. In this sense isolationism is a positive policy, involving a retraction of over-seas trade and communication and an abandonment of traditional insistence on freedom of the seas. As such it is inextricably inter-woven with the neutrality controversy of the 1930s and with popular analysis of the factors that had led to intervention in the First World War. This mood, though present, was neither strongly developed nor widely held in the earlier decade. The issues then were more confused and hazy.

In the 1920s debate over the League of Nations was largely couched in traditional terms. Supporters of the League believed that the relative geographical and political isolation enjoyed by the United States in the nineteenth century had gone, and that a new policy had to be adopted to meet changed world circum-stances. In other words they believed that the traditional environ-ment in which foreign policy had been formulated had been so transformed that a new policy had to be evolved to meet changed conditions. In the presidential election of 1920 both James M. Cox, the Democratic presidential candidate, and his running mate Franklin D. Roosevelt were ardent Wilsonians who made their campaign an appeal for a popular mandate to ratify the treaty with the covenant. They are identifiable therefore as internationa-lists, seeking to draw the United States into active participation in world politics. Their Republican opponents significantly straddled the issue. Warren Harding sometimes favoured American participation in 'an association of nations'; at others he repudiated the League and similar organisations. The implica-tions of this position are that the Republican party leaders recognised the extent to which the conventions of American foreign policy had been eroded by the war, and so did not wish to brand themselves too deeply with the traditionalist label; but that at the same time they wished to take every possible political advantage of anti-Wilsonian sentiments. It would be misleading to consider the Republican victory in 1920 as an absolute repudia-tion of the internationalists elements of Wilsonianism, and it is no paradox to argue that a rejection of the party of Wilson did not at the same time indicate total rejection of his foreign policy. As suggested in chapter 2 the country was tired of war, and the Democratic party was associated with the war. It was tired of Wilson's uncompromising morality in domestic politics. It was ready for 'normalcy': for a relaxation of strain and moral precept. The party of 'normalcy' won, but the common picture of the election of lying between Wilsonian Democrats on the one hand and isolationist Republicans on the other is not convincing. The new policy of internationalism had suffered a setback but it was not as yet opposed by an ardent isolationist group.

EUROPEAN POLICY 1921–1929

When the new president took office in March 1921 he was faced with the problem of German-American relations. Congress had tried in May 1920 to end by joint resolution the legal state of war between the two countries but Wilson, under the continuing delusion that the Senate would eventually accept the Treaty of Versailles, vetoed it. The war was officially ended when Harding approved a similar bill in July 1921, and treaties of peace with Germany, Austria and Hungary were ratified in August. However, these formal moves did not mean a greater measure of involvement in Europe. The security treaty which Clemenceau had hoped to obtain as one of the fruits of victory and as a positive testimony of British–American concern with the stability of Europe had already been rejected by both governments. Preoccupied with domestic reconstruction they did not wish to be directly associated with French fears of a resurgent and revengeful Germany, and unlike the French seemed to have no doubts of the pacific and democratic nature of the new German Republic.

Following the partial eclipse of internationalism in 1920 the United States reverted to its pre-war aloofness towards Europe. When French and Belgian troops occupied the Ruhr in January 1923, following the German default on reparations payments, Washington expressed concern; but the only positive move made by the administration was the withdrawal of American forces from the Rhineland army of occupation and the recall of the unofficial American observer on the Inter-Allied High Commission. The proposed Geneva Protocol of 1925 was viewed with disfavour, and the secretary of State indicated that the American government was neither interested in nor could be associated with the Locarno treaties, by which France sought guarantees for her eastern frontier and the creation of a *cordon sanitaire* among the new states of eastern Europe which had been created out of the Austro-Hungarian empire. The experiences of the immediate post-war world seemed to have strengthened the traditional American belief that the peace of Europe was a matter for the European instead of encouraging a new faith in the wisdom and necessity of international co-operation.

Europe entered the American consciousness in the middle 1920s largely as a haven for expatriate writers and as an area of economic and financial investment. It was not thought to demand attention for reasons of national and international security and policy continued to rest upon the traditional opposition to entangling alliances. This was demonstrated by the interesting and illuminating series of events that culminated in the drawing up of the Pact of Paris in 1928, otherwise called the Kellogg–Briand Pact after Coolidge's secretary of State Frank B. Kellogg and the French foreign minister Aristide Briand.

Late in 1927 Briand proposed to Kellogg that their two countries conclude a treaty outlawing war between themselves. In the context of the French search for security Briand's approach must be seen not only as an attempt to gain an assurance that the United States would not unilaterally attack her but, more importantly, as a guarantee that America would not join a coalition of powers against her. The proposal was ignored in Washington until mounting pressure from public opinion, organised by the proponents of universal peace and supporters of the movement for the outlawing of war, dictated a response. Kellogg met the situation by suggesting that the pact be made universal and multilateral. In this way he sought both to avoid the appearance of a Franco-American *entente* and to satisfy the peace movement at home. Briand saw no alternative, if he were to secure the compliance of the United States, to accepting the new plan. Consequently, a general treaty was drawn up outlawing war as an instrument of national policy.

As an effective instrument of international diplomacy its value was slight. It did not contain provisions for sanctions against signatory states which resorted to war, and reservations were written into the pact excluding specific areas where special interests and previous treaty commitments clashed with the general terms of the agreement. Moreover, the outlawing of war was qualified by clauses permitting recourse to war in self-defence. These exceptions substantially limited the application of the pact. The 'legalisation' of defensive war was of especial importance, for the determination and definition of such was specifically reserved to the individual signatory states. This left the way open for aggressor nations to claim the necessity of belligerent action in order to forestall imminent attack. But despite its weaknesses, and although later opinion came to believe that the Paris Pact invoked a dangerous illusion of security, it represented at the time of its conclusion an assertion of considerable moral impact. Many people still clung to the belief that the world war had been 'a war to end war'. Experiences on the western front and the promiscuous sinking of unarmed shipping on the high seas had aroused an emotional revulsion against war which found expression in the Paris Peace Pact, and the treaty helped to mobilise the conscience of people throughout the world. Moreover, it was not so dangerous a threat to national security as its critics proclaimed. The reservations which limited its own practical application also effectively minimised any adverse consequences which it might otherwise have had on the pre-existing structure of treaties and alliances. It in no way weakened the Locarno agreements, nor the League of Nations; and the moral force which it embraced might have been deployed in favour of the pacific settlement of disputes. The failure of the League to meet the threats to international stability which shortly overtook it cannot be laid at the door of the framers of the Kellogg–Briand Pact. Its causes lay elsewhere, in the unpreparedness of member governments to look beyond their own immediate national interests, and in their failure to educate their peoples to a mature understanding of the responsibilities incurred under the League covenant. In the United States, however, ratification of the pact did encourage the belief that this much having been achieved nothing more substantial was necessary to protect vital interests or to help maintain the normally precarious balance of international peace.

The strength of traditional American suspicions of foreign entanglements which the opponents of Wilson and of the League had been able to play upon in the senate debates of 1919–20 found expression later in the 1920s with reference to the Permanent Court of International Justice at the Hague. The Hague conferences of 1899 and 1907 had led to the establishment of a Court of Arbitration and, building upon this foundation, the League set up the Permanent Court of International Justice in 1920. Membership of this Court, popularly called the World Court, was open to all nations and not just to those states which had ratified the League Covenant.

The Protocols of Adherence to the Court were sent to the United States in 1921. For two years nothing was done, but in 1923 they were sent to the Senate. Hearings were held by the Committee on Foreign Relations, which in 1926 accepted ratification in principle but subject to five amendments. These varied in content but all had a similar aim: to preserve the right of independent action by the United States and to keep the national interest unimpaired. Of these five reservations the most important was the fifth, which denied the Court jurisdiction over issues in which the United States had or claimed an interest, except when the United States gave it specific authority to act.

Acceptance of such a reservation by the member-states of the Court would have imposed a serious limitation on its jurisdiction, and have established a precedent which might closely manacle its future effectiveness. Unilateral denials of jurisdiction might leave no issues of substance within the sphere of authority of the tribunal. At a conference of member-states in Geneva in the autumn of 1926 a series of compromises were worked out which sought to meet the fears of the senate without accepting the exact wording and meaning of the Fifth Reservation. These did not, however, satisfy Congress and, despite an attempt by former secretary of State Elihu Root in 1929 to draw up a formula acceptable to both sides, President Coolidge and President Hoover successively failed to secure ratification of the Protocols.

American policy towards Europe in the 1920s shows the extent to which the United States was still living in an illusion of strength through isolation. Although world conditions had changed as technological and mechanical progress and invention shortened distances and revolutionised the art of war, geographical separateness was still regarded as a guarantee of security. This belief was strengthened by the changes that the Great War had brought about in the balance of power. With Germany defeated, Russia crippled by revolution, and Great Britain and France weakened by the strains of war the might of the United States was nowhere seriously challenged nor its security threatened. Economic interdependence was growing during the post-war decade as world trade expanded, and the American share of this trade increased, but growing economic and financial ties with Europe and the rest of the world did not give rise to a change in basic attitudes. Traditional American diplomacy accompanied by the erection of a defensive wall around the western hemisphere could possibly have achieved military security for the United States but only at the cost of economic dislocation which the nation could ill afford. However, the retention of traditional attitudes towards entanglement in Europe and the continued but misplaced faith in isolation do not indicate that the United States was isolationist. As yet it was the strength of traditionalism, enhanced by an emotional revulsion against war and a sense of disillusionment with Europe, where the ideals for which they had fought seemed to have been betrayed, that inhibited acceptance of a new international role.

THE WASHINGTON TREATIES

Towards the Far East as towards Europe American policy was dictated by a determination to avoid commitment. In this area also the recent past was rejected and Theodore Roosevelt's preoccupation with the necessity of maintaining a balance of power in the western Pacific forgotten. In a series of treaties signed in Washington early in 1922 the United States effectively abdicated power to maintain its position in the Philippines.

The Washington Conference of 1921–2 was convened by the Harding administration in response to a number of very different pressures. At the end of the war there was considerable and increasingly vocal demand in the United States for a reduction of the burden of expenditure on arms. This largely economic agitation became associated with the strong popular demand for disarmament for moral and emotional reasons. In 1921 Senator William A. Borah of Idaho introduced into the Senate a resolution advocating talks with Great Britain and Japan aimed at the limitation of naval construction. It was thought that if this could be achieved a beginning would have been made towards substantial disarmament, with consequent savings in governmental expenditure and also the establishment of a degree of stability in the Pacific. As it happened this move coincided with a desire on the part of Great Britain for an *entente* with the United States. The Anglo-Japanese alliance of 1902 was due for renewal, and it was feared that in the light of tensions between the United States and Japan over Shantung, commercial rights in China, and the recent restrictive immigration legislation (see chapter 2) there might be adverse consequences for Britian should the alliance be renewed. Prominent in the minds of British statesmen was the undefended frontier between Canada and the United States which made the prospect of conflict between the two nations unthinkable. Rather than renewal of the alliance a wider pact would clearly be advantageous for all countries concerned. The idea of a conference was therefore widened to include all nations with interests in the western Pacific and political issues as well as matters concerned with the limitation of armaments were included on the agenda.

Representatives of nine powers assembled in Washington in November 1921. Out of their meetings came three interrelated treaties of considerable importance for the future of the Pacific region. As a direct substitute for the Anglo-Japanese Alliance a Four Power Treaty was adopted by the United States, Great Britain, France and Japan by which they agreed to respect each other's possessions in that area and to consult with each other should these rights be threatened. China was a problem as a result of the ineffectiveness of the republican government and the continuing problem of concessionary rights enjoyed by many European powers. A solution was sought by the adoption of a Nine Power Treaty between China, the United States, Great Britain, France, Italy, Japan, Belgium, the Netherlands, and Portugal. They agreed to respect the territorial and administrative integrity of China and to uphold the principles of the Open Door. This treaty extended the unilateral declaration issued by secretary of State William Jennings Bryan in 1915 after Japan's presentation of Twenty-One Demands to the Chinese government claiming rights in China which would have amounted to the establishment of a protectorate over the country. The Four Power and the Nine Power Treaties represented an attempt to prevent serious future political differences in the western Pacific.

The naval armament problem and the prospect of a naval arms race was directly confronted by secretary of State Charles Evans Hughes at the first plenary session of the conference. He proposed an immediate beginning of disarmament by acceptance of a ten-year holiday in the building of capital ships and stablisation of the number of battleships possessed by the United States, Great Britain and Japan in the ratio of 5:5:3 with an agreed maximum total tonnage. The plan involved scrapping some ships already built and many which were under construction. One observer commented that the plan involved the destruction of more shipping 'than all the admirals of the world have sunk in a cycle of centuries'. This dramatic gesture caught public opinion, and it was eventually embodied in a Five Power Treaty between the United States, Great Britain, Japan, France and Italy, establishing ratios of $5:5:3:1·75:1·75$, or a tonnage of capital ships for Britain and America of 525,000, with 315,000 for Japan and 172,000 for France and Italy. The treaty also contained a self-denying ordinance by the western powers that they would not fortify their Pacific bases beyond existing limits.

Two important points need to be emphasised about the three treaties which stemmed from the Washington Conference. The first is that, significantly, they contained no provisions for sanctions against breach of faith. The treaties contained the germs of a security system without its substance. Secondly, although they were designed to stabilise the situation in the Pacific and to act as a restraint upon Japan, which was known to have expansionist tendencies, the practical result of the treaties was to give Japan a preponderant position in the western Pacific. In naval terms, although Japan accepted a lower ratio than either Britain or America, the concentration of her fleets when compared with the world-wide dispersal of the other navies gave her a position of immense superiority in home waters. Furthermore, the agreement by Great Britain and the United States not to fortify their island bases in the Pacific beyond existing limits crippled still further their strategic position. Without adequate fortified naval stations and supply bases in the Far East the western fleets would be unable to operate effectively in that area against a strong opponent.

Although superficially therefore the summoning of the Washington conference and the conclusion of the treaties that came out of it have an appearance of positive action and of commitment to international co-operation by the United States, there had in reality been no departure from the traditional policy of non-entanglement. A somewhat naïve idealism had committed the country morally to a course of action for which there were no legal sanctions and which it would be almost impossible to support with the necessary force should need arise. Against this Britain had relieved herself of an embarrassing alliance, and the Japanese empire had received tacit recognition of a superior position in the western Pacific. Already under the Harding Administration the chief characteristic of American policy throughout the 1920s was taking shape: a commitment in principle to internationalism, with at the same time a retention in practical terms of established policies of non-involvement and non-intervention. However, in the winter of 1921–2 the testing of principle was not yet demanded. It was not to come until the early 1930s when Japan invaded Manchuria and launched a positive expansionist policy on the Asian continent in flagrant defiance of the treaty structure.

ABANDONMENT OF 'THE BIG STICK' IN LATIN AMERICA

In relations with the Latin American Republics, however, the hestitant moves towards a new policy of international co-operation found stronger expression. During the nineteenth century American policy in the western hemisphere had been based upon the Monroe Doctrine of 1823. British acquiescence in this unilateral statement by President Monroe had preserved Latin America from political interference by European powers, except for two instances during the American Civil War. In 1861 Spain had attempted to regain control of Santo Domingo and the French tried to install Maximilian of Austria as emperor of Mexico. With the collapse of this imperial scheme in 1867 political interference from Europe was largely restricted to the remaining European colonies on the mainland and in the Caribbean. Economic imperialism through investment and the development of natural resources was rampant in Latin America throughout the nineteenth century but political intervention remained at a minimum. In the first decade of the twentieth century the Roose-velt Corollary to the Monroe Doctrine represented a change in American policy. From being a passive onlooker the United States undertook a role of active intervention in the domestic affairs of the South American Republics in order to preserve peace and stability and to expand American economic interests. Even Woodrow Wilson actively intervened in Mexican affairs to pro-tect American investments. However, Elihu Root, secretary of State in Roosevelt's second administration, had tried to evolve a policy of friendly co-operation between the republics of North and South America whilst at the same time maintaining American predominance.

This policy was revived by Harding's secretary of State Charles Evans Hughes. He stated in an address of December 1922 that:

The Government of the United States has no ambition to gratify at your expense, no policy which runs counter to your national aspirations, and no purposes save to promote the interests of peace and to assist you, in such manner as you may welcome, to solve your problems to your own proper advantage. The interest of the United States is found in the peace of this Hemisphere and in the conservation of your interests.

Hughes sought to expand the Monroe Doctrine into a programme for mutual advantage and defence which would remove the suspicion of American aims and aspirations that generally prevailed south of the border. Setbacks occurred under Hughes's successor Frank B. Kellogg and there appeared to be a reversion to the older policy when the marines were sent into Nicaragua in 1927. But economic troubles with Mexico were peacefully resolved through the skilful diplomacy of the American ambassador Dwight Morrow and in general the 'big stick' diplomacy of Theodore Roosevelt was on the wane. The new trend was accentuated during the presidency of Herbert Hoover. After his election but before the inauguration, Hoover went on a tour of Latin America during the course of which he repudiated the use of force to maintain economic interests and stated that 'we must clothe faith and idealism with action'. A memorandum drawn up by a State Department official J. Reuben Clark in 1928 and published in 1930 emphasised the repudiation of Roosevelt's policy:

So far as Latin America is concerned, the Doctrine is now, and always has been, not an instrument of violence and oppression, but an unbought, freely bestowed, and wholly effective guaranty of their freedom, independence, and territorial integrity against the imperialistic designs of Europe.

Although Clark's reference to past American attitudes might have raised a cynical smile in Latin America, the clear statement of present policy and future intent was an auspicious sign for the future course of United States relations with the countries to the south. When the marines were finally withdrawn from Haiti in 1932, together with the last of the troops from Nicaragua, the 'good neighbor' policy seemed to be already under way. This policy did not spring unheralded from the mind of Franklin D. Roosevelt and his advisers in 1933. It had its origins in the Republican administrations of the 1920s. However, it was Roosevelt who symbolised the new approach with a slogan that caught men's imagination. In his inaugural address of 4 March 1933 the new president stressed that in the field of foreign relations the United States would follow the policy of 'the good neighbor'. At the Inter-American Conferences held at Montevideo (1933), Buenos

Aires (1936) and Lima (1938) it was evident that the United States was intent on winning the confidence of the southern republics. Stress was laid on co-operation for mutual aid and defence and the United States relied on explanation and persuasion rather than on compulsion. The new American insistence on the equality of the states of the western hemisphere could not of course conceal their basic inequality of development, nor the predominant power of the United States, but at the same time the proceedings bear witness to the sincere desire of the administration to place relations on a sound basis of good faith and mutual respect.

MANCHURIA

On the world scale the greatest test of American policy since the end of the world war came when the Japanese invaded Manchuria in 1931. This province, although technically under the suzerainty of China, had long been a bone of contention between the Japanese and the Russians, both of whom had concessionary economic rights and privileges in the area. For Japan, whose population had almost doubled since 1870, Manchuria represented a valuable source of primary products, a market for industrial goods, and an increasingly important area for the resettlement of surplus population. Full control of Manchuria would greatly increase Japan's competitiveness in increasingly competitive world markets. For some years an army had been based in Manchuria to protect the Japanese economic investment and to maintain a strategic hold over the region. This army became increasingly restive in the late 1920s as the Chinese began to reassert claims to full possession of the region. Civilian control from Tokyo over the Kwantung army in Manchuria was weakened following the assassination of Premier Hamaguchi in April 1931, and the generals began to claim the right to decide the future of the Japanese foothold in East Asia. After an explosion near Mukden on the South Manchuria Railroad on 18 September 1931, a confused situation developed between the Japanese and the Chinese authorities which was used as a pretext for full-scale war for control of Manchuria, although war was not officially declared by either side.

This Manchuria 'incident' tested the good faith of the signatory powers of the Nine Power Treaty of 1922. In that treaty they had declared their support of the territorial and administrative integrity of China. Despite the concessionary rights of foreign powers, Manchuria was technically a part of China. Both Japan and China were, moreover, signatories of the treaty. The events of 1931 and the war which followed were to display whether the treaty was merely a form of words without substance, or an agreement which would be regarded as binding. President Hoover and his secretary of State Henry L. Stimson appear to have differed in their response to the situation. Hoover consistently opposed intervention on behalf of China, but Secretary Stimson seems to have wavered between verbal condemnation of Japan and a mild sanctions policy. Sanctions, however, met with opposition not only from the president but also from the British foreign secretary Sir John Simon. The League showed a similar wariness, and appointed an investigating commission under Lord Lytton which did not issue its report until October 1932. By then the Japanese had consolidated their position in Manchuria and had declared the province reconstituted as Manchukuo, an independent state but associated with Japan. By this time too Stimson had promulgated the doctrine which, although it originated in the mind of the president himself, has come to bear his name. The Stimson Doctrine stated that the United States would not recognise the fruits of aggression, nor any territorial changes which were the result of resort to armed force. It was a unilateral statement, later adopted by the League Assembly, which established the moral position of the United States but was completely ineffective in any real sense. The Japanese smiled and gobbled up their gains.

The Manchurian crisis illuminated many of the weaknesses of inter-war diplomacy. The American unwillingness to undertake positive commitments overseas which might, in the last resort, involve the use of armed force was matched by a similar disinclination on the part of other nations whose traditional foreign policies had been very different from those of the United States. Both the United States and the European powers had trading and strategic interests in the Far East which were implicitly threatened by Japanese expansion. Yet none of the powers were prepared to enforce the principles which they had themselves erected to preserve the *status quo*. Moreover, this paralysis among the nations did not reflect the decline of national assertiveness in favour of international co-operation through the League of Nations. Although the United States was not a member, Britain and France were two of the dominant powers in the League organisation. They used their influence in Geneva to check a move towards sanctions which might have had a restraining influence on Japan. If isolationism means unilateralism, and furthermore unilateral rejection of positive action in the defence of asserted principles of policy, then not only was the United States isolationist in 1931; so was Britain; so was France; and because they were so inclined the smaller League powers were forced to follow suit. The precedent was established in 1931 that military aggression by an expansionist power would be met with words and not with countervailing force. It is unlikely that this lesson was lost upon Germany and Italy in the mid 1930s. In a very real sense therefore the world was on the slope that led finally to the Second World War.

THE CHIMERA OF DISARMAMENT AND SECURITY

The gulf between principle and practice was not confined to the question of the enforcement of international agreements. Parochial nationalism, and preoccupation with short-term national interests rather than with long-term international security also inhibited progress towards disarmament. Although the restrictions on battleship tonnage established at the Washington Conference were extended by the London Naval Conference of 1930 to other types of vessels, notably cruisers, the dominant French fear of a revived Germany prevented international agreement where land forces were concerned. The French were only prepared to accept a reduction of their land forces if they received as a *quid pro quo* a security treaty with Britain along the lines of the proposed treaties of 1921. Such a treaty, involving the commitment of British forces to the continent of Europe, the British government was not prepared to make. British aversion to involvement on the continent and the understandable French passion for security came into direct conflict at the League disarmament conference at Geneva in 1933. General obeisance to the principle of disarmament was shattered by the irreconcilability of these two positions. For the United States President Hoover had repeatedly emphasised the political impossibility of an American commitment to aid France should the peace of Europe be threatened by Germany and so no progress was made.

At Geneva the nations waited for evidence of what the policy of the new president, Franklin D. Roosevelt, would be. Roosevelt's chief representative at Geneva, Norman H. Davis, broke the suspense on 22 May 1933. In a major speech he put forward on behalf of the administration the concept of parallel action: a policy whereby, should other states decide on collective measures against an aggressor, the United States would 'refrain from any action tending to defeat the collective efforts which these States may thus make to restore peace'. Two months before Roosevelt's inauguration, Adolf Hitler had come to power in Germany, and the president had no illusions about the nature of the new régime. This conditional offer put forward by Davis, moderate though it was, represented a revolution in American policy. It was designed to remove any doubts possessed by the European democratic nations about American policy in the event of conflict. Although the concept of parallel action short of military intervention was designed to rebut the politically dangerous charge that the traditional American policy of non-entanglement had been compromised, in effect it implicitly rejected the historic patterns of foreign policy by associating the United States with the undefined action of foreign powers in conditional circumstances. The idea did not come to fruition, for European suspicions of America's willingness to act were not removed by Davis's statement to the conference. The British continued to refuse a treaty of mutual guarantee with France, and the French therefore insisted on the impossibility of disarmament without specific pledges of assistance. After faltering through 1933 and the spring of 1934, the conference went into what became permanent adjournment in the autumn of 1934. Thereafter the prospect of achieving a substantial measure of disarmament became illusory. Although the London Naval Conference of 1930 had extended ratios of naval tonnage to various categories not covered by the Washington Conference, the subsequent meeting in London in 1935 failed to reach any agreement.

INTERNATIONAL ECONOMIC PROBLEMS

Apart from questions of disarmament the Roosevelt administration inherited in 1933 other problems of international importance which required immediate attention. Prominent among these was the World Economic Conference which was due to meet in London in May. In the summer of 1932 a group of economic experts had recommended that such a conference be called to work out concerted measures to relieve the depression which was by then affecting most nations of the world.

World economic difficulties were in many ways the result of the world war. The very fact of war had prevented many normal economic adjustments from being made and concentration upon war production had led to imbalance in the domestic economies of many countries as well as in their export trade. In the United States this was true of both the industrial and the agricultural sectors. In the mid west, for example, agricultural production had risen to ever-increasing heights to satisfy European demand, European production having been considerably dislocated by the patterns of war, and by the end of the war tremendous surpluses of primary products had accumulated. American industry was also stimulated to greater expansion than normal conditions would have allowed by the demands of the armed forces and the volume of Allied export orders. In 1919 the country was therefore faced not just with the problem of industrial reorganisation for peacetime production, but with surplus productive capacity. Great though these problems were for the American government they were multiplied by the fact that the position of the United States in the international market had radically changed. Whereas in 1914 it had been a debtor country in terms of international trade and international exchange, by 1918 it had become a creditor nation. Great amounts of gold and foreign exchange had flowed into the country during the war as the Allied powers paid for their war purchases. When the Allies had spent their reserves the United States extended billions of dollars in loans. The immediate post-war problem was therefore how the debtor countries were to pay their debts: they could only pay if they could earn dollars or other foreign exchange which was convertible into dollars.

Solution of this problem was made more difficult by the growth of economic nationalism in the 1920s. One of the results of the peace settlement had been the fragmentation of the large trading areas of central Europe by the establishment of the 'succession' states. These states sought to preserve their newly won political independence by the creation of economic independence. To do this they pursued autarkic economic and financial policies. The United States, faced with large agricultural and industrial surpluses, followed the same policy and the Fordney–McCumber tariff of 1922 raised a tariff wall around the United States. Although this had the short-term effect of protecting home production, it had the important corollary that foreign nations seeking to trade with the United States were placed at a competitive disadvantage. They were therefore unable to earn dollars with which to pay their debts. The imbalance of the world economy continued.

The situation was for some years masked by the prevalence of large-scale American loans to Europe and other areas. The Dawes and Young Plans of 1924 and 1929 to scale down reparations and stabilise the German currency were largely financed by American capital. By this means debtor countries were enabled to pay some of the interest on old loans with the dollars acquired through new loans. Much of this money was, however, short-term loan, called 'hot money', Hot money is always a potential threat to the stability of the international financial structure because it is likely to be recalled if substantially better investment opportunities appear at home. With the boom on the New York Stock Exchange in the middle and late 1920s this happened. The withdrawal of many of the short-term loans to Europe grievously weakened the European economy. In the Hawley–Smoot tariff of 1930 the United States raised its tariff barriers even higher, so increasing the difficulties of foreign exporters in trading with the American market. Following the failure of the Credit Anstalt Bank in Vienna in 1931 the insecurity of the European economic structure finally took shape in a profound depression which, together with the economic collapse in America itself, brought about a world wide economic crisis.

High tariffs were a normal reaction of states in economic distress, and were not confined to the United States. The British Empire concluded in 1932 the Ottawa Agreements which consolidated an imperial trading bloc protected from outside penetration by a tariff wall. However, it was clear that the earlier American barriers to free trade had done nothing to help solution of the economic problems consequent upon the world war and in 1932 economic thinking began to turn seriously towards the idea that lower rather than higher tariffs might stimulate domestic economic recovery by promoting a greater measure of international trade. This belief formed a part of the climate of opinion in which the London Economic Conference met in 1933. The timing seemed auspicious, for Roosevelt's secretary of State, Cordell Hull, was known to be a vigorous free trader who had been committed throughout his public career to lowering impediments to world trade and commerce. But tariffs were not the only item on the agenda at London. One effect of the depression had been to drive a number of countries including Britain and later the United States, off the gold standard. France alone of the major European nations remained on gold. Violent fluctuations in international exchange rates resulted from the abandonment of gold and the question of the stabilisation of currencies was to be discussed at London.

The London Economic Conference is often taken to be a test of the foreign policy attitudes of President Franklin Roosevelt. It has been argued that the president's commitment to either internationalism or isolationism can be detected by an examination of the proceedings of the conference, and the conclusion often drawn is that by his actions Roosevelt displayed the extent to which he had departed from the internationalism of his earlier career. It is often stated that Roosevelt destroyed the conference with the 'bombshell' message of 1 July 1933 in which he rejected stabilisation of currencies in order to leave himself free to manipulate the dollar in the domestic market. It is true that Roosevelt believed that the best way to cure the depression in the United States was to raise the level of domestic prices, and that he sought to do this partly by manipulating the dollar. It is undeniable that on 1 July 1933 he rejected stabilisation. But at two earlier stages in the London Conference he had rejected the idea of stabilisation. He was suspicious of the apparent attempt by European delegations to drive him into a stabilisation agreement which seemed merely a device to keep France on the gold standard, and he was not prepared to accept stabilisation considered in isolation from the other items on the agenda. He insisted that he favoured international co-operation on tariffs and quotas, and also on foreign exchange, but that the time was not ripe for a general stabilisation of currencies on the lines proposed in London. He believed that in order to achieve a stable international economic order a start had to be made at the domestic level, and that in order to achieve domestic recovery he needed freedom to devalue the dollar if such a step proved desirable. Roosevelt's economic thinking was not very sophisticated, but in the context of his total policy rejection of the tentative stabilisation agreement cannot be taken as conclusive proof that he had abandoned his former ideals. After the immediate domestic emergency had been faced the Reciprocal Trade Agreements Act of 1934 reversed the high tariff trend and a limited stabilisation agreement was concluded in 1936.

ROOSEVELT CONFRONTS THE ISOLATIONISTS

Roosevelt had been a committed internationalist since 1920 when he fought for election to the vice-presidency on a League of Nations ticket. His belief in the necessity of international co-operation was sustained during the 1920s, although he moved away from the assumption that the League of Nations was the best instrument for achieving world peace. In February 1932, as part of his campaign to obtain the Democratic party presidential nomination, he finally repudiated his former belief that the United States should ratify the covenant and become a member-state of the League. He retained, however, a passionate conviction that the United States should be brought into the world community and should play a positive role in international policy. He wrote to a friend:

Ideals do not change, but methods do change with every generation and world circumstances. Here is the difference between me and some of my faint-hearted friends: I am looking for the best modern vehicle to reach the goal of an ideal while they insist on a vehicle which was brand new and in good running order twelve years ago. Think this over! And for heaven's sake have a little faith.

As a matter of political reality he could not be prepared to com-promise American freedom of action by joining an overseas alliance system, and he was not sure of the ways in which the influence of the United States could be brought to bear on a unilateral basis, but throughout the 1930s he sought for a formula which would make possible the fulfilment of his aim.

The concept of parallel action short of the use of armed force that Davis placed before the Geneva Disarmament Conference was one possibility. Related to it was the president's growing belief that in the highly industrialised modern world, where countries were increasingly interdependent, aggression could be forestalled, or at worst contained, by the use of economic sanctions. Throughout his complex and sometimes apparently confused policy in the 1930s this belief runs as a consistent thread.

One of the most violent political battles waged on Capitol Hill during the inter-war years was that fought over neutrality legisla-tion. Since the beginning of the twentieth century bills had been introduced into Congress for the preservation of American neutrality in the event of war breaking out overseas. A number were put forward in the seventy-third Congress which assembled in March 1933. They varied in their specific provisions, but they possessed one feature in common: although they professed to seek to maintain the neutrality of the United States, they proposed to do so by the abandonment of traditional neutral rights. The administration shared in the national abhorrence of war, and shared in the desire to keep the country from becoming involved in wars which did not threaten substantial national interests, but the type of neutrality envisaged by the administration differed in one significant particular from that advocated by the isolationists. Whereas the latter wanted to preserve the neutrality of the United States by isolating the country from conflict, Roosevelt wanted to use the position of an official neutral to benefit the victims of aggression. He wanted to embargo trade with the aggressor nation or nations whilst allowing full trade with the states against which aggressive action had been taken. Under Roosevelt's plan the United States would be neutral in that it would not actively participate in hostilities, but would be un-neutral in that discrimination would be exercised between the belligerents. He believed that in this way the horror of war would be avoided whilst at the same time the economic power of the United States would be wielded to the full in the defence of democratic right. Such a policy was not that of an isolationist. It was that of a man who wanted to avoid war but at the same time was passionately convinced that the United States could not stand aside and let aggression go unpunished.

Roosevelt failed in 1935 to get neutrality legislation of the discretionary type that he favoured. The widely publicised hearings of a senate committee under the chairmanship of Senator Nye of North Dakota, which was investigating the munitions industry and the effect that arms shipments had on American policy in the world war, encouraged popular belief in the devil theory of war. The Nye Committee sought to prove that armaments manufacturers had a vested interest in war for the consumption of their product, and that the United States had been tricked into intervention. An isolationist policy evolved whereby the non-involvement of the United States would be maintained in the event of foreign war by the complete embargoing of trade in munitions and weapons to the belligerents. The newspaper proprietor William Randolph Hearst and Father Coughlin, a priest who conducted a radio programme from Detroit which had national distribution, directed their immense national following behind the new isolationist theories. Partly as a result of the lobbying of senators and congressmen by their supporters Congress passed a neutrality bill which made no distinction between the aggressor and his victim. Roosevelt's policy had suffered a decisive setback. The bill was re-enacted in 1936 and not until 1937 did the president gain a significant victory. In that year the exportation of strategic materials other than arms and munitions to belligerent powers was made subject to a cash and carry provision. This meant that shipments could be made provided that the purchaser paid cash for the goods and shipped them in his own vessels. In this way the United States would not become associated through a creditor relationship with the belligerent powers, nor would American shipping be engaged in direct trade in contraband materials with the belligerents, thereby running the risk of maritime incidents. The introduction of cash and carry into the neutrality acts represented a victory for the administration in the political struggle with Congress. Roosevelt and Hull believed that the provision would assist the democratic nations of Europe in the event of war breaking out with Germany, for Britain was a maritime nation whose strategy in war had always been the imposition of a blockade against the continent of Europe. Cash and carry therefore would allow Britain freely to exploit the industrial resources of the United States whilst denying the same privilege to Germany.

The first test of neutrality came in 1935 when the Italians invaded Ethiopia. The Neutrality Act was invoked by presidential proclamation. In Geneva the Council of the League of Nations was considering the possibility of economic sanctions against Italy, and Roosevelt and Hull were anxious that if such a policy were implemented it should not be evaded by increased trade between Italy and the United States. They wanted, however, to avoid the appearance of being guided by League action, which would have provided ammunition for the isolationists. Shortly before the League sanctions list was issued the president therefore appealed for a moral embargo on the exportation to Italy of strategic materials other than those direct weapons of war listed in the neutrality proclamation. Furthermore, the presidential proclamation included oil, which the League list did not. Although the American embargo was a moral embargo only, and could not be absolutely enforced, when taken together with the provisions of the neutrality act it represented an attempt by the administration to make its position on military aggression clear to the nations of the world. It was an attempt to parallel the action taken by the League powers.

When civil war broke out in Spain in 1936 between the Republican government and the Falange the United States was again presented with a diplomatic challenge. The Neutrality Act did not automatically apply to Spain as the war was a domestic conflagration, in theory at least, and not an international war between independent states. However, when Great Britain and France formulated a non-intervention policy which was ratified by the League, the United States extended the neutrality provisions to Spain. When, following German and Italian unofficial intervention on behalf of the Falange, domestic pressures developed for abandonment of official neutrality and aid for the Republican government, the administration resisted them. This was in large part due to a desire to keep in step with the official policies of the Western European democratic states. Parallel action again seemed to be the dominant impulse of the administration.

Threats to international peace came also from the Far East. Following an incident at the Marco Polo Bridge in 1937 Japan invaded North China. As in 1931 the signatory states of the Nine Power Treaty of 1922 were unwilling to get embroiled in a Far Eastern conflict for which there was no easy solution and which might easily ramify into a world war. The Brussels Conference in the autumn of 1937 underlined the problems that all nations faced, and resulted in no concerted action other than the expression of pious hopes. In many ways the problems of Europe so dominated statesmen that they failed to appreciate the underlying significance of the Far Eastern situation, and they were, in any case, unprepared and unwilling to go to war.

In the formulation of foreign policy the president was restricted by two factors, one domestic and the other external. The political strength of isolationism dominated the domestic scene. In part isolationism represented a natural horror of war, and the determination of the American people to avoid involvement except when obvious territorial interests were threatened. In this sense it was based on traditionalism, and on a conservative concept of the national interest. In part isolationism represented the reaction of rural areas to the dominance of the city in American life. In this sense it was a conservative response to the presumed interest of manufacturers and industrialists in war. In part isolationism represented the reaction of hyphenate Americans to intervention on the world scene against their original homelands. It was strongest in the middle western areas which had a preponderance of German-Americans, Italian-Americans, and Scandinavian-Americans who were traditionally opposed to involvement in war. The American political system which gives an overweighting to rural areas in the national legislature gave these groups a greater voice in Congress than their numbers perhaps warranted and made them a political force which the president could not ignore. The final failure in January 1935 to ratify the World Court Protocols was a direct result of isolationist pressure on the senate. Domestic economic and social problems in the mid 1930s were so great that the president was unwilling to run the risk of losing political support for his domestic policies by an overt challenge to the isolationists over issues of foreign policy. One of his few attempts to rally popular support for his theory of economic sanctions was made in October 1937 at Chicago. He spoke of the interdependence of nations and of the threat to all countries by a breach of the peace in any one area. He likened 'world lawlessness' to an epidemic of physical disease, and said that when physical disease starts to spread the 'community approves and joins in a quarantine of the patients in order to protect the health of the community against the spread of the disease'. Internationalists approved the tone of the speech, but the reaction of isolationists against it was vehement, so vehement that Roosevelt perhaps misjudged their strength. Not until his annual message to Congress in January 1939 did the president again present a direct challenge to isolationism in the country at large. In the meantime Hitler had annexed Austria, and the Munich agreements of the autumn of 1938 had sanctioned the dismemberment of Czechoslovakia.

The second factor inhibiting Roosevelt's tentative foreign policy was an external one. The democratic nations of Europe were themselves unwilling to commit themselves to a forceful policy against German expansion. In part this was dictated by their own domestic problems. The policy of appeasement had strong popular support as well as the sanction of governments. But in part it arose from a genuine feeling that the co-operation of the United States could not in the last resort be relied upon. This deadlock became unresolvable. The American administration could not enter into military guarantees with foreign powers because of the traditions of policy and the strength of the isolationists. The European powers were unwilling to undertake a militant policy against aggression without the positive support of the United States. In this context Roosevelt's attempted policy of parallel action was doomed to failure because, quite apart from the problem of internal American dissent, the powers with whom he hoped to become aligned were themselves following a policy of appeasement.

By the end of the 1930s, however, issues had been clarified. Within the United States, although parts of the traditional attitude towards foreign relations remained intact, and in particular the aversion to commitment within multi-national alliance systems, two clear groups had emerged. On the one side were the main stream of internationalists, among whom the president must be ranked, who wanted to assert the power of the United States as a force for peace, stability and the restraint of aggression. On the other were the isolationists, who wished in the event of war to withdraw from world politics and who falsely invoked tradition to sanction their position. As war clouds gathered in Europe in the summer of 1939 the struggle between these two groups was to become the dominant issue in American national politics.

4

DEPRESSION, NEW DEAL AND
WAR PROSPERITY

CAUSES OF THE GREAT CRASH

Superficially the dominant characteristic of the 1920s was its un-inhibited exuberance; but exuberance and optimism overlaid profound anxieties about the state of society and concealed, as the literature of the period indicates, grave concern about America's cultural identity. This dualism was paralleled in the economic sector. Despite the boom there were many within the increasingly affluent society who did not share in its general prosperity. Moreover, the unprecedented rise in stock exchange prices was as much a psychological phenomenon as an index of economic advance; there were fundamental instabilities in the economic order both at home and abroad which would be exposed once public confidence was shaken, and in the absence of governmental controls a fall in the market was likely to bring the entire economic structure crashing to the ground.

Two groups in particular found that their incomes were failing to keep pace with the demands of a constantly rising standard of living, and that their relative share of the total national income was steadily declining. Farmers suffered from over-production, high costs, and restricted export markets; and in the industrial sector profits and dividends rose at a greater rate than wages. The absence of stock exchange controls, together with Republican taxation policies, encouraged speculative use of increased profits and stock values soared far above the level justified by industrial profitability and expanded production.

The international financial situation was also out of balance. During the war the United States had become a creditor nation; its new role was reflected in its gold reserves, which rose from less than 25 per cent of the world's supply in 1913 to almost 40 per cent in 1921. In the post-war world high tariffs made it difficult for foreign countries to pay the interest on outstanding loans through increased exports, and gold continued to flow into the country. A way out of the dilemma that was frequently employed was to meet existing obligations through new American loans, but this was at best a temporary expedient as it increased the total burden of indebtedness and meant financial collapse should American investors find greater speculative possibilities elsewhere. Weakness in the system was increased in 1925 when Great Britain returned to the gold standard at a rate which overvalued the pound. Other countries followed Britains' example and based their currencies on foreign exchange as well as gold, so increasing their dependence on the dollar.

In 1925 the Federal Reserve Board lowered interest rates in an attempt to check the flow of gold from Europe by stimulating investment prospects within the United States. This more than any other act contributed to the rise in stock prices from 1925 to 1929. The Florida land boom of 1923–6 had already demonstrated the extent to which a naïve 'get-rich-quick' mentality existed and this speculative mania was transferred to the New York Stock Exchange. In May 1924 the *New York Times* industrial averages stood at 106; by the end of 1928 they had risen to 331 and in August 1929 stood at 449. Stocks which had never paid a dividend and yet stood high on the exchange underlined the fact that the market was being forced up by speculation instead of being a reflection of economic growth.

The supreme self-confidence of the investing public was made the more dangerous by two peculiarities of the business world. The ability to buy on margin, which meant that only a fixed percentage of the price of stock had to be paid on purchase, with the balance covered by brokers' loans, enabled the investor to make considerable purchases out of a small working capital. He hoped to sell at a profit before his debts became due and as long as the market continued to rise the expectation of profit was considered sufficient guarantee. Bewitched in this way by the prospect of quick and continuing profit the investor gambled so far beyond his resources that by September 1929 outstanding brokers' loans stood at the fantastic figure of $7,000 million. The situation was dangerous: a collapse of the market would result in widespread financial panic because obligations would have to be met from current assets. The second weakness was the absence of control which allowed the growth of holding companies and investment trusts often run by unscrupulous speculators who exploited a gullible and unsuspecting public. The pyramids of such companies which were a feature of the 1920s depended for their stability on the prosperity of the base company; any weakness there would be reflected in the financial structure superimposed above it and could, as was shown in 1929, result in complete collapse.

In mid-September 1929 confidence in the market began to crack. After uncertain weeks in which the Stock Exchange index alternately slid down and then edged back up the market broke on Black Thursday, 24 October, when thirteen million shares changed hands. Attempts were made to buttress the market but the price level continued to decline and on Tuesday, 29 October, almost sixteen and a half million shares were traded at falling prices. *New York Times* Industrials went down to 224 on 13 November and as the depression deepened they collapsed to a floor of 58 in July 1932.

It is difficult if not impossible to say why the crash occurred when it did. A year earlier it had been evident that the commodity price level had begun to fall, that productive capacity was not being fully utilised, and that construction had declined. Market prices in Europe had begun to dip whilst the American boom was in full spate. These previously ignored omens may suddenly have come to the attention of investors and destroyed their belief in the cornucopia of the market. Whatever the reason for its timing, when the crash came it toppled the financial structure and dragged with it the entire economy. Prices, production, and employment dropped and the ramifications of the American recession spread throughout a world already suffering from basic economic problems of its own. The era of the great depression had begun.

HOOVER AND THE GREAT DEPRESSION

In November 1928, almost exactly a year before the crash, former secretary of Commerce Herbert Hoover was elected president of the United States, soundly defeating the Democratic candidate Alfred E. Smith. Smith, who had served for four terms as governor of New York, represented the urban wing of the Democratic party; he was a Catholic, a liberal, a 'wet', spoke with a nasal twang and wore a brown derby or bowler hat. His defeat strengthened the prevailing belief that a Catholic could not be elected to the presidency, one that John F. Kennedy had to overcome in 1960, but although his religion undoubtedly alienated sections of the Bible Belt his other qualities were equally obnoxious to rural America. Everything about him proclaimed the city and he seemed to symbolise the new America which was so unpalatable to the old. However, to put Smith's defeat into perspective it must be remembered that any Democratic candidate would have found it difficult to beat the Republicans in 1928. The party of 'normalcy' was still popular and Herbert Hoover seemed to represent all that was best within it. He had great ability, an impressive reputation, an attractive although aloof personality and was a difficult man to defeat as long as the economy seemed to be soundly trimmed.

Born in West Branch, Iowa, Hoover was a graduate of Stanford University, an eminently successful mining engineer, a millionaire philanthropist, and an efficient and highly respected cabinet member. His personal career represented the triumph of American individualism in a *laissez faire* society; he had raised himself by his own efforts and talents and believed in the absolute virtue of individual enterprise untrammelled by government intervention. Whilst in the cabinet he had emphasised the principle of voluntarism, and approached the formidable responsibilities of the presidency according to the philosophy which had guided his earlier career. The tragedy of his administration was that as the depression deepened this approach proved to be totally inadequate to meet the challenges of his new office. The ravages of depression had been sorely felt in the past in a more agrarian society; in urbanised America private enterprise and charity could neither absorb nor adequately relieve the problems of unemployment and distress.

Statistics bleakly indicate the extent of the economic collapse. The index of manufacturing production fell 28 points between 1929 and 1932; gross national product measured in 1929 dollars fell from a peak of $104,400 million in 1929 to $74,200 million in 1933; automobile factory sales dropped from 4,455,178 in 1929 to 1,103,557 in 1932; unemployment rose from just over one and a half million in 1929 to 12,830,000 or 24·9 per cent of the labour force, in 1933. The consequences of these figures in terms of social misery were catastrophic. Families and entire communities were depressed to the verge of starvation; packs of men, women and children roamed the land looking for work and food; shanty towns constructed of cardboard and rubble rose on the outskirts of most cities and were ironically dubbed Hoovervilles; apple sellers appeared on the street corners of downtown New York offering apples for sale in the attempt to salve their pride by appearing not to beg; breadlines which sometimes stretched for entire city blocks queued at charity stations for relief; scavengers sorted the rubbish at city dumps looking for edible scraps.

At first Hoover believed that the collapse represented merely a temporary period of adjustment following the boom and almost daily expressed his confidence that the corner had been turned. As his optimism was betrayed by events he came to believe that although there were some structural flaws in the domestic economic machinery the major responsibility for the depression was to be found in forces outside the United States. This change of emphasis was paralleled by an increasing sense that the government had to cease being a somewhat casual partner in the economy and should undertake a more active role. Always, however, his acceptance of intervention was limited by the traditional Republican fear of big government and by his belief in voluntarism rather than coercion.

This sense of limitation marked the essential difference between Hoover and Franklin D. Roosevelt, at that time governor of New York, in their anti-depression policies. What was to become the New Deal was foreshadowed in Hoover's policies as well as in those of Governor Roosevelt but whereas the latter was prepared to intervene with all the force of government, believing as he had said in 1912 that the liberty of the individual must sometimes be subordinated to the liberty of the community, Hoover clung to more traditional views and accepted the necessity for federal action only as a last resort and on a limited scale. As the depression deepened, however, he did begin to chart a new course and in areas of traditional federal activity was prepared to create government expenditure as an instrument of economic revival. In the first half of 1931 the mileage of highways under construction was doubled and many conservation projects, such as measures for the control of pests and rodents, surveys of wild life, and the opening of forest roads and trails were undertaken. Appropriations were made for new public buildings, for river and harbour improvements and for the construction of Boulder Dam to harness the power of the Colorado river. Although beneficial such schemes were inadequate to cope with the extent of the emergency and Hoover's one great innovation showed the same sense of limitation. The Reconstruction Finance Corporation was created in January 1932; it was a new departure in government financing but in its methods of operation conformed to Mellon's general theories that relief at the top of the economic pyramid would benefit all sections of the community as its benefits filtered down to the local and individual level. The corporation gave loans to banks, agricultural credit agencies and other financial bodies, and to railroads; its function was to secure capital, not to create it, and although it was partly successful in supporting threatened institutions its limited funds and restricted role prevented it from playing a decisive part in re-establishing financial and industrial stability. The difference between the Hoover and Roosevelt policies was a matter of degree which perhaps eventually amounted to a difference in kind. President Hoover was never prepared to accept massive deficit spending and always seemed to be dominated by theories of the balanced budget. His successor was prepared to make half-hearted obeisance to such theories in principle whilst flagrantly disregarding them in practice. Hoover's budgets did not balance largely because of falling revenue; Roosevelt's failed to balance at a time of rising revenue because of mounting expenditure.

Higher tariffs were a traditional response to depression, for it was believed that protection of domestic industry and agriculture would raise the level of domestic prices and stimulate production. The Hawley–Smoot Act of 1930 continued the trend set by the tariff of 1922, imposing duties far above the level necessary to remove the difference in production costs between domestic and imported goods. It did nothing to help agriculture, whose problem was still one of over-production. The Farm Board established by the Agriculture Marketing Act of 1929 likewise failed to help the farmer, because with a limited budget it sought to maintain prices without requiring a reduction of acreage. In the industrial sector the 1930 tariff led to reprisals from foreign countries but Hoover regarded these as retrogressive steps which interrupted the flow of world trade, and this illogicality helped to confirm his growing belief that American troubles had their origin in external forces for which he held little responsibility. Once he was so convinced, however, he displayed a genuine desire for international co-operation in the face of economic disaster, declared a moratorium on debts and supported the proposal being discussed in many countries for an international conference to discuss common economic problems. Here he seemed to be more enlightened than his successor. Roosevelt in 1933 was just as determined to raise the level of domestic prices as the first step towards recovery but appeared to accept the necessity of moving in the direction of economic nationalism as a temporary expedient.

The major difference between the two men, however, lay in their attitude towards the unemployed. Unlike Roosevelt, who believed that that state had a direct responsibility to provide a living for the individual citizen, Hoover clung to the belief that if a man was out of work it was somehow his own fault. In his view responsibility for relief lay with private charitable institutions such as the Red Cross and the Community Chests. The unemployed had the right to expect charity, and this he felt should be freely given, but state relief might stifle the springs of private generosity and diminish individual initiative. Wheat and cotton could be provided by the federal government for distribution to the poor, but payment of a regular dole from federal funds was to him an un-American practice, denying one of the fundamental freedoms of the American people. He failed to appreciate that by May 1932 relief payments in New York City averaged only $2.39 per week per family, and that in many cities relief funds were completely exhausted. The president also, despite his many protestations, failed to appreciate the human predicament of the poor. He allowed himself to be photographed whilst feeding his dog and used troops against the B.E.F. In the summer of 1932 a number of unemployed war veterans, calling themselves the Bonus Expeditionary Force, marched to Washington to lobby Congress for early repayment of their outstanding war bonuses. They camped in a Hooverville on Anacostia Flats along the Potomac river. For two months the administration ignored their presence but after a clash with the District of Columbia police in which two of the B.E.F. were killed, Hoover sent the army under General Douglas MacArthur to evict them. Their tents and huts were burned, tear gas was used and a baby died. The Republican administration never recovered from this disastrous blow to its public image.

However, the slight upturn in the economy in the summer of 1932 seemed to Hoover to testify to the success of his efforts in the fields of economic policy and exhortation. When the decline set in again in the winter he attributed it to reaction against the victory of Franklin Roosevelt in the November presidential election and to fears about the rise of a dangerous radical threatening the very foundations of traditional American society.

4

ELECTION OF ROOSEVELT AND THE CHARACTER
OF THE NEW DEAL

Roosevelt's re-election to the governorship of New York by unprecedented majorities in 1930 made him automatically a leading candidate for the Democratic nomination in 1932, and through his agent James A. Farley he had quietly built up support throughout the country in preparation for the national convention. Sliding over the inflammatory issues of prohibition and religion which had fissured the party in the past Farley emphasised social and economic questions, and from the base in New York built up a new rural-urban coalition of professional people and politicians, workers and struggling farmers. However, although the Roosevelt forces went to the Chicago convention with considerable strength behind them the nomination was bitterly fought. Their candidate was opposed by the Al Smith group which Roosevelt had alienated through his independent policies in Albany, by eastern conservatives under Jowett Shouse and J. J. Raskob, and by support from the south and south-west for the speaker of the House of Representatives John Nance Garner of Texas. As it seemed clear that any Democratic candidate could win against Hoover, who had been easily but listlessly re-nominated at the Republican convention, there was a danger that the political ambitions of the various Democratic aspirants might effectively deadlock the convention. However, in February 1932 Roosevelt had renounced his former advocacy of American entry into the League of Nations (cf. chapter 3) and this apparent capitulation to William Randolph Hearst and the isolationist and traditionalist wings of the party helped to pave the way for a deal with the Garner forces. The Texan and Californian delegations threw their support to Roosevelt in exchange for the selection of Garner as vice-presidential candidate. The bargain having been made Roosevelt secured nomination on the fourth ballot.

After a vigorous campaign the Democrats won the presidential election, taking 42 of the 48 states. In his acceptance speech to the Democratic convention Roosevelt had pledged himself to a new deal for the American people, but the details of his programme were not clear except in terms of what he had accomplished as governor of New York. He had pioneered direct relief of the unemployed, supported state exploitation and conservation of natural resources, extended controls over banks and other financial institutions and strengthened labour and industrial legislation. His campaign speeches contained many contradictions and obscurities: there is a well-known story of the candidate being presented with two incompatible farm policies and telling his advisers to put the two together in a compromise incorporating the best points of each. But although his policies were vague his aims were not. In April 1932 he had spoken of 'the forgotten man at the bottom of the economic pyramid'; in a speech to the Commonwealth Club of San Francisco in September he had outlined his dream of a society in which every man had the right to a comfortable living and in which business and government would cooperate to their mutual advantage. There was and perhaps could be no clear route towards the attainment of this ideal. In May he called for 'bold persistent experimentation', and such pragmatism dominated his policy thinking. Following the election Hoover tried to secure Roosevelt's endorsement of his antidepression measures; for the president-elect this was not only politically unthinkable but also practically undesirable. He kept free of all commitments which might impair his freedom of action.

It was known that he would not be afraid of using the full powers of government in his attempt to establish the New Deal, and that he was open to advice from all quarters on the ways in which these powers should be used. When he moved to Washington in March 1933 he carried with him not only substantial majorities in both houses of Congress but also his Braintrust, the group of advisers gathered largely from the universities that he had assembled during the campaign. The progressives had brought intellectuals into politics around the turn of the century, harnessing their particular skills to the attack on social and economic problems, and Roosevelt expanded this device, creating a crowd of talent the like of which was not to be seen again until John F. Kennedy entered the White House in 1961. Its most early prominent members were Raymond Moley, Rexford Tugwell and Adolf Berle, Jr., with Felix Frankfurter of the Harvard Law School in the background supplying an endless stream of brilliant young men, later known as the 'happy hot dogs', to staff the new government agencies in Washington. These advisers were sometimes more influential in the formulation of policy than were members of the cabinet, but although the composition of the administration reflected traditional political pressures and the repayment of past obligations it was by no means without distinction.

Frances Perkins, secretary of Labor and the first woman cabinet member, had long been active in industrial welfare work in New York and had influenced Roosevelt's policies in Albany. Henry A. Wallace, secretary of Agriculture, came from a well-established mid-western progressive farm family. The secretary of the Interior, Harold Ickes of Chicago, embodied the urban progressive tradition. Secretary of State Cordell Hull of Tennessee, although a man of limited intellectual quality, was an outspoken exponent of Wilsonian internationalism and a devoted advocate of low tariffs in the interests of improved international trade and better understanding. The progressive liberal element in the cabinet predominated and it was to this same tradition that most of the Braintrust themselves belonged.

It is customary to divide the New Deal programme into two phases. In the period down to the beginning of 1935 the administration's attention is said to have been focused upon recovery whilst later preoccupation was with the enactment of fundamental reform legislation aimed at transforming society. The difference is sometimes expressed as a move from the 'corporativism' of the 'first New Deal', in which the government welcomed and encouraged the formation of large economic units in order to create a balanced trinity of government, capital and labour, to the adoption in the 'second New Deal' of a Brandeisian policy, named after Justice Brandeis of the Supreme Court and representing an emphasis upon reform accompanied by an attack on big business and capital.

There are, however, dangers in trying to codify Roosevelt's programme into ideological boxes, for the essence of the New Deal was its pragmatism. The aim, of providing a decent environment and decent living and working conditions for all Americans, was constant. The methods by which the aim was to be fulfilled changed according to changing circumstances. Roosevelt was no theoretician making a blanket rejection of the established order; he merely tried to make it work in accordance with the long-established principles of freedom and democracy as he understood them. In so doing he perpetuated one revolution in American life, but only one, and that consisted of a quickening of historical processes rather than an abandonment of the past: he accelerated the speed at which the federal government assumed direct responsibility for the lives and dignity of its citizens. This adoption of responsibility meant a greater intervention by government in society. The changing tactics of policy and the varied forms of intervention employed reflected changing conditions in the country at large. The administration's legislative programme throughout the six years between inauguration and the outbreak of war in Europe can be treated as a whole, with no significant change of direction after the initial honeymoon period was over. Policy stumbled towards the expressed ideal, veering slightly from side to side according to prevailing economic and political facts but retaining not only a remarkable consistency of intent but also of practice. Much of the legislation of the 'second' New Deal had its roots in the acts of the 'first'; much of the 'first' New Deal remained intact after 1935 and provided a base for future advance. Politically there was a difference in emphasis after 1935 as opposition to the original programme developed, but the rising temperature of the political debate was not followed by a wave of 'radical' legislation.

THE NEW DEAL IN ACTION

In March 1933 the immediate crisis confronting the administration was the imminent danger of complete collapse of the nation's banking and financial institutions. Thousands of banks had failed and more were on the verge of failure. Roosevelt acted decisively, ordering a national bank holiday which was followed by the re-opening of only those institutions certified to be sound. Extension of the rediscount powers of the Federal Reserve Banks and authorisation of the Reconstruction Finance Corporation to buy bank stock, hence providing new capital, helped to guarantee the stability of these re-opened banks. Three months later the Glass–Steagall Act created a new federal corporation to guarantee small bank deposits and confidence in the banks was restored. The act also separated investment from deposit banking functions, and the Federal Reserve Board was given powers to regulate speculative activity by member-institutions. Restrictions on the export of gold and repudiation of the gold backing of the currency had already taken the United States off the gold standard. The sum of these measures was the depreciation of the dollar on the international exchange market and a slight but continuous rise in the domestic price level. Official devaluation took place in January 1934 with the passage of the Gold Reserve Act fixing the price of gold at $35 an ounce. The administration's silver policy was confused, but subscribed to the demand of western mining states for the purchase of silver. Such purchases helped to raise the domestic price level but had disastrous effects overseas. Silver policy did not become coherent until 1939 when a new Silver Purchase Act was passed as a purely sectional measure to relieve the producing states, unhampered by theories of its relation to the causes of domestic inflation.

Roosevelt's financial policy in 1933 was completed by passage of a Securities Act, which was later expanded as the Securities and Exchange Act of 1934. This set up a Securities and Exchange Commission with powers to regulate the securities market. The aims of policy were to bring order and confidence to the banking and financial system whilst securing a degree of controlled domestic inflation in the belief that a rise in the domestic price level was the best answer to depression. It was in this context that discussions at the World Economic Conference in July 1933 broke down (cf. chapter 3).

The desire to produce controlled inflation also dominated industrial policy during the hectic 100 days with which the Roosevelt era began. The National Industrial Recovery Act required the drafting of codes of fair competition to establish prices, production levels, wage rates and conditions of work and labour. These codes had the unfortunate and unforeseen effect of helping big business to the detriment of small companies, and so helped to support later charges that Roosevelt was toying with ideas of a corporate state dominated by a partnership of big business and big government. However, although in many ways the codes represented government sponsorship of methods employed by the trade associations of the previous decade, the N.I.R.A. was a genuine attempt to strengthen all parts of industry whilst recognising that big business was one of the basic features of the nation's economic life.

The programme was placed under the direction of General Hugh Johnson, who waged an effective publicity campaign under the sign of the Blue Eagle which was displayed by firms subscribing to the conditions of the N.I.R.A. codes. However, the disillusionment of the small business men began to be felt in 1934, when the policy became popularly known as the National Run Around, and at the same time large corporations which had been enthusiastically in favour of the act became resentful at production quotas and of those sections of the N.I.R.A. which encouraged labour organisation. Even before the act was declared unconstitutional by the Supreme Court in the Schechter case in 1935 it had become unworkable because of business opposition. However, in the light of the debate over the two New Deals it is significant that following the court's decision in 1935 the Guffey–Snyder Act in effect re-enacted the bituminous coal code, and when this was itself thrown out by the Court parts of it were reformulated in the Guffey–Vinson Act of 1937. Similarly in the period of the 'second' New Deal the Connally Act (1935), the Walsh–Healey Act (1936), the Robinson–Patman Act (1936) and the Miller–Tydings Act (1937) reasserted with respect to particular industries and business practices parts of the N.I.R.A. provisions. It should also be remembered that the original N.I.R.A. would have expired in 1935 even had the courts upheld its validity. It was a temporary measure to meet an immediate emergency and did not envisage the permanent suspension of the Anti-Trust Acts.

Roosevelt's acceptance of the Wagner Labor Relations Act of 1935, to which he had earlier been opposed, is often taken as one of the signs marking a shift towards reform. However, the collapse of the N.I.R.A. meant the collapse of section 7(a) which recognised the right of union organisation and collective bargaining. In its place some other measure was necessary if the new wave of union activity which had begun in 1933 was to be protected. Roosevelt was personally hesitant about some aspects of Wagner's bill, but with the invalidation of N.I.R.A., and when the bill appeared to have the support of labour leaders he accepted it. It replaced 7(a) as labour's charter, and in 1938 the minimum wage and maximum hours provisions of N.I.R.A. were redefined in the Fair Labor Standards Act.

Despite such legislative sanction the labour movement did not survive the 1930s without internal dissention. The traditional craft bias of the American Federation of Labor was alien to the needs of workers in the new mass production heavy industries. John L. Lewis of the United Mine Workers formed a Committee for Industrial Organisation within the A.F. of L. in 1935 to try to open up the new industries by vertical union techniques. Steel was one of the major targets and here, after a period of bitter strikes and violence, the new industrial unions gained a considerable measure of success. In so doing, however, the split with the A.F. of L. was consolidated and the Committee for Industrial

Organisation, member unions of which had been suspended by the A.F. of L. in 1936, was reorganised as the Congress of Industrial Organisations and emerged as the leading rival of the older federation.

In the agricultural sector the administration was also presented in 1933 with immediate problems that had to be faced. The result was the Agricultural Adjustment Act which, like the N.I.R.A., embodied policies which had been argued throughout the previous decade. It accepted the concept of parity, by which the farmer was to be given purchasing power equivalent to that which he had enjoyed during the base period from 1910 to 1914. Price supports were to be paid out of a processing tax, and were to be distributed to those farmers who reduced production according to quotas laid down by the administrator of the act. The programme represented a genuine attempt to deal with the problem of farm surpluses which had been the major cause of the collapse of farm prices in the 1920s, and with its accompanying legislation, the Emergency Farm Mortgage Act and the Farm Credit Act, relieved the mortgage burden of the farmer and contributed to a revival of agricultural prices and farm incomes. Like the industrial programme, however, the A.A.A. was also bedevilled by unforeseen and worrying consequences. In order to put the acreage and crop reduction requirements into operation during its first year millions of acres of growing crops were ploughed under and millions of hogs were slaughtered at a time when thousands of families were living on the verge of starvation. Even though over one million pounds of pig meat was distributed to people on relief this policy created an unfortunate public impression, and it later became evident that acreage reduction meant the dispossession of share croppers and Negro tenant farmers and encouraged mechanisation on large-scale production units. The droughts of 1934 and 1936 and the enlargement of the dust bowl brought home the fact that despite the increase in farm prices agriculture was still a major social problem and a continuing challenge to government. The classic account of farm distress in John Steinbeck's novel *The Grapes of Wrath* is not over exaggerated.

When the Supreme Court declared the A.A.A. to be unconstitutional secretary of Agriculture Wallace sought new palliatives. Conservation had been a significant part of the programme from the start and the Taylor Grazing Act of 1934 represented an attempt to prevent over-exploitation of the range. This principle was extended and expanded in the Soil Erosion Act of 1935, the Soil Conservation and Domestic Allotment Act of 1936 and by the policy of the Resettlement Administration. Reduction of production did not, however, solve the problem of cyclical surpluses and shortages and in the second Agricultural Adjustment Act of 1938 Wallace instituted the 'ever normal granary' system under which the government guaranteed purchase of surplus crops at maintained prices with the intention of selling them when market conditions allowed. A Surplus Marketing Administration was also set up to distribute crop surpluses to the urban unemployed, thereby avoiding the necessity of wholesale destruction of farm products.

Roosevelt's farm programme, like his industrial policy, did not solve the problem with which it sought to deal. Not until the war years did the American economy rise out of depression into a new prosperity. But it did achieve significant results and mitigated the distress of the American people. In its methods it underlined the fundamental characteristics of the New Deal: belief that the raising of the level of domestic prices was an essential prerequisite of recovery; willingness to try ideas which had been long agitated, and the desire to do something in the hope that eventually a solution would be found.

Important though these policies were, however, the greatest immediate problem in 1933 was that of the unemployed. These, according to some estimates, numbered over fourteen million. In the face of this emergency Roosevelt employed the methods he had tried in New York State and which President Hoover had tentatively embarked on. The N.I.R.A. included a section establishing a Public Works Administration which was placed under the authority of secretary of the Interior Harold Ickes. A number of large-scale projects were started, but planning and administration under the careful guidance of Ickes meant that the programme only slowly came into being, and to attack the immediate crisis the Civil Works Administration was set up under Harry Hopkins to provide jobs during the winter of 1933–4. A Civilian Conservation Corps was also established to give employment to young men on forestry and conservation projects. Valuable though these agencies were, they did little to help the vast majority of the unemployed of whom there were still over eleven million in 1934. The following year Hopkins was given control of a new agency, the Works Progress Administration, which, acting as a genuine relief organisation, deliberately created work to fit the particular skills of the men and women on its register. Its scope was far ranging, and included the sponsorship of plays and the employment of artists to decorate buildings. But radical though the idea was it was motivated by the traditional belief in the dignity of work and rested on the assumption that it was better to pay wages for marginal activity than to give a dole.

The logical alternative to the alleviation of unemployment through direct relief and created work was insurance, and according to Frances Perkins's testimony Roosevelt had agreed before his inauguration that public insurance schemes should be examined. This research bore fruit in the Social Security Act of 1935 which, for the first time in the history of the United States, launched a national system providing benefits not only for the unemployed but also for the aged, for dependent children, for the care of the blind, and for the expansion of public health facilities. Parts of the programme were to be administered entirely by the federal government; others were to be federal–state enterprises that established a new relationship between the federal and state authorities. The original act did not cover all categories of workers, but it laid a broad foundation on which the expanded coverage of later years could be based. The role undertaken by the federal government in the field of social security represented a new departure in the patterns of American development, and marked one of the enduring transformations of the American scene which were a legacy of the New Deal. The act is often invoked as one of the major pieces of legislation belonging to the 'second' New Deal, but the evidence suggests that the president was personally committed to some form of insurance from the beginning of his administration.

Among the many acts of the hectic hundred days is one which stands alone both in the grandeur of its conception and in the scope of its application. Like so much of the New Deal, however, it was revolutionary in scope rather than in its underlying concepts. Since the time of Theodore Roosevelt the government had been engaged in the conservation of natural resources. During the world war a federal dam had been built at Muscle Shoals on the Tennessee river for flood control and for the production of hydro-electric power to serve government owned and operated nitrate munitions plants. Throughout the 1920s attempts to sell these facilities to private corporations had been thwarted largely through the efforts of Senator George Norris of Nebraska, a leader among senatorial progressives. Roosevelt had become an exponent of public development of such projects and during his terms as governor of New York had advocated joint exploitation with Canada of the resources of the St Lawrence. During the 1932 presidential campaign he expounded the concept of regional planning and emphasised the extent to which this would facilitate the social and economic rehabilitation of depressed areas.

The Tennessee Valley Act of May 1933 established an authority which was intended, in the words of the president, to plan 'for the proper use, conservation, and development of the natural resources of the Tennessee River drainage basin and its adjoining territory for the general social and economic welfare of the Nation'. Its administrator David Lilienthal described its operation as 'centralized large scale production combined with decentralized, grass-roots local responsibility'. Within ten years the valley was transformed from an eroded, poverty stricken region subjected to periodic flooding, into a fertile and prosperous agricultural and industrial area in which the promise of American life seemed to have been amply fulfilled. The administration had extended the traditional interest of the federal government in internal improvements and projected it to cover the comprehensive rehabilitation of an entire region. The production of cheap power acted as a yardstick to bring down the price of private electricity and stimulated the work of the Rural Electrification Administration. In the case of *Ashwander v. T.V.A.* in 1936 the Supreme Court upheld the constitutionality of the authority under the commerce and war powers of the constitution. The great experiment in planning had passed the judicial test.

The legislative record of the New Deal in the creation of its 'alphabetical' agencies was phenomenal. During the hundred days bills were rushed through Congress at an unprecedented rate, and the absence of significant opposition provides one of the best indications that the course charted by the New Deal was not alien to American traditions. Even in the later period measures like the Social Security Act were passed with large majorities and without crippling amendments. The secret of Roosevelt's success lay in the pragmatic way in which he moved towards fulfilment of his general aims, and in his acute sense of the shifting currents of public opinion. He was a practical politician, not an ideologue. In

1936 his efforts bore fruit in re-election by the astounding total of 46 states against the 2 which voted for his Republican opponent Governor Landon of Kansas.

Although he so convincingly retained the support of the electorate the honeymoon period of 1933 was over. Apart from the Republican party, organised opposition to the New Deal had congealed in a number of widely different groups. Conservative opposition to its financial policies, the disillusionment of businessmen with the N.R.A., and the increasingly uneasy membership of the Smith–Shouse wing of the Democratic party in the Roosevelt coalition, resulted in 1934 in the formation of the Liberty League, which thenceforth carried on a continuous campaign of bitter criticism of the administration. A new acrimony entered into political debate, and it became clear that the co-operation of business which Roosevelt had hoped for in 1933, and which at that time had been freely given, was no longer possible. This change in the political climate was not, however, the trigger for a violent swerve of policy towards 'the left'.

Nor is it clear that the rise of demagogues which was a feature of the mid 1930s fundamentally effected the course of the New Deal. Father Coughlin, the Detroit radio priest of the Shrine of the Little Flower whose following numbered millions in the Middle West, at first supported the administration but then moved in the direction of socialism and advocated nationalisation of banks, public utilities and natural resources. Dr Francis E. Townsend, an elderly doctor in California, advocated a system of federal pensions of $200 a month for people over 60 which, having to be spent within the month, would immediately stimulate purchasing power and hence increase production. Upton Sinclair, with a programme to End Poverty in California (E.P.I.C.), wanted to institute a self-supporting production system for the unemployed. Governor Huey Long, the Louisiana Kingfish whose story is told in Robert Penn Warren's novel *All the King's Men*, advocated a 'share the wealth' programme under which the rich would be heavily taxed and every family provided with a guaranteed annual income and a farm. In the elections of 1934 these several groups posed a considerable political problem but Roosevelt's non-intervention policy minimised the threat. Apart from in Louisiana, where Long controlled the Democratic machine, their candidates made little headway. Long was assassinated in 1935 and in 1936 the only significant potential threat was the Coughlin–Townsend movement which fell apart through internal dissension.

The great importance of the demagogues is that they brought into debate policies which, however impractical, enlarged the spectrum of political discussion. The amount of support they generated helped Roosevelt to determine where, if anywhere, the national consensus lay, and helped to confirm his instinctive and long standing concern for the 'one-third of a nation ill-housed, ill-clad, ill-nourished' (second Inaugural Address). But there is little real evidence that they acted as a positive force impelling him into new directions. The Public Utility Holding Company Act of 1935 instituted controls which had long been advocated, and the Revenue Act of 1935 which increased surtaxes and raised the rate of the graduated income tax merely extended the taxation principles which had been followed by Theodore Roosevelt and Woodrow Wilson. In his budget message of January 1935 the president had indicated that he foresaw no need at that time for increased taxation, and his advocacy of the new bill in June may have been dictated by his awareness of an increasing 'social unrest and a deepening sense of unfairness' (Tax message, 19 June 1935) but this extension of existing practice is not a radical diversion of the New Deal. In his first inaugural he had spoken of the money changers fleeing from the temple of American civilisation. By 1935 the increasing antagonism of business, as well as the increasingly vocal opposition of the demagogues, seemed to indicate that the money changers had returned. The Revenue Act of 1935 was perhaps partly a reaction to this situation but it should be remembered that the Revenue Act of 1934 had also raised the level of income and inheritance taxes and that the particulars of the 1935 bill do not support the charge that it was a particularly vicious 'soak the rich' act. In his acceptance speech to the Democratic convention in Philadelphia in June 1936 Roosevelt referred to his conservative critics as 'economic royalists' who denied his ideal of a just society. It was political rhetoric of the highest order, 1936 was election year, and his slogans met with an immediate and electrifying response. But they were not followed up in the new Congress by radical new legislation moving the New Deal into unaccustomed policies.

At a time of great depression the American people were prepared to accept innovation within the general framework of the American tradition, but this same tradition itself militated against radicalism and acted as a restraint upon excessive experimentation. Throughout the New Deal programme Roosevelt skilfully kept within the limits beyond which he would have aroused both the public and politicians to concerted opposition and there is no evidence that he ever wished to break through them. His two great mistakes were tactical errors rather than ideological blunders.

When much of the New Deal was struck down by the Supreme Court in 1935 he believed that the majority of the justices were acting according to their personal economic and political prejudices instead of seeking to apply judicial objectivity to the questions at issue, and he accused the court of trying to take the country back to 'the horse and buggy days'. His electoral success in 1936 encouraged him to put forward a plan for judicial organisation which would have given him the power to appoint additional justices whose votes would have outweighed those of some of the older and some of the more conservative members. Although there were precedents for increasing the size of the Supreme Court these were so far in the past that he appeared to be meddling with one of the hallowed institutions of American life in order to gain political advantage. This was a serious political mistake, which was not helped by his deviousness in pleading the necessity of reform in the interest of judicial efficiency instead of admitting his true purpose, which was to gain judicial acquiescence with the acts of the elected legislative representatives of the people. Reaction against the scheme was such that he was forced to abandon it. An attempt to purge conservative Democrats in the congressional elections of 1938 suffered a similar failure. Perhaps through over-confidence, possibly through uncertainty about the future path of the New Deal, Roosevelt seemed to have lost his political touch.

Normally however, his handling of people and politics was masterly. He used the political powers of the presidency in an unequalled manner and deployed his own cheerful optimism and engaging manner as two of his major political assets. He instituted regular press conferences in which these gifts found full expression, and extended them to the country at large through the 'fireside chats', informal radio talks which became one of the most persuasive weapons in his political arsenal. He had rallied the nation in 1933 with the statement that 'we have nothing to fear but fear itself', and this epitomised his psychological attack upon the depression. His success is borne out by the remark of a bystander as his coffin passed through Washington D.C. in April 1945 on its way to burial at Hyde Park: 'He hoped me!'

Success in rallying people's spirits was not, however, enough. On the economic front the New Deal achieved only qualified success. The decline which set in again following the cut back of government spending on the W.P.A. in the winter of 1937 underlined the fact that normal economic processes were not yet sufficient to create a genuine economic revival. Massive W.P.A. spending was promptly restored, but the episode underlines one other important fact about Roosevelt: he was not in any theoretical sense a convinced exponent of Keynesian economics although he engaged in deficit spending as a practical expedient. Despite the resumption of deficit spending in 1938 recovery in 1939 had still not reached the level of prosperity of 1929. After six years of New Deal expenditure and experimentation individual distress had been relieved but the fundamental weaknesses of the economy had not been cured. There were still thousands of men who, except for some miracle, could not hope to work again, and for thousands of school leavers there was no prospect of normal employment. In 1939 17.2 per cent of the civilian labour force, representing almost nine and a half million workers, was unemployed; the index of manufacturing production was still three points below the level of 1937 and one point below that of 1929. The miracle which ended the depression was the unhappy one of war in Europe and tensions that were to result in war in the Far East. Large-scale defence spending began in 1940 and with this a boom really got under way.

ROOSEVELT BREAKS A POLITICAL TRADITION

When the economy began to fall into gear in 1940 Roosevelt's second term was drawing to its close. The precedent established by George Washington in the early days of the Republic that a president should not offer himself for a third term had never been breached, but after some hesitations Roosevelt made it known that he would accept re-nomination. He believed that the dangers inherent in the international situation necessitated a continuation of his policies but was no doubt also influenced by his own well-developed political ambitions. Popular support for the president in the country at large was still overwhelming and so despite the bitterness of the many aspirants for the succession some of whom he himself appears to have encouraged, the convention broke with the past and renominated on the first ballot the only candidate whom many of the delegates thought could win. The real battle came over the vice-presidential nomination. Roosevelt wanted Henry A. Wallace, his secretary of Agriculture, whom he felt was a reliable liberal whose mid-western connections would appeal to the farm belt. Within the party, however, Wallace had the reputation of being a mystic philsopher with a passion for strange theories, and only the full use of presidential influence was sufficient to force his nomination upon the reluctant convention.

When the Republican party made the unexpected choice of Wendell Willkie, a liberal who rejected the isolationist wing of his party, a possible head-on collision between the parties over foreign policy was averted and the Republican campaign, although hard fought, focused upon Democratic inefficiency and the third-term issue. Only in the last month before the election did Willkie raise the foreign policy question and accuse the president of trying to lead the country into war. The political effectiveness of this charge was diluted by Roosevelt's earlier foresight in bringing two prominent Republicans, Henry L. Stimson and the former vice-presidential candidate Frank Knox, into the administration as secretaries of War and Navy (June 1940) and the president managed to quieten these fears (cf. chapter 5). His triumph by substantial although reduced majorities was a tribute both to his individual political appeal, despite the third-term issue, and to the extent to which he held his coalition together.

After the Japanese attack on Pearl Harbor in December 1941 party politics went temporarily into abeyance, but in the mid-term elections in 1942 the Republicans won surprising victories in both houses of Congress and in the states. The vote probably represented a reaction against the uneven military fortunes of the summer of 1942 and the imposition of wartime controls over American society, plus a growing resentment against what appeared to be one-party rule.

In 1944 the harmonious choice of the Republican national convention was Thomas Dewey, who had won the governorship of New York state in 1940. Roosevelt again indicated that he was prepared to run on the Democratic ticket and despite opposition from the south his nomination was never in doubt. Opposition focused, as it had in 1940, on the vice-presidential nomination.

The incumbent vice-president, former secretary of Agriculture Henry Wallace, seemed to be the popular choice but he had strong political enemies and Roosevelt failed to support him openly. During a confused convention battle it seemed at one moment that Wallace might be successful, but the president allowed it to be known that he favoured either Senator Harry S. Truman of Missouri or Justice William O. Douglas as his running mate and Senator Truman, with the support of the south which wanted above all to see Wallace defeated, gained the nomination. In the election of 1944 as in 1940 there was little difference between the candidates on foreign policy and the Republicans fought the campaign on charges of big and tired government in Washington. Although he lost ground in the south and in the farm belt Roosevelt once again piled up sweeping majorities. Despite the burdens and strains of twelve years of office, the further breach with tradition, and widespread realisation that his health was less resilient than it had been, his personal magic and political agility continued to exercise their customary sway over the electorate.

THE ECONOMY AT WAR

The period from the fall of France in May 1940 to the end of the year saw the beginning of economic mobilisation for war. Between June and December 1940 ten and a half thousand million dollars worth of defence contracts were placed, a sum nine times greater than the total expenditure for military purposes in the fiscal year 1937–8. The federal budget of over $13,000 million in 1941 was $4,000 million greater than in 1940 and 62 per cent of the total was allocated for defence expenditure. By 1945 the budget was running at almost $100,000 million, 80 per cent of it for defence and security purposes. One of the effects of this enormous expenditure was the doubling of the index of manufacturing production and a rise in the gross national product from $91,100 million in 1939 to $213,600 million in 1945.

America's industrial potential had risen to the challenge. The president's targets of 60,000 airplanes, 45,000 tanks, 20,000 anti-aircraft guns and 8,000,000 tons of shipping in 1942 were met, and these construction figures were surpassed in 1943 and 1944. The rate of industrial mobilisation and technological advance can be illustrated by the increasing speed of construction of the Liberty ship, a utility freighter. In 1941 it took 355 days to complete one ship; in 1942 this was cut to an average of 56 days and one of Henry Kaiser's Oregon yards turned out a Liberty ship in the record time of 14 days. Such industrial feats were, moreover, carried out at a time when twelve million men and women were being drafted into the armed forces under the Selective Service Act of 1940, and these included many of the most able and skilled of the nation's manpower resources. However, the reservoir of unemployment meant that until 1943 there were few labour shortages. Between June 1940 and December 1941 unemployment dropped from nine to four million, and by September 1943 it had reached about the irreducible minimum. As the unemployed, including many of those thought to be unemployable, together with women and retired men went into the factories the working force rose from 46,500,000 to over 53,000,000. With full employment a shortage of workers was felt in the new industrial complexes on the West Coast, and elsewhere in industries which paid relatively low wages and offered poor working conditions. Although a War Manpower Commission was appointed controls were never very stringent and the high turnover rate of industrial workers presented a continual problem.

In general, however, the tremendous volume of defence production was made possible only by large-scale and widespread planning. The war years, like the New Deal period, were characterised by the proliferation of 'alphabetical' agencies geared to harness the nation's economic and human potential behind the war effort. As early as August 1939 the president had set up a War Resources Board but this had a short life, being dissolved following Roosevelt's rejection of its plan for the appointment of a single economic 'czar' with powers over the entire economic structure. In May 1940 the president established an Office for Emergency Management to assist him in the co-ordination of the defence agencies. Most of the new organisations originated as units of this office. The following month Donald M. Nelson was appointed Co-ordinator of National Defense Purchases and the president was empowered by statute to order priorities in the delivery of Army and Navy contracts. Metals Reserve, Rubber Reserve, and Defense Plant and Defense Supplies Corporations were set up and further agencies followed in 1941, the most important of which were the Office of Production Management and the Office of Price Administration whose objectives were the establishment of a priorities system for defence materials and the prevention of spiralling price inflation as shortages developed in civilian consumer production. Later a Supply Priorities and Allocations Board under Nelson was superimposed over the O.P.M. to determine the main lines of policy. A small but typical example of the type of restrictions imposed by the Board was prohibition of the use of chrome for automobile fittings and on perambulators. In January 1942 the War Production Board inherited the powers of the O.P.M. and the Supply Priorities and Allocations Board, and in May 1943 the Office of War Mobilization was given extensive powers to oversee and co-ordinate the whole programme, powers so extensive that its director J. M. Byrnes was often called the 'Assistant President'.

The transportation system had also to be made capable of sustaining the war effort. An Office of Defense Transportation was established in December 1941, followed by a War Shipping Administration in 1942. The railroads retained their independence but the systems were integrated to increase efficiency. Tyres were rationed and after experiments on the East Coast, where gasoline was in short supply owing to the disruption of the sea lanes from the Gulf of Mexico by German submarine activity, national gasoline rationing was enforced in the autumn of 1942.

In the agricultural sector the United States entered the war with plentiful supplies of most home-produced commodities. Federal stocks had accumulated under secretary of Agriculture Wallace's 'ever normal granary' programme and these were sufficient to meet the immediate needs of the rapidly expanding armed forces. However, in 1943 shortages developed, reflecting the dwindling of certain imports, the demands of America's allies through the Lend Lease programme (cf. chapter 5), and the increased prosperity of the American consumer. War production and restrictions had removed many consumer durables from the market, and as the discretionary income of the American worker reached pre-Depression heights he had a greater surplus than ever before to spend on food. Meat, butter, sugar and some other commodities were rationed but this increased demand for non-rationed products. The administration was less successful in its agricultural programme than in most other areas of economic life. Although a Food Administration was established it ran into opposition from the powerful Farm Bureau, which represented organised farmers, and was at first unable to prevent the ceiling on farm prices from rising to 110 per cent of parity, a level demanded by the Farm Bureau but one incompatible with the attempt to control inflation. Not until passage of the Stabilization Act in October 1942 was the 110 per cent parity clause dropped, and as there was then substituted a provision giving 'adequate weighting' to farm labour costs, prices remained high. The parity ratio of farm prices, that is the ratio of prices received by the farmer to prices paid by him, including interest, taxes and wages, rose from 77 in 1939 to a peak of 113 in 1943. The Food Administration also found difficulty in controlling production: luxury products which commanded high prices were grown to the detriment of essential commodities, and production of main crops fluctuated according to price changes instead of remaining at a stable level. Despite the shortage of labour, general restrictions, high costs and a 17 per cent decrease in the farm population, the index of farm output rose 16 points between 1939 and 1945. Net cash income of farmers almost trebled between 1939 and 1945 whereas the average earnings of workers in production industries less than doubled.

Apart from the stimulation of production, economic policy during the war years subscribed to the general programme that Roosevelt presented to Congress in April 1942. Aimed at stabilising the cost-of-living index it advocated heavy taxation, ceilings on prices, rents and dividends, stabilisation of wages and prices, rationing of all essential commodities in short supply, and the discouragement of credit and instalment buying. Efforts to check war profiteering in industry were successful: James V. Forrestal, the assistant secretary of the Navy, pointed out in 1943 that the electrical, steel, rubber and other manufacturing industries which in 1939 had $4.26 of current assets for every dollar of current liability had now only $1.86 of assets against each dollar of liability. The levelling process of war was quickened by new tax laws which helped to redistribute incomes. Although low incomes were taxed for the first time in the Revenue Act of 1942 the tax rate on the highest earnings was increased to 94 per cent. War prosperity stimulated private savings, and the changes in the tax structure helped to ensure that these savings were distributed throughout the greater part of the population.

THE NEGRO, CIVIL LIBERTIES AND THE ATOM

The plight of the American Negro had not been a major concern of the administration during the pre-war years although there had been attempts in the relief programmes to break down discrimination, but wartime changes made the problem more visible. Economic mobilisation stimulated a movement of Negroes out of the south as it had during the First World War. About one million Negroes left to work in new factories in the north and west and by 1944 over two million Negroes were working in defence plants throughout the nation. This migration and the increased affluence of the coloured population helped to break down the economic barriers of racial segregation but also helped to carry racial tensions into areas which formerly, with relatively insignificant Negro minorities, had been free from active prejudice. In the northern industrial cities which had been faced with steadily increasing Negro populations since the civil war the new migration intensified existing problems. In 1943 serious rioting occurred in Detroit and New York and Negro leaders threatened to march on Washington. This was only narrowly averted by Roosevelt's appointment of a Fair Employment Practices Committee with a mandate to seek ways of preventing discrimination in industry.

The presence of increasing numbers of Negroes helped to aggravate an already difficult labour situation. With the increase in industrial activity there was a parallel increase in the number of industrial disputes. The National Defense Mediation Board which was set up in March 1941 proved ineffective and was superseded in January 1942 by a National War Labor Board which was given authority to arbitrate disputes in industries concerned with war production. In 1943, however, it was unable to resolve a strike of 400,000 coal miners and the federal government was forced to take over the mines for a period of five months.

Although on the domestic front the necessary concomitant of war was the extension of restrictions and controls, in some sensitive areas of national life the traditions of the American past militated against effective regulation. Freedom of the press was a liberty dearly prized and the Office of Censorship which was established in December 1941 was given no powers of compulsion over the press and radio but relied upon voluntary persuasion. To the credit of the news media this system proved fairly effective.

There was at first no central office of information similar to George Creel's Committee on Public Information in the First World War and a number of competing public relations and information agencies served the various government departments. In the preparedness period before Pearl Harbor an Office of Facts and Figures was established to co-ordinate defence information. A Co-ordinator of Information was later appointed with responsibility for assembling intelligence materials and transmitting information abroad through the press and through a subordinate agency, the Voice of America, but during the war period there was considerable confusion in the handling of information because of the multiplicity of agencies. Roosevelt's characteristic predeliction for competing agencies rather than powerful single offices continued during the war emergency. In general, however, the use of federal power to control *laissez faire* which had been the major feature of the New Deal continued. Such controls were necessary for efficient economic and military expansion and always stopped short of dictatorial methods. Indeed many of them might have been better conceived and applied had the ideological foundations of American society sanctioned authoritative federal action. In one episode, however, the emergency powers of the government were put to unhappy use.

Although the nation had matured since 1917, and Americans of German and Italian descent went largely unmolested, there was one exception to this pattern of tolerance which reflected a degree of hysteria comparable to the revulsion against German-American culture in the earlier period. In February 1942 the extensive Japanese-American colony on the West Coast was forcibly removed to relocation camps in the hinterland. The removals were done at short notice and many citizens suffered not only personal hardship but also serious financial loss. Suspicion of the Japanese stemmed from a racial prejudice against oriental immigrants dating from the late nineteenth century which was strengthened by the emotional shock and hatred generated by the surprise bombing of Pearl Harbor in December 1941. The policy was justified at the time, and later confirmed by the Supreme Court, on the grounds of war necessity, but the manner in which it was done was unnecessarily harsh, and the incident, together with a number of cases in which, at a time of national danger, military authority was held to overrule civilian processes, seemed to represent a grave threat to civil liberties.

These shadows over the liberty of the citizen were accompanied, as the United States moved into the post-war world, by another and more ominous cloud. One of the greatest achievements of American science and technology during the war years was the harnessing of the power of the atom and its unleashing in the bombs which were dropped on Hiroshima and Nagasaki in August 1945 to end the war in the Pacific. In the 1930s and during the early years of the war the United States, like Great Britain, had provided sanctuary for European scientists fleeing from fascist persecution. Among them were a number of nuclear physicists and a group of these men, working with their American colleagues, produced the first controlled atomic reaction in laboratories at the University of Chicago in 1942. Development of a bomb was then entrusted to the top secret Manhattan Project. Nearly $2,000 million and the energies of thousands of scientists and technicians, including many from Great Britain and the Allied countries, were poured into the work. Giant plants were built at Oak Ridge, Tennessee, and at Hanford, Washington, to produce fissionable material, and the bomb itself was developed at Los Alamos, New Mexico, by a group under the direction of J. Robert Oppenheimer. The new weapon was first tested on 16 July 1945. It worked.

The promise of the New Deal, with its emphasis upon the dignity of the individual, had been fulfilled in economic terms only by the coming of war. The war, fought for the preservation of democracy, eventually gave freedom to subject nations at the cost of curtailment, albeit temporary, of the individual liberties of many Americans. The controls of the New Deal period had been extended by war, and exploitation of the atom was a testimony to intelligence, courage, imagination, teamwork and centralised direction. But a question mark hung over the United States as peace was made: it was uncertain whether the country would move further in the direction of a planned society or whether there would be a reversion to *laissez faire*. Equally uncertain was the way in which the power of the atom would be used.

5

INTERVENTION, WAR AND AN
UNEASY PEACE 1939–1950

The profound economic and social changes of the years from
1939 to 1945 resulted from a transformation in the world role of
the United States that was consolidated and extended in the post-
war period. By 1939, despite the efforts of President Roosevelt, the
nation had adopted a defensive posture which, as embodied in the
neutrality acts, represented an attempt to insulate itself from
overseas conflagrations and defined the national interest ex-
clusively in hemispheric terms. Between 1939 and 1941 Roosevelt
pursued a policy which ran counter to this attitude. He reiterated
his own larger conception of the national interest and initiated a
policy which brought the United States into active association
with the victims of aggression in both Europe and the Far East.
From the end of 1941 until 1945 the United States was a full
belligerent and one of the major supporters of the idea of a
United Nations organisation. It became a founder-member of the
United Nations on its establishment in 1945 and between 1945 and
1947, having demobilised its great armies, pinned its faith in that
organisation as an instrument for the peaceful resolution of
international disputes. Realisation in 1947 of the significance of
the Iron Curtain which had fallen across central Europe marked
the beginning of a period of cold war in which the United States
sought to contain Communism by launching an ideological
campaign accompanied by massive programmes of technical and
military aid to threatened countries. This activist policy was
consolidated by a revolution in American diplomacy: the United
States joined in a system of regional alliances designed to protect
the 'free world' against Communist aggression. The testing of the
new international policy came in 1950 when the cold war moved
into a new phase; South Korea was invaded from the North and
the United States, in accordance with its interpretation of obligations under the United Nations charter, went to the aid of the
South Koreans.

Within the short space of eleven years the United States had cast
off deeply rooted traditions of foreign policy, had abandoned
both neutrality and isolation and emerged as the self-appointed

protector of anti-Communist movements throughout the world. Arguments based on material interest had failed in the past to do what was now accomplished by the ideological division of the post-war world. To this challenge the American responded with courage and determination, for in his conception of democracy and the rights of man lay his very identity as an American. In defence of this identity he was prepared to accept the burdens of the cold war and, in the last resort, to fight.

THE ROAD TO WAR

European policy 1939–1941

When Roosevelt delivered his annual message to Congress on 4 January 1939 he took the opportunity to warn the American people of the dangers that threatened as a result of the international situation. He spoke of the common interests of all democratic nations, urged that the United States look to its defences, and reiterated his misgivings about the form of the neutrality acts which he believed might operate unevenly to the advantage of aggressor nations. Already he had begun to ask for increased appropriations for defence and had instituted an enlarged naval building programme. The German occupation of Prague in March and Italy's seizure of Albania in April strengthened his conviction that the democratic states of Europe were in imminent danger. An attempt to revise the neutrality laws was, however, lost in the face of isolationist opposition.

Not until the outbreak of war in Europe did opinion in Congress and throughout the country at large swing massively behind presidential policy. The shock of the German and Russian invasions of Poland on 1 September 1939, and the declaration of war against Germany by Britain and France two days later produced sufficient reaction for Roosevelt to be able to call Congress back on 21 September for a special session to consider a revision of neutrality. The president hoped to secure changes that would enable belligerents to purchase arms and munitions as well as raw materials on a cash and carry basis according to the 1937 formula. The administration's campaign was carefully conducted, and it was emphasised that the extension of cash and carry would in no way imply eventual American participation in the war, but the isolationist opposition, led by Senators Borah of Idaho, Nye of North Dakota and Johnson of California, pointed out that non-belligerency of the type proposed would in fact if not in theory represent a retreat from neutrality in that it was specifically designed to help Great Britain. They were, however, defeated when Roosevelt exploited to the full the shift in public opinion and managed to amass enough political support to secure majorities in both houses of Congress.

After the collapse of Poland the war in Europe entered its 'phony' phase and throughout the winter of 1939–40 there was no further military activity on the part of Germany. Russia's invasion of Finland in December 1939 aroused strong emotional reaction within the United States but had little effect on policy. In his annual message of January 1940 Roosevelt again stressed the impossibility of complete isolation from war but made no positive proposals for action. The strangely quiescent war still seemed remote and unreal. This air of illusion was not broken until April 1940, when Germany invaded Denmark and Norway. The tempo quickened when Holland and Belgium were conquered in May, and the following month France collapsed. With France fallen Britain stood alone, and whilst Roosevelt had no intention of active intervention he was determined to do all that was within his power, short of war, to try to ensure British survival. He regarded the British Empire as the last bastion of democracy before the advancing 'gods of force and hate' which threatened to engulf the non-American world.

Politics as well as policy dictated emphasis upon a determination to stay out of the war. 1940 was presidential election year and although the Republican candidate Willkie represented the internationalist element of his party the president realised the necessity of avoiding agitation of the possible implications of his foreign policy. For a time he was successful and the question of aid to Britain short of war did not emerge as a significant campaign issue until shortly before polling day. He was then forced, however, when pressed about his foreign policy, to make the famous speech in Boston in which he emphasised again and again that American boys and girls would not be sent to fight in foreign wars. This attempt to still doubts about his intentions was effective, but he later admitted to being ashamed of the speech, a confession which appears to support the view that he expected war to follow at some time in the future. However, it served immediate purposes, he was re-elected, and despite the political tensions of the autumn of 1940 the policy of aid short of war continued.

Already in September 1940 an agreement had been made to transfer 50 over-age American destroyers to the British government in exchange for bases in Newfoundland and the West Indies. This destroyer deal was of benefit to both parties but was particularly valuable to the British as the ships were urgently needed for use against German U-boats which threatened to disrupt the Atlantic sea lanes upon which survival depended. But aid of this type, although essential, was not adequate. The flow of food and war material from the United States rested, under the provisions of the neutrality act, on Britain's ability to pay cash, and she had already spent two-thirds of her dollar resources. If aid were to continue some way out of the dilemma had be to found. Early in December 1940 the British prime minister warned the president that Britain's reserves were almost exhausted. In a press conference on 17 December Roosevelt responded with a tentative exploration of the possibility of lending material to Britain on the understanding that it would be returned after the war, thereby getting rid, as he said, of 'the silly, foolish old dollar sign'. In a fireside chat to the nation at the end of the month he began to place the idea before the public. Reviewing the whole international situation he identified, in clearer terms than any he had used before, the security of the United States with the continued survival of Britain. He stressed also the urgent need for expanded defence production and stated his conviction that America must be 'the great arsenal of democracy'. In his annual message to Congress on 6 January he spoke in similar terms and four days later a bill to give effect to the scheme was introduced, bearing the symbolic number H.R. 1776, the year of the revolution against Britain. This bill authorised the president to transfer, exchange, lend or lease any article of defence potential to any nation whose own defence he thought vital to the security of the United States. After two months of congressional hearings and debate it passed Congress, was signed by President Roosevelt on 11 March, and $7,000 million, a sum greater than Great Britain's dollar reserves at the beginning of the war, was immediately appropriated as the first instalment of the programme.

The lend-lease bill was not simply an act of magnanimous generosity, despite the president's strong desire to help the European democracies in their fight against Germany. It was based upon the firm belief that German victory in Europe would not only result in absolute control of that continent but would also pave the way for a German advance into India, Africa and Latin America; and that quite apart from the economic consequences of such an empire for the United States German penetration into Latin America would mean a direct military confrontation. The bill reflected the president's belief that National Socialism was an expanding force that could only be halted by superior strength. He was convinced that Britain was fighting what must inevitably become America's war, and that it was therefore in the interest of the United States to support Britain in every way possible in order to secure maximum advantage at minimum cost.

Definition of the possible changed as public attitudes within the United States swung towards acceptance of the president's analysis. Military staff talks were held with British and Commonwealth officials to determine common strategy in the light of future contingencies. In March and April 1941 Roosevelt allowed British vessels to be repaired in American shipyards, seized German shipping in American ports and enlarged the Atlantic zone in which American ships were authorised to search for German submarines and to warn Allied shipping of their presence. Greenland was made a temporary protectorate of the United States and in July 1941 American troops were stationed in Iceland. This series of events culminated in a meeting between Roosevelt and Churchill at Argentia, Newfoundland, in August and out of this meeting came the joint statement called the Atlantic Charter, a significant declaration by the leader of a country that was still officially a non-belligerent. In September American naval vessels were authorised to take all action necessary to protect merchantmen in areas deemed necessary for America's defence, and Congress revised the neutrality laws to permit the arming of American merchant ships and their voyage to belligerent ports. The United States had moved even further towards open war, and was in danger of being caught in a situation from which there might be no escape but war.

But despite the change in public opinion these measures were not taken without violent and impassioned debate within the country at large. The debate was not conditioned by party allegiance, for official party attitudes had, by 1941, come to agreement on the policy of aid to Britain short of war and even, following the German attack on the Soviet Union in June 1941, on the extension of lend-lease aid to Russia. Roosevelt had stimulated the move towards bipartisanship by bringing Knox and Stimson, into his cabinet in 1940. In 1941 difference of opinion over American policy was focused around the activities of two rival committees, the America First Committee and the Committee to Defend America by Aiding the Allies.

The America First Committee began as a student movement at Yale University under the leadership of Douglas Stuart of the Law School. He and his associates emphasised the necessity of strong hemispheric defences, did not oppose cash and carry, but firmly believed that even if Britain were on the verge of defeat the United States should refrain from active intervention in the war. Stuart attended the party conventions in 1940 and enlisted the support of a number of prominent isolationist senators. He also found support among mid-western businessmen and in September 1940 the America First Committee was set up in Chicago. Its platform contained four major planks: that American defences should be built up; that a prepared America was immune from attack; that American democracy could be preserved only by keeping out of the European war; and that aid to the Allies short of war weakened national defences and threatened to involve the country in the overseas conflict. The committee secured the endorsement of Charles A. Lindbergh, hero of the trans-Atlantic flight of 1927, and of General Hugh S. Johnson, former director of the N.R.A. By December 1941 it had gathered approximately 850,000 members, organised in 450 chapters spread throughout the country but strongest in the middle west around Chicago, where mixed ethnic and religious groups holding strong traditional attitudes towards foreign policy offered a fertile field for propaganda. Although the committee exploited the confused feelings and emotions of the American heartland it should not be forgotten that it was motivated by the deepest patriotism and could appeal to the beliefs which had dominated American foreign policy before the first great war, beliefs that the American people, blessed with abundant natural resources and insulated by the sea from Europe need have no concern for the affairs of that continent. The movement had solid historical traditions behind it but it was out of date. Circumstances had changed, and attitudes were changing with them, moving in the direction epitomised by the title of Wendell Willkie's book of 1943, *One World*. However, during its short life, the committee fought valiantly against Roosevelt's foreign policy, attacking the destroyer deal, the lend-lease bill and revision of the neutrality acts.

It was opposed by the Committee to Defend America by Aiding the Allies. This committee developed out of a Non-Partisan Committee for Peace through Revision of the Neutrality Laws which had been formed under the chairmanship of William Allen White, the Emporia newspaper editor, at the time of Roosevelt's attempt to secure modifications of the neutrality legislation in September 1939. It was revivified after the collapse of Denmark and Norway in April 1940 and represented what was probably, according to the public opinion polls, the majority view within the United States at the time. In his editorials throughout the 1930s White had frequently stated his belief that the security of the United States was inseparable from that of Europe, and after the fall of France he became convinced that Nazi victory in Europe would be followed by an attack on the Americas. He favoured helping the Allies by all means short of war in order to gain a breathing space for the United States to build up its own defences, but he would not carry this argument to its logical conclusion and accept the necessity of direct American participation in the war. Neither he nor his group favoured such intervention and they had strong doubts of the wisdom of some of the president's policies, but their support was invaluable in helping to secure legislative acceptance of the lend-lease act and in the general task of helping to mould public opinion away from isolationism. Without the assistance of the Committee to Defend America by Aiding the Allies Roosevelt's task would have been the more difficult.

By the summer of 1941 the battle for public opinion had been won but events seemed to be outpacing accepted policy, and it seemed possible that the president might soon be tempted to play upon incidents on the North Atlantic in order to take the country over the brink into war. In December, however, the situation was simplified and clarified by the disaster which struck in the Pacific. The choice of war or peace was resolved for the American people by the Japanese attack on Pearl Harbor and the subsequent declaration of war by Germany and Italy, but in the pattern of events leading up to this attack the policies of the American government were not without influence.

Far Eastern Policy, 1939–1941

Although the United States officially pursued a policy of non-intervention in the Sino-Japanese dispute of the late 1930s the sympathies of most Americans lay with the Chinese, who were regarded as the innocent victims of aggressive militarism. The desire to keep out of war was, however, stronger than admiration for China and the *Panay* incident of December of 1937, in which an American gunboat on the Yangtse river was sunk by Japanese aircraft, underlined the caution with which the Far East was approached at that time. Diplomatic protests were made but when Japan accepted full responsibility and offered to pay an indemnity no further action was taken. The United States still adhered to the principles of the Open Door, which meant equal opportunity to exploit the economic resources of China, but confined itself to attempts to protect the persons and property of American nationals in China by diplomatic action.

Even after the Japanese proclamation, in November 1938, of their intention of creating a Greater East Asia Co-Prosperity Sphere implying the reduction of China to vassal status within the Japanese empire, there was no change in the American position. However, as the Japanese thrust deeper into China and diplomatic protests found no response from Tokyo the American administration moved towards a policy of economic sanctions in general conformity with Roosevelt's belief that aggression could be halted and contained by economic action. In July 1939 six months' notice was given of abrogation of the Japanese-American Treaty of Commerce and Navigation (1911).

The outbreak of war in Europe raised fears of a German-Japanese attempt to seek world domination which were strengthened in the spring of 1940. The collapse of France and the other western European states created a power vacuum in the Far East and opened their colonial possessions to the danger of Japanese attack. The agreement of September 1940 by which Vichy France gave Japan advance bases in Indo-China did nothing to allay such fears. The conclusion of the Tripartite Pact between Germany, Italy and Japan in the same month appeared to signal the creation of an offensive alliance between the three powers, an alliance which, moreover, in the light of the clauses assuring mutual assistance in the event of attack on any of the signatories by a power not already involved in the war, seemed to be directed against the United States. The possibility that after the conclusion of the Nazi-Soviet Pact in 1939 Japan's traditional rivalry with Russia in the Far East dictated an *entente* with Germany in no way qualified American suspicions. In the light of their territorial ambitions the Japanese dilemma was as acute as that which confronted the American administration, but attitudes were hardening on both sides and the diplomatic moves made by the Japanese were paralleled by increasingly severe American restrictions on trade with Japan. The National Defense Act of July 1940 had empowered the president to restrict export of strategic materials, and Roosevelt used its provisions to embargo the export of high grade scrap iron and aviation fuel. In September 1940 this embargo was extended to lower quality materials.

1941, however, was a year in which both sides engaged in serious diplomatic conversations in an attempt to negotiate their differences and at first there seemed some hope of success. But success depended on both sides being prepared to compromise, and it quickly became clear that the United States was not prepared to moderate its attitudes. Japan was almost eager to disclaim any offensive intention in the Tripartite Pact and seemed ready to withdraw from Indo-China, but continued to insist on the retention of hegemony over the Republic of China and was not prepared to abandon the gains of four years of arduous war. On this point the negotiations reached impasse, for the United States was equally adamant that the Japanese armies must be withdrawn from China and the situation restored to the status quo of 1936.

Critics of the administration have suggested that American policy was based upon assumptions of dubious validity; that it presupposed that the Kuomintang government of Chiang Kai-Shek had been in effective control of the country before the Japanese invasion and disregarded the fact that China had been engaged in a civil war which the Communists showed signs of winning; that it failed to recognise the existence of a power vacuum in China into which if not the Japanese then the Russians might move; that it exaggerated the extent of American interests in China and presumed that under Japanese control the China market would be closed to American goods. They have argued that moral principles were substituted for a rational analysis of the national interest and that such principles led to the mistaken policy of trying to elevate China under Chiang Kai-Shek into a strong counter-balance to Japan instead of allowing Japan to emerge as the natural check to the Soviet Union in this area of traditional Russian interest. Roosevelt and Hull certainly equated Japanese policy with expanding militarism, and were determined that such militarism should not be given full rein. They subscribed to the legalistic and moral traditions of American policy which denied the right of nations to resort to aggression to achieve their aims. But the president, and to a lesser extent Hull, did not completely ignore the realities of power, and did not wish to engage in any sort of crusade which ignored the American national interest as they conceived it. They believed that if Japan were allowed freedom of action in China and succeeded in consolidating its position it would then try to expand into South-east Asia, and that if China were abandoned the rest of the Far East would inevitably fall to the Japanese empire. They believed that in the modern world the United States could not ignore what went on outside the western hemisphere and that if Germany and Japan were encouraged by American inaction to conquer the areas upon which their immediate sights were set their ambitions would eventually grow to embrace the American continents themselves. This was the concept of 'one world' and it led to a policy of acceptance of part responsibility for the course of events in both Europe and the Far East. In so doing the American leaders did not seek war, but they also did not shrink from the possibility of war resulting from their assumption of common interests between the United States and the victims of aggression.

WAR 1941–1945

The result of the 'hard' American policy of economic action, combined with an insistence on Japanese withdrawal from China, was that Japan was placed in a dilemma from which there was no resort but war. Pride buttressed by fear of possible Russian expansion made withdrawal from China and abandonment of the Greater East Asia Co-Prosperity Sphere policy impossible. Whilst talks were still going on in Washington a Japanese task force struck at the American naval and air bases at Pearl Harbor in the Hawaiian Islands. This surprise attack on 7 December 1941 represented a desperate gamble, an attempt to cripple American power in the Pacific so that the simultaneous attack on South-east Asia and the East Indies could be successfully completed before the United States recovered from the blow. In Japanese eyes the gamble was both provoked and justified by the nature of American Far Eastern policy; to the Americans it was despicable treachery. But although the Pearl Harbor attack was a military setback of the first magnitude for the United States it clarified the political situation and seemed to justify the administration's belief that Japanese militarism was untrustworthy, imperialistic and profoundly dangerous. It united the country behind the president and, being followed by declarations of war by Germany and Italy, brought the United States into a war for self-defence and the maintenance of democratic rights against the tyranny of the Tripartite Pact.

The immediate military situation in the Pacific in the spring of 1942 was, however, grave. The American commander in the Philippines, General Douglas MacArthur, was forced to evacuate his position on the Bataan peninsula and to withdraw to Australia, vowing that he would return. The Japanese swept through the East Indies and took Malaya. Their first reverse did not come until the battle of the Coral Sea in May but when this was followed by their defeat at the battle of Midway the next month it became clear that the United States was beginning to recover from Pearl Harbor and that its superior economic and technological potential was beginning to be felt. The Japanese advance was halted, and there began the slow and painful process of recapture of Japanese-held islands with the aim of fighting through the western Pacific to the Japanese homeland itself. Between the summer of 1942 and the spring of 1945 strange new names, Guadalcanal, Tarawa, Iwo Jima, Okinawa and many others were added to the roll of American battle honours. The campaign was costly, the capture of Okinawa alone resulting in 11,260 dead and 33,769 wounded, but it was successful, and American forces approached to within 360 miles of Japan itself.

In the European theatre the first priority was an intensification of naval activity to keep the supply lanes of the North Atlantic open. Although Allied losses to German submarines continued to rise until mid 1943 there was new hope that the tide could be turned, and the flow of men and materials across the ocean became so great, despite the losses, that it quickly became possible to move from defence to attack. Although the Soviet Union was pressing hard for a second front in Europe to relieve the strain upon the Russian armies to the east it was eventually decided to launch operation Torch in North Africa. Allied forces landed at Casablanca, Oran and Algiers in November 1942 with General Dwight D. Eisenhower as supreme commander and caught Rommel's German army in a trap, contained to the east by Montgomery and the British Eighth Army. Victory followed in May 1943. In July Sicily was invaded and in September landings were made in Italy itself. Mussolini had already been overthrown by a domestic revolution, and the new government under Marshal Badoglio opened negotiations for surrender, but the Germans took control of Italy and the war continued. Each mile of the Allied advance up the peninsula had to be dearly bought. By June 1944 the Russians were advancing rapidly on the eastern front and the long-awaited Allied invasion of the fortress of Europe took place. Landings were made in Normandy on D-Day, 6 June, catching the German forces completely by surprise. The massive amphibious undertaking was brilliantly successful, despite bad weather and unexpectedly heavy opposition at Omaha Beach, and within six weeks the Allied armies had broken out of the beachhead into Brittany and were moving across the northern French plains towards Paris. The fate of the war was no longer in doubt for Germany was encircled in a grip which was continually being tightened. In March 1945 the Rhine was crossed; Hitler committed suicide on 30 April, and on 8 May 1945 victory in Europe was complete.

The atomic bomb

In the Far East the war continued, and it was estimated that continuation of the island-hopping tactics would cost almost a million more American casualties before Japan finally fell. In these circumstances Truman, who had succeeded to the presidency on the sudden death of President Roosevelt from a massive cerebral haemorrhage on 12 April 1945, felt that he had no alternative but to use the atomic bomb. The new weapon was dropped on Hiroshima on 6 August 1945, killing between seventy and eighty thousand of its inhabitants. Despite this demonstration of the terrible destructive power of the bomb the expected Japanese surrender did not follow and a second bomb was dropped on Nagasaki three days later. On 14 August Japan capitulated.

The war was over but the problems of peace remained. The ways in which these problems would be approached had already been largely determined by what had happened on the diplomatic front during the years of war, for the experience of war had transformed America's traditional attitudes towards foreign relations and had led to the creation of a bipartisan foreign policy in which the assumption that the United States could not once again retreat into isolationism was no longer seriously questioned.

CONFERENCE DIPLOMACY

The demands of global war had created a new type of diplomacy in which heads of government and senior ministers met to discuss in person the common problems inherent in their united effort. Such conference diplomacy helped to establish working relationships between Roosevelt, Churchill and Stalin which considerably eased the burdens of their task and minimised the sometimes profound differences over policy, tactics, and post-war aspirations which emerged as the war continued. Following the meeting between Roosevelt and Churchill in August 1941 which produced the Atlantic Charter a series of conferences embracing different combinations of the Allied leaders and ministers met at frequent but irregular intervals throughout the wartime period. In 1943 for example there were major conferences at Casablanca, Quebec, Moscow, Cairo and Teheran. At the first of these, in January 1943, Roosevelt and Churchill agreed that they would continue the war until they received the unconditional surrender of the enemy and that a second front in Europe should be mounted as soon as possible. Many other questions of military and political consequence were on the agenda at this and subsequent meetings and on some of these issues the two powers differed widely.

One of the major disagreements between Roosevelt and Churchill stemmed from their widely different views on colonialism and gave rise to conflicting interpretations of the scope of that section of the Atlantic Charter which declared that at the end of the war oppressed and subject peoples should be given the right of self-determination. When Roosevelt indicated that he believed that this provision applied to colonial peoples, as well as to the victims of military aggression, the British prime minister vehemently rejected this broad interpretation in a famous declaration that he had not become the king's first minister in order to preside over the dissolution of the British Empire. The breach was temporarily patched over but Roosevelt's anti-colonialism was to be a continuous source of irritation between the two men during the whole series of conferences in which they were involved and the president's distrust of traditional British policy also complicated discussions of military strategy.

Outside of the Americas he rejected not only colonialism but also the concept of spheres of influence. Suspicion that the British were anxious to carve out such a sphere in the Balkans led to the American refusal to countenance a second front in that area, and after the landings in Europe had taken place, and the march towards Berlin was in full swing, political factors were deliberately excluded from decisions taken on the pace of the advance. British arguments that the armies should move into eastern Europe as quickly and as deeply as possible in order to contain the extent of the Russian advance westwards were rejected. Roosevelt and his advisers showed a healthy fear of British ambitions but at the same time displayed an unhealthy confidence in the good faith and democratic instincts of the Soviet Union. A certain naïvety pervaded America's relations with both the British and Russian governments, a naïvety that perhaps reflected both a relative lack of experience in diplomatic dealings with rival world powers and a traditional optimism and faith in the rule of moral law.

Despite the experiences of the past twenty years the United States appeared to revert during the Second World War to a Wilsonian belief that in post-war Europe power politics and naked national interests would be of minimal importance. Great faith was placed in the proposed United Nations, which it was hoped would prove to be an effective instrument for the pacification and regulation of disputes and foster the creation of a genuine sense of mutual world interest. Only with respect to the Far East was American policy recognisable in terms of customary non-American traditions, and it has been Far Eastern policy which has been most severely and continuously attacked by domestic critics since 1945.

At the Yalta conference with Churchill and Stalin in February 1945 Roosevelt secured Russian confirmation of the promise which had been given in October 1943 that they would enter the Pacific war at the end of the fighting in Europe. However, in return for this agreement, to take effect within three months of peace in Europe, Stalin exacted concessions in the Far East. The Soviet Union was to be given the Kurile islands, southern Sakhalin, Dairen and Port Arthur and economic rights in Manchuria. In addition the United States and Great Britain were to recognise the autonomy of Outer Mongolia and secure the acceptance by Chiang Kai-Shek of these provisions. In all of these areas Russia had some historic claims, and the Yalta agreements represent an acceptance by Roosevelt of traditional European diplomatic practices and the abandonment of the principle of self-determination which had been written into the Atlantic Charter. This was the price exacted and accepted for the Russian pledge to honour the earlier promise of intervention in the war against Japan.

Concessions were also made at the Yalta conference with respect to eastern Europe, but in this area the position was less negotiable. Russian armies were already in control and could dictate the form of settlement. However, although it was agreed that parts of eastern Poland were to be transferred to the Soviet Union, with Poland receiving compensation from eastern Germany, concessions were not made by the western powers alone. Stalin, who also participated in this curiously old-fashioned conference, agreed to reconstitute the puppet Lublin government in Poland by the inclusion of representatives of the Free Polish government in London. Free elections were to be held in Poland and the rest of eastern Europe, and a modification of his position on representation and use of the veto in the United Nations Organisation was obtained. These concessions, however, were less substantial than those made by the western powers and application of the provisions relating to eastern Europe in particular depended entirely upon future Russian good faith.

THE UNITED NATIONS, A REVOLUTION IN AMERICAN POLICY

Like Wilson before him Roosevelt believed that any defects in the post-war settlements could be rectified through an international assembly, and the establishment of such an organisation became one of the cardinal points of American foreign policy during the war period. As early as 1 January 1942 a declaration affirming the principles of the Atlantic Charter had been signed in Washington by representatives of twenty six nations, and in 1943 a bipartisan movement was launched by members of both the major American political parties with the object of securing American participation in a post-war international organisation. The Fulbright–Connally resolution to this effect had passed both houses of Congress by the end of the year, and a conference at Dumbarton Oaks in the autumn of 1944 worked out a draft charter for a United Nations structure which formed the working basis for the San Francisco conference in April–June 1945. The details were worked out in San Francisco by delegates from fifty nations and as finally approved set up a bi-cameral organisation consisting of a General Assembly and a Security Council with associated agencies such as the Trusteeship Council, the Economic and Social Council and the International Court of Justice. The United States, which together with Great Britain, the Soviet Union, France and China, was given a permanent seat on the eleven-nation Security Council, had reached a turning-point in its history. When the Senate accepted the United Nations treaty in July 1945 a revolution in American foreign policy was formally sealed. The dreams of 1919 which had been blighted by partisan political rivalries seemed at last to be offered their chance of fulfilment. Acceptance of an internationalist role in world affairs was buttressed by massive American participation in the International Monetary Fund and in the International Bank for Reconstruction and Development which were set up following the United Nations Monetary and Financial Conference at Bretton Woods in July 1944.

1945–1947, THE WORLD DIVIDES

Sole possession of the atomic bomb gave Americans a feeling of confidence in foreign affairs at the end of the war. The great armies were demobilised and reconversion of the economy to peacetime production gave rise to sufficient problems to preoccupy the public mind. The nation's enemies had been defeated and qualified optimism encouraged belief that the wartime association with the Soviet Union would continue despite all difficulties. This illusion did not long remain intact. Proceedings at the last of the wartime conferences, held at Potsdam in July 1945, had already indicated that Russian suspicion of the West, temporarily subordinated since 1941 to common dangers and common needs, once again dominated Soviet policy and that the coalition was splitting apart at the seams. President Truman's first meetings with Stalin underlined the fact that diplomatic relations between their two countries would be neither easy nor pleasant. Already the Soviet Union seemed intent on blocking agreed policies whenever these policies conflicted with Russian political ambitions, and the history of the years from 1945 to 1947 confirmed the extent to which the world was once again divided.

The Soviet Union gave strong support to Communist parties in eastern Europe, encouragement to Communist guerrillas in Greece, and retained troops in Iran. The peace treaties which were concluded reflected neither a harmony of interests between the united nations nor the American aspirations towards self-determination, but instead incorporated the realities of power politics and the traditional concept of spheres of influence. Those with Finland, Hungary, Bulgaria and Rumania favoured Soviet interests whilst the treaty with Iran displayed Western influences. No agreement at all could be reached between the Soviet Union and the Western allies on the details of peace settlements with Austria and Germany, and the Four-Power Allied Control Council which was set up to work out satisfactory solutions to the German problem succeeded only in hardening the divisions between east and west. Boundaries between the Russian zone of occupation and those controlled by Britain, France and the United States became armed frontiers, and eastern Germany became a Russian-dominated satellite. The particular problems of Berlin, which although located within the Russian zone had been partitioned among the occupying powers, gave rise to constant irritations and difficulties. Western access to the city by defined land and air corridors was at all times vulnerable to Russian interference. Berlin epitomised the optimism of the West during the period of conference diplomacy and in the post-war world came to symbolise the cleavage between the Communist and non-Communist worlds.

After trying to work out a satisfactory relationship with Stalin Truman eventually came to the conclusion that effective co-operation between the United States and the Soviet Union was impossible. It was with the president's encouragement that Winston Churchill made the historic speech in Fulton Missouri in March 1946 in which he described 'the iron curtain' which had descended across the continent of Europe, from Stettin on the Baltic to Trieste on the Adriatic, and warned the West that the Russians regarded military weakness as evidence of lack of will and paid heed only to military strength. The Fulton speech marked a turning-point in international relations. The concept of 'one world' was abandoned and in its place emerged the idea of a divided world in which the Soviet bloc confronted the 'free world', a heterogeneous group of states united only by their immediate rejection of communism.

CONTAINMENT AND COLD WAR

Collapse of the grand partnership of the Second World War had profound strategic implications for the United States which, in the light of the history of the inter-war years, were assimilated with surprising rapidity. A policy to meet the new situation was publicly expounded in an article in the journal *Foreign Affairs* (July 1947) by an anonymous author, later identified as the prominent American diplomat and expert on Russian affairs Mr George Kennan. From the premise that Communism is a dynamic expansive force aiming at world domination he argued that it must be contained by the application of counter-force around the perimeter of the Russian empire. This theory of 'containment' gave a new word to American diplomatic vocabulary but its underlying concept was already being applied by the Truman administration. Truman had already come to terms with the new situation and three months earlier, in March 1947, had asked Congress for an appropriation of four hundred million dollars in military aid for the armed forces of Greece and Turkey in an attempt to buttress the Greek and Turkish governments against the danger of Communist subversion and possible Russian attack. The request was specific, but in presenting it to Congress Truman propounded the general doctrine that 'it must be the policy of the United States to support free peoples who are resisting attempted subjugation by armed minorities or by outside pressure'. The 'Truman doctrine' was accepted by Congress in the interest of national security and became one of the fundamental assumptions behind American foreign policy in the cold war period.

The logical corollary of military assistance was general economic aid. In June 1947 the secretary of State George Marshall formulated a plan, denounced by the Soviet Union as an example of American imperialism, which provided for an extensive programme of economic aid to Europe in the hope that speedy economic recovery would promote the conditions necessary for survival and the strengthening of democratic institutions. A Committee of European Economic Co-operation was formed in Western Europe and, following the Communist coup in Czechoslovakia in April 1948, Congress established the Economic Co-operation Administration to channel American aid to Europe. Within the next three years $12,000 million were spent by E.C.A. Not only was this an act of generosity unparalleled in peacetime; it was also a realistic attempt by the United States to build a coherent policy to meet the new challenges of world politics. Truman's Point Four programme of economic and technological assistance to underdeveloped countries, announced in his second inaugural address of January 1949, represented the next stage in this policy. As European recovery began to gather momentum the continent became less vulnerable to Communist infiltration and the underdeveloped areas of the world became the weak points in the Western defence perimeter. It seemed clear that they might quickly fall to the allurements of Communist promises unless the capitalist countries demonstrated their concern and good faith. Point Four was an attempt to meet this threat.

The virility of communism and of the Western counter-attack had created a state of cold war, and there seemed little danger of 'hot war' as long as the United States retained sole possession of the atomic bomb, but the determination of both sides was frequently tested. The most serious crisis developed in 1948 when the western powers decided that, as a common solution of the German problem was for the time being impossible, a Federal Republic of West Germany should be created out of the British, French and American zones of occupation. Reaction from the Soviet Union was swift; land communications between Berlin and the West were cut and the Western part of the city was threatened with starvation or surrender. The American dilemma was acute. President Truman was adamant that Berlin should not be abandoned, but was equally opposed to an attempt to force supply convoys through the Soviet zone by the land corridors, thereby incurring the risk of a direct confrontation between the United States and the Soviet Union and the danger of war. The dilemma was resolved by flying necessary supplies into the beleaguered city along the air corridors which the Soviet Union allowed to remain open. Throughout the winter of 1948–9 and into the spring of the new year this unprecedented operation lifted over two and a half million tons of food, fuel and other materials into Berlin. Vigorous response to the Russian challenge achieved its purpose: Stalin's bluff was met, the blockade raised, and in October 1949 the Federal German Republic came into being. The episode represented a considerable tactical victory for the United States but also underlined the perilous state of world politics and the ever present risk that any miscalculation or mistake in policy could result in war.

Although the United States had undertaken an activist role, and through its extensive programmes of economic and military aid had become associated with many other states, it remained, with one exception, outside any alliance system. The exception was the collective security arrangements made for the western hemisphere in the Treaty of Rio de Janeiro in 1947. Signed by the United States, Canada, Mexico and the Latin American Republics the treaty provided for mutual assistance in the event of attack upon any one of their number. The following year the Organisation of American States was set up to provide machinery for inter-state consultation. This example of collective security on a regional basis seemed to offer wider possibilities and during the winter of the Berlin air-lift negotiations were held between the United States and the Marshall Plan countries which resulted in the conclusion of the North Atlantic Treaty of 1949. A military alliance with guarantees of mutual assistance it was patterned on the Rio treaty and provided for the establishment of a North Atlantic Treaty Organisation. When the senate accepted the NATO treaty in July 1949 the second post-war revolution in American foreign policy was complete. Not even during the two world wars had the United States concluded treaties of alliance with its associates, but under pressure from the threats of the cold war it had now entered two multi-lateral systems and accepted obligations which effectively limited its own freedom of action in the future. Not only did isolationism appear finally to be dead; with it had disappeared the long tradition of neutrality.

Disclosure on 23 September 1949 that the Soviet Union had exploded a nuclear device and that the United States no longer possessed a monopoly of this dangerous weapon helped to confirm belief in the wisdom of the new policy. In 1951 the joint military forces which had been envisaged in the NATO treaty came into existence under an American supreme commander, General Eisenhower, and it was clearly recognised that the United States now regarded the security of Western Europe as an essential part of its global strategy.

PERILS IN THE FAR EAST, 1945–1950

Whilst these important developments were taking place in Europe the fortunes of American policy in the Far East fluctuated. Success in Japan was accompanied by failure in China.

After the surrender of the Japanese empire to General MacArthur on the battleship *Missouri* in Tokyo Bay (August 1945) American troops remained in Japan until the end of the decade. Rejecting the Russian demand for participation in the occupation Truman appointed MacArthur his personal representative in charge of the process of demilitarisation and democratisation of Japan, responsible nominally to an eleven-nation Far Eastern Commission in Washington and a four-power Allied Council in Tokyo. Neither of these bodies had any significant influence over the general who became, in effect, the omnipotent overlord of Japanese rehabilitation. His arrogance was enlightened by his policies and he was signally successful in the execution of his mandate. Realising that the authority of the emperor had to be maintained, in order that the stability of the state might not be prejudiced, much of the imperial mystique was left intact but at the same time representative institutions were strengthened in order to create a check upon imperial power. The military were rigidly controlled but responsibility for domestic order was gradually transferred to Japanese authorities. War industries were dismantled but MacArthur realised that the economy would collapse unless supported by an efficient industrial machine, and so no attempt was made to reduce Japan to agrarian status. Under MacArthur's guidance the foundations were laid for Japan's recovery and re-emergence as a great Far Eastern and world power.

By contrast, however, the situation in China in the post-war years went from bad to worse and ended in disaster. In 1945 continued support for Chiang Kai-Shek remained the keystone of the American policy and Kuomintang troops were air-lifted from the western to the eastern provinces in order that Chiang and not the Chinese Communists might receive the Japanese surrender. This attempt to boost the power of the Nationalists did not, however, strengthen the régime sufficiently for it to be able to crush the Communists, and the civil war which had gone underground during the war with Japan flared out again. A series of American missions to China reported that the only hope of survival for the

Kuomintang régime lay in the rapid inauguration of basic economic reforms accompanied by the creation of a political coalition with the Communists. An attempt was made to make American aid dependent upon reform, but although some progress was made Chiang Kai-Shek refused to accept Communist demands that their armies remain intact as separate units of the national army and that they receive a significant percentage of higher ministerial posts. With Chiang's rejection of these terms attempts to create a coalition were abandoned and full-scale war broke out again. Chiang's incompetence and unpopularity made Communist victory inevitable. A mission to China led by George Marshall in 1947 was still-born from the outset and during 1948 the Communists gained control of most of the country. In 1949 the Nationalist government fled to Formosa, where Chiang had established a stronghold from which he hoped to be able eventually to launch an invasion of the mainland.

Creation of the Chinese People's Republic under Communist rule was not only a serious blow to American prestige in the Far East; it also produced within the United States a serious challenge to the bipartisan foreign policy which had been followed since 1941. The 'China lobby' which emerged in Washington in the late 1940s was not an isolationist lobby. The opponents of President Truman and his new secretary of State Dean Acheson did not want the United States to withdraw from the Far East: quite the opposite, they wanted greater intervention and a more active policy of opposition to Communism. They charged that the administration had effectively betrayed Chiang Kai-Shek by failing to give him massive economic and military aid during the period from 1945 to 1947 and was therefore responsible for the collapse of China. This emotional reaction to the advance of Communism in Asia was in marked contrast to the realistic attitudes of the White House and the State Department. Both Truman and Acheson understood that local conditions in China since 1945 had been such that only full military intervention by the United States could perhaps have saved the Kuomintang, and both believed that large-scale American participation in the Chinese civil war had never been either politically possible or militarily certain of success. The anti-Communist howl that was heard in Washington over the defeat of Chiang Kai-Shek was to have important domestic consequences but it was not loud enough to divert the administration from its realistic approach to world problems. Nor did it threaten the general policy of internationalism and containment. Essentially the only difference between the administration and its critics lay in definition of the frontiers of the 'free world' behind which the ultimate stand against communism should be made.

In 1950, however, this difference suddenly became of paramount importance, for in January Acheson issued a statement defining the American defence perimeter in the Far East. It did not include the island of Formosa, nor Korea, and it was on this relatively unknown peninsula that the cold war developed a heat which threatened to drag the whole world once again into total combat.

6

THE BURDENS OF WORLD LEADERSHIP

CRISIS IN KOREA

In the post-war period Korea, like Berlin, had become a visible symbol of the divided world. When the Soviet Union entered the war in the Far East in August 1945, according to the agreements made at Yalta in February, Russian troops moved into Korea and at the time of the Japanese surrender had reached the 38th parallel. There they met the American advance north. The peninsula had been occupied by Japan since 1910 but during the war the Allied powers determined that it should be restored as an independent sovereign state. In the first flush of victory the United States believed that the Soviet Union would co-operate, that a Korean government would be formed and that the occupation forces would then be withdrawn. However, despite agreement between the British, Russian and American foreign ministers in December 1945 to set up a provisional government on democratic principles, under the aegis of a joint Russian-American commission, no further progress was made. This failure was followed by the establishment in the northern zone of a Communist People's Republic in which, with Russian help, an army of 150,000 men was trained and equipped. The American response was to form an interim government in South Korea and then place the whole question before the United Nations. A United Nations Temporary Commission was sent to supervise free elections throughout Korea and oversee reunification of the peninsula. It was, however, denied access to North Korea and had to be content with elections in the American zone. A constitutional assembly was convoked, a constitution drafted and accepted, and Syngman Rhee was elected first president of the Republic of Korea. His government was recognised by both the United States and the United Nations as the only lawful government in Korea. At first there appeared some hope for the future. By June 1949 the American occupation forces had been withdrawn from South Korea and the Russians had announced that their own withdrawal from the North would soon be completed. However, developments in the South Korean Republic caused some concern in Washington, for Rhee's government had little popular support and was dominated by wealthy landowners and military groups. Unwillingness to seem overcommitted to such a régime resulted in a cut back in American aid which, together with Acheson's statement in January 1950, may have contributed to the events that followed.

On 25 July 1950 North Korean forces crossed the 38th parallel and launched a full-scale invasion of South Korea. American reaction to the crisis was immediate: on President Truman's instructions the secretary of State immediately brought the situation to the attention of the Security Council which condemned the invasion, branded it as aggression, and called for the withdrawal of the North Korean forces. Such swift decision was made possible by the absence of the Soviet delegate, who was boycotting all meetings because of the Council's refusal to seat a representative of Communist China. In addition Truman authorised General MacArthur to supply arms to the South Koreans and to use naval and air cover to assure their delivery; the Seventh Fleet was ordered to the Formosa Strait to isolate Formosa both from attack and from participation in the conflict. Two days later the American Far Eastern Command was instructed to give military support to the South Korean forces. This action was taken by the president after consultation with his advisers, including congressional leaders, but Congress itself was only informed officially after the event. As an example of executive leadership in the field of foreign affairs, for which he had direct responsibility under the constitution, Truman's decisive and immediate action was unparalleled in recent American history; it was also a clear and unmistakeable sign of determination to accept the Communist challenge and face the burden of leadership of the 'free world'. On the day that American forces were committed to Korea the Security Council, on a motion from the United States, expanded its original resolution and called upon all members of the United Nations to render assistance to the beleaguered republic. A United Nations command was set up, the American government was asked to nominate a supreme commander, General MacArthur was appointed, and nineteen member-nations including Great Britain quickly sent support to the Far East.

Military circles were at first optimistic that the United Nations force would be more than sufficient to stem the invasion, for the size and scope of the North Korean movements were unknown. However, during the summer campaigns MacArthur's army was thrust back to the south-eastern corner of South Korea, and although the base at Pusan was strongly defended there was grave danger of a complete collapse of the position. Only reinforcements on a massive scale enabled MacArthur to break out of the beachhead. The tide turned following landings at Inchon far behind the North Korean lines and this skilfully executed flanking operation paved the way for a drive back up the peninsula to the 38th parallel. By 1 October all the ground lost during the summer months had been regained and MacArthur was poised for a counter-invasion of North Korea itself.

At this point a new factor entered the situation. During the war in the south little had been heard from the Chinese Communists, but after the successful United Nations recovery the Chinese foreign minister warned that if North Korea were invaded China would not stand apart from the struggle. This threat was not seriously regarded by the United Nations or its Supreme Commander and on 7 October 1950 the General Assembly authorised General MacArthur to move north and establish control over the whole country. President Truman, however, recognised that the possibility of Chinese intervention had to be faced and repeated earlier instructions to MacArthur that he was not to take military action against targets in China without authorisation from Washington. In order to reiterate personally this policy and to gain MacArthur's first-hand observations on the situation President Truman flew to meet the general on Wake Island in the Pacific on 15 October. During the talks he was assured that there was little danger of Chinese participation in the war, received confirmation that the declared policy of the administration would be observed and heard MacArthur's optimistic belief that any Chinese assistance to the North Koreans could be quickly crushed by the forces under his command. At first this confidence seemed justified and all fears groundless. The United Nations armies encountered little resistance as they moved steadily northwards, but as they approached the Yalu river which marks the boundary between Korea and China they ran into heavy concentrations of Chinese troops. A failure of intelligence had not indicated the existence of 850,000 Chinese troops massed along the line of the Yalu. The advance was halted and then fell into retreat to the 38th parallel with very heavy losses.

Despite these reverses the administration was determined not to take any action which might result in the war spreading beyond the borders of Korea itself. This policy was now seen to conflict with the views of the United Nations supreme commander, who believed that military considerations dictated bombing Chinese bases in Manchuria. At the Wake Island meeting MacArthur had been warned not to make provocative statements with political implications, but after active Chinese intervention had been established he issued a number of policy statements which ran counter to official American and United Nations strategy. These caused grave concern in Washington and he was ordered to desist. His advocacy of total victory became even more embarrassing when the United Nations dropped its original aim of reuniting the whole of Korea under a democratically elected government and settled for the maintenance of the security and independence of South Korea alone. When General Ridgway managed to stop the North Korean advance slightly to the north of the 38th parallel, and it became clear that he could hold this position, the concept of fighting a limited war for limited objectives became established in New York and Washington. A general war with China would have been, as General Bradley said, 'the wrong war at the wrong place, at the wrong time and with the wrong enemy'. The new strategy adopted was to hold the lines against attack, inflict such casualties upon the enemy that they would have no inclination to press southwards, and hope for a negotiated peace. MacArthur was unable to accept such limited objectives. On 25 March he issued a further public statement, and in reply to a letter from Joseph W. Martin, the Republican party leader in the House of Representatives, claimed that there was no substitute for victory and that the war was one to defeat communism in the Far East. This open challenge to presidential authority could not be ignored and on 11 April 1951 President Truman relieved MacArthur of his commands. General Ridgway was appointed to succeed him.

The dismissal of General MacArthur was not only an example of Truman's courage but was also, at a time of great emotional strain for the American people in their fight against communism, a tribute to the American tradition of keeping military authority subordinate to the civil power. It underlined the executive responsibility of the president in formulating the foreign policy of the Union, revealed a maturity of judgement in the White House and a convincing realism in American strategy. But the general was not persuaded of the wisdom of the administration's policy and on his return to the United States made a triumphal progress across the country to Washington where he addressed a joint session of Congress. The Senate Armed Services Committee held hearings to investigate the dismissal in the context of the whole Far Eastern policy. Judicious management by Democratic congressional leaders kept the political situation under control, cooled tempers, and brought about a recognition that full-scale war with China, involving the possibility of Russian participation, was not to be welcomed or encouraged lightly.

However, although it was reluctant to provoke a wider war the administration was determined to make the Chinese realise that aggression, according to the American definition, does not pay. The United Nations approved an embargo on the export of strategic materials to China, and branded China an aggressor in Korea; and the United States made it clear that it would oppose the entry of Communist China into the United Nations with all the influence at its command. A peace treaty, accompanied by a defence treaty providing for the continuation of American bases, was signed with Japan in the hope of building up its position in the Far East as a counter-weight to China. Mutual security treaties were concluded with the Philippines, Australia, and New Zealand in an attempt to construct a strong alliance system in the western Pacific.

Whilst these measures were being negotiated the communists began to make tentative overtures towards a peaceful solution of the war. Jacob Malik, leader of the Russian delegation to the United Nations, indicated that a settlement could be made in terms of a cease fire and agreement to withdraw United Nations military forces to the 38th parallel. General Ridgway opened negotiations with North Korean and Chinese representatives on 10 July, and on 27 November the first real hopes of an armistice were raised when the Communists modified their original demands and accepted the existing military lines as a basis for negotiation. Progress was, however, slow and in October 1952 the talks at Panmunjom temporarily broke down over the question of repatriation of prisoners: the Communists demanded the return of all prisoners, even those who had indicated that they did not wish to go back to the North, and this demand was rejected. The talks were not resumed until March 1953, after the inauguration of the new American president Dwight D. Eisenhower. During his campaign Eisenhower had promised that he would go to Korea. He did, but it is doubtful whether the trip influenced the negotiations in any way. The greatest threat to their successful conclusion came from President Syngman Rhee himself, who released northern prisoners without arranging for their repatriation, and threatened to remove his own troops from the United Nations command and resume fighting. Indeed until American pressure was brought to bear upon him Rhee refused to accept any armistice which allowed Chinese forces to remain in North Korea. When negotiations were finally concluded in July 1953 he would not sign the agreement, although in return for American promises to train and equip twenty South Korean divisions, provide economic aid, and conclude a mutual security treaty with South Korea, he was reluctantly prepared to support it.

The war in Korea had cost the United States over 120,000 casualties. It had secured the first objective of restoring the independence of South Korea but had failed to achieve the second aim of the United Nations: reunification of Korea under one freely elected government. American determination to resist the advance of Communism had been demonstrated and the swift initial response to the invasion underlined the fact that, despite congressional prerogatives, the federal system enabled a strong president to take effective action. The peculiar circumstances of the cold war had if anything strengthened traditional executive powers, for in any move against aggressive Communism the president could appeal to a clear national consensus which was prepared to accept military action in the defence of liberty; liberty which, in the post-war world, was identified with the support of all types of non-Communist government. At the same time the president had shown responsible caution in resisting the urgings of extremists and, in accepting the Communist challenge, had established the possibility of fighting a limited war for limited objectives. Wise leadership on both sides had managed to contain the fighting to the Korean peninsula but by demonstrating the possibility of limited war for local objectives the Korean example may also have established a pattern for future Communist policy.

REPUBLICAN FOREIGN POLICY: THE STRATEGY OF EISENHOWER AND DULLES

With victory in the 1952 presidential election the Republican party returned to power after twenty years in the political wilderness. To most observers the new president, despite the massive reputation which he had built up during the Second World War, and during the short period from 1951 to 1952 when he had been supreme commander of the NATO forces in Europe, seemed to be overshadowed in the fields of diplomacy and military calculation by his secretary of State John Foster Dulles. Until Dulles's death in 1959 the president gave him more complete authority in the conduct of foreign relations than had ever previously been exercised by a secretary of State.

Eisenhower had complete confidence in Dulles, whom he believed to be unequalled in his knowledge of world affairs and diplomatic practice, and saw his whole career as a preparation for the highest office in the State Department. The grandson of President Harrison's secretary of state, and nephew to Wilson's secretary Robert Lansing, John Foster Dulles had assisted at the Paris Peace conference in 1919 and had helped to negotiate most of the international agreements, including the United Nations Charter, which marked the revolution in American foreign policy since the Second World War. He had worked closely with all the Democratic secretaries since 1933. Eisenhower's confidence in Dulles's training and ability led him to trust the secretary's judgement, and although the memoirs of members of his administration emphasise that Dulles was always careful to keep the president completely informed and never exceeded his constitutional authority, it is also clear that Dulles, who always had the ear of the president at any hour of the day and night, exercised unparalleled power in the functions of his office.

Dulles was an energetic moralist. Communism was atheistic Communism and he could not readily accept the necessity of living with it in a divided world. The foreign policy planks of the Republican party platform of 1952, which he had largely written himself, denounced 'the negative, futile and immoral policy of "containment"'. In its promise of independence for the 'captive peoples' of the Communist satellites, in its repudiation of all secret agreements such as those made at Yalta, in its talk of total victory against Communism, the platform seemed to herald the coming of an administration committed to a policy of liberation, of rolling back Communism until it eventually succumbed to the forces of light. The fact that Dulles had himself helped to shape the Democratic policies which were now so vigorously denounced appeared to have been overlooked even by Mr Dulles himself.

Dulles's greatest weakness was the way in which, despite his legal and diplomatic training, his enthusiasms led him to use high-sounding phrases which did not stand up to analysis and to issue promises that were frequently unattainable. After he took office he modified many of the positions adopted in the platform, recognised the wisdom of much of the Democratic foreign policy and redefined liberation to mean, not actual physical and political liberation, but a large-scale ideological offensive exerting constant pressure upon the Communist world in an attempt to weaken the allegiance of satellite states to the Soviet Union. However, despite these qualifications, his free use of language continued to create a public image which was always to some extent at variance with his actual policy. For example in an interview for *Life* magazine in 1956 he outlined his famous 'brinkmanship' theory, asserting that the necessary art of diplomacy is the ability to get to the brink of war and stare it in the face without fear. Coupled with earlier statements about massive retaliation this helped to develop a picture of a trigger-happy secretary of State who might at any time let loose an atomic holocaust. This was unfortunate, for brinkmanship was only a spectacular description of policies traditionally followed in international affairs: no power can ever afford to abandon the possibility of ultimately defending its interests by war, which must always form part of its calculations. However, his honesty and ingenuous frankness does not mitigate the fact that, as he stated in January 1954, he relied more upon the nuclear deterrent than upon strong local traditional forces.

Such reliance upon nuclear power commended itself to the president and to the cabinet, for it meant that the military establishment could be cut down, an appealing possibility to a Republican administration which hoped to be able to balance the budget. The concept was also attractive to the American people who, at the end of the Korean war, were experiencing the normal reaction of wishing to demobilise the troops and bring them back home. The new policy, which relied upon the atomic bomb and its more powerful successor the hydrogen bomb, both to be carried in the airplanes of the Strategic Air Force, became popularly known as 'more bang for a buck'. However, despite the economic savings which could be envisaged the policy had serious military and diplomatic defects. Although perhaps ideally suited to a major confrontation between the great world powers, and perhaps a real deterrent therefore against direct Soviet aggression, it failed to provide for the sort of war that had been fought in Korea and which seemed likely to become the prototype for Communist probes in the future. Moreover, the circumstances under which the ultimate deterrent would be used in the Dulles strategy were never exactly defined, and perhaps could not be so defined without appearing to abandon much of the non-American world. It was generally accepted that it would only be employed in the event of a Russian offensive against the United States itself, Latin America, and probably western Europe. It was doubtful if it would be used against China in the case of war in South-east Asia, or even in the defence of Formosa. The security of India and of the African states also posed fundamental questions of strategy which the atomic deterrent did little to solve. On the other hand, it could also be argued that the very uncertainty of the circumstances in which atomic weapons would be used made the deterrent effective.

Although President Eisenhower accepted the main outline of Dulles's foreign policy thinking there is evidence to believe that he tenuously subscribed to a more flexible concept of international politics. Although it was eclipsed until the death of Dulles in May 1959 his consuming desire for peace was continually being exerted to modify his secretary's over-exuberant pronouncements. When Dulles talked of liberation during the campaign he was reiterating with significant omissions Eisenhower's speech to the American Legion, in which the presidential candidate had called for the freeing of subject peoples by peaceful means. When Dulles spoke of liberation without qualification Eisenhower quietly rebuked him by stressing in Philadelphia that he meant to 'aid by every peaceful means, but only by peaceful means, the right to live in freedom'. However, although Eisenhower promised, in his first state of the union message, a new and positive foreign policy his growing admiration for Dulles and his strong belief that somehow the United States had to stop the slow erosion of the 'free world' prevented him from doing more than correcting Dulles's verbal excesses and occasionally following his own instincts, as in the 'Chance for Peace' speech in April 1953. The new positive policy appeared to be that of Dulles, over whom the president cast a benevolent supporting shadow. Only in the last year of his presidency, after Dulles had been removed by death, did the president seize the initiative in foreign affairs. The fact that he then failed to alter in any significant sense the patterns of international politics neither justified nor condemned the Dulles policy, for Soviet-American relations during the final months of Eisenhower's presidency were afflicted by particular difficulties for which the president himself was largely responsible.

DIPLOMATIC FAILURES IN THE FAR EAST

Even as the foreign policy of the new administration was being enunciated its limitations were exposed by a crisis in South-east Asia. In Indo-China the French were retreating before the advance of Communist-Nationalist forces and were threatened with the loss of the whole of their eastern empire. The critical situation came to a focus at the fortress of Dienbienphu, where French and loyal Vietnamese troops were besieged and heavily outnumbered by the rebels. Defeat at Dienbienphu would open the way to Saigon and result in the overthrow of French authority over the whole of Indo-China. Although the United States had been underwriting much of the cost of the war by economic aid to France, it became clear, as the siege of Dienbienphu continued, that only large-scale military support could save the French position. Accepting the 'domino' theory that the fall of Indo-China would inevitably mean the collapse of the rest of South-east Asia Eisenhower wanted to act but rejected unilateral American intervention of the type proposed by Admiral Radford, chairman of the joint chiefs of staff, and by William Knowland, Republican leader in the United States Senate, which would have meant bombing the Vietminh bases. Dulles inclined towards the Radford plan but many congressional leaders and White House advisers, and the president himself, saw the dangers of getting involved without support in a war similar to that which had been fought in Korea. On the other hand, it was generally felt that France could not be abandoned, particularly in view of American anxiety to secure French acceptance of the proposed European Defence Community. A compromise plan was finally evolved by which the United States agreed to commit troops to Indo-China under specific conditions, chief among which were British and Commonwealth participation and a French undertaking to guarantee independence to Vietnam, Laos and Cambodia. Reluctant French consent was obtained and it seemed that the British would participate, but Churchill and Eden then decided to wait until consultations had been held with the Russians and with Communist China at the forthcoming Geneva conference. This delay meant that American policy was overtaken by events and Dien-bienphu fell before the conference met. At Geneva in July 1954 the facts of the situation had to be recognised and French Indo-China was divided into its component parts of Laos, Cambodia and Vietnam, which was partitioned into a Communist North Vietnam and non-Communist South; the four new states were given their independence. The deterrent had failed because its use was never seriously envisaged, and diplomacy had failed because all of the Western powers were disinclined to get involved with France in a costly conventional war.

In the long term perhaps failure is too harsh a word, in that from the beginning the only possible solution in Indo-China was that finally reached. The tendency of nationalist groups to accept Communist support in their fight against colonialism has been repeatedly demonstrated in the post-Dulles period and the later situation in South Vietnam underlined the particular difficulty of trying to buttress non-Communist régimes in South-east Asia. However, the contemporary impression was that American and Western policy had failed decisively.

This sense of failure was accompanied by a growing realisation in Washington that a capacity for massive retaliation was not in all circumstances an adequate deterrent against aggression and could never be a safeguard against internal subversion. Slowly but consistently the administration began to prepare for what came to be called selective retaliation, and Dulles reverted to the concept which had dominated the foreign policy of the Truman admini-strations since the beginning of the cold war period, one which he had himself helped to formulate and which, somewhat incon-sistently, had been endorsed by the Republican party platform in 1952. He sponsored the creation of a South-east Asia Treaty Organisation on the model of NATO in the hope of containing Communism through a mutual security system. In its very com-position, however, SEATO embodied one fundamental weakness which distinguished it from its predecessor: whereas the member-ship of NATO consisted of the states of Western Europe which believed themselves to be threatened none of the Far Eastern countries most exposed to a Communist take-over joined SEATO. It contained none of the new states established at the Geneva conference; India, Burma and Indonesia refused to join, and it became an association of the United States and the former colonial powers of Great Britain and France, together with

Australia, New Zealand, Pakistan, Thailand and the Philippines. Nationalist China might have been a member had it not become ineligible through the withdrawal of British recognition. SEATO appeared to be a viable organisation but only because it did not embrace the countries most likely in the immediate future to become the areas of conflict between the Communist and non-Communist worlds. Its possible effectiveness was reduced by its air of unreality.

This weakness in Western policy was accompanied in other sectors by a lack of definition which also sowed the seeds of future tension. The mutual security treaty which was signed by the United States and the Chiang Kai-Shek government on Formosa towards the end of 1954 made no mention of the off-shore islands of Quemoy and Matsu. These were occupied by the Nationalists but were so close to the shores of Communist China that their existence was a visible assertion of Chiang's pretentions. Action against the islands was to be expected, and a massive bombardment was launched by the Communists in the winter of 1954–5. For the Eisenhower administration the attack posed a dilemma which admitted to no easy solution. An explicit removal of Quemoy and Matsu from the American defence perimeter would appear to be a confession of weakness and would undermine the prestige of Chiang Kai-Shek, whilst a guarantee of Nationalist control of the islands could be militarily effective only through use of atomic weapons. An unsatisfactory answer was found in leaving the question unresolved in order to keep the Communists guessing. In January 1955 Congress, at the president's request, passed a resolution authorising him to employ the armed force of the United States in any way he deemed necessary to protect Formosa; uncertainty about American policy had the desired effect and the Communist bombardment slackened off. The situation had been a gamble for both sides but initiative, and hence direct responsibility for the course of events, had been given to the Communists. This vague defensive posture was to become a familiar characteristic of American diplomacy as the United States moved out of the short period of hard nuclear diplomacy. But on one issue the administration stood firm: it rejected British arguments for recognition of Communist China and refused to accept the possibility of Communist China's entry into the United Nations.

In 1958 the bombardment of Quemoy and Matsu was resumed

at a time when the United States was heavily preoccupied in the Middle East. Eisenhower was subjected to strong domestic pressures advocating abandonment of the islands and to counterpressures, in which Dulles participated, for strong defensive action. He resisted both, but made clear his determination not to retreat in the face of threats and provocation. At the same time Dulles assured the Chinese Communists that Chiang Kai-Shek would not be allowed to attack the mainland from Formosa. This represented a reversal of the policy hinted at in the president's first message to Congress in 1953 when, at Dulles's instigation, he had announced that the American Seventh Fleet would no longer be used to prevent operations being staged from Formosa against the Chinese mainland, thereby cancelling Truman's order made at the beginning of the Korean war. The episode illuminated the extent to which roll-back had been abandoned in favour of containment. There is also evidence to suggest that Dulles tried to persuade the Nationalists to abandon the islands, or at least to agree to their demilitarisation in exchange for a Communist agreement to stop the shelling, but in this he failed and the uneasy and dangerous situation was continued.

Although face had been saved, and the Communists had made no territorial advances in this sector, the Western position in Asia as a whole had deteriorated during Dulles's years in office. The Chinese had consolidated their hold over Tibet and extended their influence in the new states created out of the former French empire. Although officially neutral, Prince Sihanouk in Cambodia was moving more and more closely towards the Communist world, and in Laos Souvanna Phouma had formed a coalition government which included members of the Communist Pathet Lao. In Malaya the authority of the British administration was threatened by internal subversion stimulated by the Chinese. The complete military picture demonstrated the need for building special forces which could be effective in jungle warfare and underlined the limitations of the sophisticated deterrent. Politically American policies were becoming identified by the local populations with continuing white economic and political influence and the prospect of being able to establish strong pro-western governments in South-east Asia became increasingly remote.

EUROPEAN AND MIDDLE EASTERN
POLICY 1953–1959

In his European as well as in his Far Eastern diplomacy Dulles was forced to abandon the grandiose phrases of the Republican party platform and walk well within the accepted limits of established policy. As early as June 1953 talk of liberation was exposed as a hollow dream. Stalin had died in March and there was hope that his successors would adopt a more conciliatory policy towards the West. This hope may have encouraged the East German revolt against Communist rule which broke out in June. However, whilst the world waited to see what action the United States would take, the Soviet Union moved with speed, crushed the revolt and restored the authority of the Ulbricht régime. The United States did nothing more than set up food kitchens along the border between East and West Berlin. Although positive intervention in East Germany might have been the trigger for world war, the realism of Dulles's reaction to the crisis did not disguise the fact that the speciousness of his earlier promises had been exposed. He had, in fact, become the victim of his own enthusiasms. Although it is unlikely that he had ever envisaged 'roll-back' and 'liberation' in military terms, he had been so carried away by his denunciation of Democratic policies that it now seemed that he had been forced to back down.

His fondness for slogans also affected relations between the United States and the countries of Western Europe which were trying to form a European Defence Community to unify their defence activities. The establishment of a European army would remove the necessity for the continued stationing of large numbers of American forces in Europe and at the same time solve the problem of West German rearmament by incorporating the military forces of the West German Republic into the E.D.C. The scheme was supported by the West German chancellor, Dr Adenauer, by the British government, and by the Eisenhower administration, both on its own merits and as the first step towards a united Europe. The French, however, rejected the E.D.C. treaty, and during the course of the debates Dulles made the 'agonising reappraisal' speech in which he suggested that American policy towards Europe might have to be revised if the Europeans failed to agree among themselves on the questions of a European army and the relationship of Germany to the West. At the Brussels conference in 1954 it was the British foreign secretary, Eden, not Dulles, who produced a plan for resolving the dilemma, finding in the Brussels Pact of 1948 a device for arming West Germany and bringing it into NATO through the reinvigoration of the Western European Union to take the place of the E.D.C. Pressure from Dulles in support of the Eden proposal may have contributed to its successful adoption, but the secretary of State did not emerge from the confused negotiations with particular public credit.

However, despite the events of June 1953, Soviet-American relations after the death of Stalin entered a new phase. The explosion of the first Russian hydrogen bomb in August 1953 may have given the Soviet Union a sense of confidence in international affairs which, together with the change of leadership, resulted in a thaw in the cold war. Diplomatic relations were established with the West German Federal Republic, a peace treaty was signed with Japan, overtures were made to the dissident Communist state of Yugoslavia, and negotiations for a peace treaty with Austria were resumed. These signs of a relaxation of tension produced a climate in which Eisenhower's benevolent foreign policy attitudes could be deployed and tentative moves were made towards calling a summit conference of world leaders. The president was always more optimistic than Dulles about the possibility of establishing amicable working relations with the Soviet Union, and instead of emphasising ideological differences favoured practical gestures such as the 'Atoms for Peace' proposal which he placed before the United Nations in December 1953. He then suggested that the nuclear powers pool their knowledge and donate fissionable material to be used in a co-operative programme for peaceful ends under the supervision of the United Nations. Although the Soviet government at first responded favourably, it then backed away, and when the International Atomic Energy Commission was eventually set up in 1956, its membership was composed entirely of non-Communist powers. However, the general policy of 'peaceful co-existence' which Malenkov had instituted was continued when he was replaced by Bulganin and Khrushchev in 1955. The treaty with Austria was finally concluded, the idea of a summit conference was welcomed by Moscow, and Eisenhower's dream of successful high-level diplomacy seemed to be at last close to fulfilment. Secretary Dulles, however, was opposed to the idea and only grudgingly accepted the plan for a face-to-face meeting of British, French, Russian and American leaders at Geneva in July 1955.

The absence of positive results perhaps justified Dulles's doubts. The only new idea put forward at Geneva was Eisenhower's devastatingly simple 'open skies' proposal that the major powers should permit extensive photo-reconnaissance flights over their territory so that military concentrations could be detected. Adoption of this policy would, he believed, remove the fear of surprise attack which overshadowed international relations and change the mood of the world from one of overt hostility and suspicion to mutual trust and good faith. The speech was generously received, and hopes spread that a new era of peace had been launched, but it is significant that the scheme came from a study group led by Nelson Rockefeller and not from Dulles, the professional, who remained sceptical about its reception by the Russians. Events justified the secretary's cynicism. At the Foreign Ministers' Conference in October 1955, the Soviet Union rejected the proposal and his conviction that no permanent accord with the Soviet Union could be reached, except on the basis of Western acceptance of the division of Germany and Russian domination of Eastern Europe, was strengthened. But although only an idealist could have expected an immediate settlement of east-west problems to come out of the Geneva Conference, it was not without significance. That the meeting took place at all was a sign of relaxing tension, and the 'spirit of Geneva' remained a beacon of hope for Eisenhower and for those who shared his determination to seek for means of breaking down the inflexible division of the world into two armed camps.

It was, however, soon overtaken by the dynamics of world politics and hidden by new tensions between the Communist and non-Communist blocs, this time in the Middle East. Since the creation of the Jewish State of Israel in 1948 the precarious stability of the whole of the eastern Mediterranean had been threatened by Arab-Israeli frictions which a United Nations Conciliation Commission had been unable to resolve. Partly through conscience, partly because of politically significant domestic Jewish minorities, relations between the West and Israel had been cultivated without too fine a regard for Arab sensibilities. Although the signing of the Baghdad Pact between Turkey and Iraq early in 1955, later to be joined by Great Britain, Iran and Pakistan, was a significant landmark in the policy of building defence organisations around the perimeter of the Communist states, internal tensions behind this barrier mounted.

The fulcrum was Egypt. A nationalist revolution in 1952 had overthrown King Farouk, and power passed into the hands of Colonel Gamal Abdel Nasser. The Anglo-Egyptian Treaty of 1936 guaranteeing British occupation of the Suez Canal Zone had been renegotiated in 1951, but after the revolution relations between Egypt and Britain began to deteriorate. American policy was ambivalent. Although Washington sympathised with the demands of the Arab nationalists it was anxious to keep the Canal open and concerned lest the weakening of British influence threaten the stability of the Middle East. In 1954 the British government agreed to withdraw the remaining British troops from the Canal Zone by 1956, and Dulles tried to strengthen American influence in Egypt by promises of economic aid and financial assistance in building the proposed Aswan High Dam for control of the Nile. However, Nasser was simultaneously flirting with the Communist bloc, and when it became clear that Egypt was being supplied with large quantities of modern armaments from Czechoslovakia and the Soviet Union Dulles made one of the sudden gestures which characterised his black and white approach to international politics and withdrew support for the Dam. This unexpected move completed Nasser's alienation from the West, and gave him an excuse for nationalising the Suez Canal Company on the grounds that he needed extra revenue to finance his economic programme. As four-fifths of Europe's oil supplies passed through Suez, seizure of the Canal gave him a stranglehold over Western Europe. The convention of 1888 guaranteed free and unrestricted traffic through the Canal, but Israeli shipping was already forbidden to use the waterway, and it was feared that Nasser might discriminate against any nation with whom his relations were uneasy. The situation was critical and became worse when the Israelis sought to turn Nasser's preoccupations to their own advantage. With the probable collusion of the British and French governments they invaded the Sinai Peninsula, determined to solve once and for all the border disputes which had imperilled Israeli-Arab relations since 1948. Their army was completely victorious and moved rapidly towards the Canal itself. Direct British and French intervention followed: Egyptian bases were bombed and a joint invasion launched with the aim of occupying the Canal Zone on the pretext that the waterway had to be kept open. These military operations were moderately successful, but the slowness of the advance south gave the Egyptians time to block the canal and expose the futility of the excuse.

For Dulles, and for the American people, the invasion represented wanton aggression which betrayed the ideological position of the free world and exposed it once again to the charge of colonialism and militaristic imperialism. Anglo-American relations in particular faced the gravest crisis they had met since the First World War, for it was made quite clear that the administration fundamentally disapproved of Anglo-French policy and would use all the diplomatic resources at its command to cause it to be stopped. However, this diplomatic offensive was skilfully conducted and although the Atlantic alliance was strained it did not break; for whilst the United States was calling upon Britain and France to withdraw from Egypt, arrangements were being made to send emergency supplies of oil to Europe. The extent of American indignation and sorrow at the course of events only underlined the fact that the wide community of interests between the United States and Western Europe gave the alliance a meaning which enabled it to survive immediate tensions. Its continuance was in fact more seriously threatened from the European side of the Atlantic, for the refusal by the United States to countenance the Suez venture was regarded as a stab in the back by a trusted friend rather than a realistic attempt to preserve the moral position of the West, prevent general war, and maintain the authority of the United Nations. The unfortunate episode ended with the setting up of a United Nations commission and withdrawal of the Israeli, British and French forces. Its lessons were clear: Israeli military strength had been demonstrated and Egyptian weakness exposed; gun-boat diplomacy by European states outside their rapidly diminishing spheres of influence was shown to be outdated, and the impossibility of successful unilateral European action without American support underlined. Two months after the invasion of Egypt a revolution in Hungary was crushed with great brutality by Soviet forces and the West was impotent; even its moral position had been eroded by the premature Suez operation.

Middle Eastern tensions offered a fertile field for Communist activity. The administration slowly came to recognise this danger and also the necessity of backing words with action. In a special message to Congress delivered a few days before his second inaugural address the president announced what came to be known as the Eisenhower Doctrine: a promise that the United States would give immediate economic and military aid, including the use of American armed force, to any Middle East nation that asked for such aid in order to defend itself against direct attack or internal subversion by 'international Communism'. In opening the possibility of direct American involvement in Middle East politics the doctrine was a revolutionary departure from previous policy and explicit recognition of the spread of the cold war. It also underlined the break with reliance upon the deterrent and the evolution of a flexible policy reflecting the realities of power. Within three months the Eisenhower Doctrine was tested and proved: in April 1957, in response to a request for support from King Hussein of Jordan, the Sixth Fleet was rushed to the eastern Mediterranean. This show of strength helped Hussein to keep domestic control and was followed by a promise of economic aid.

The tenuous stability of Jordan, supported by an American arms lift in September 1957, was not, however, repeated throughout the Arab world. A military coup in Syria resulted in closer ties with the Soviet Union, and the creation by Jordan and Iraq of an Arab Union in February 1958 was matched by the formation of the United Arab Republic of Egypt and Syria. The Union collapsed after a revolution in Iraq in July 1958, and General Kassim's new Iraqi government made a mutual defence pact with the United Arab Republic. Internal subversion also threatened the Lebanon and only the landing of American troops enabled President Chamoun to preserve order. These events led to a clarification of American commitments in the Middle East under the Eisenhower Doctrine and in March 1959 mutual security agreements were made with Turkey, Iran and Pakistan. Later that month Iraq withdrew from the Baghdad Pact, and its new role as a Western defence structure mid-way between NATO in the west and SEATO in the east was underlined when, in August 1959, its name was changed to the Central Treaty Organisation.

Preoccupation with the Middle East did not mean that the United States forgot its older allies. Following the Suez debacle vigorous efforts were made to repair the damage which had been done to European–American relations. The Rome Treaty of March 1957 which formally established the European Economic Community, or Common Market, was welcomed in the United States as the beginning of a positive move towards European unity.

Although Great Britain did not sign the treaty the retirement of Anthony Eden, with whom Dulles had never been in personal sympathy, facilitated a *rapprochement* with the United States. When the new prime minister, Harold Macmillan, and his foreign secretary, Selwyn Lloyd, met Eisenhower and Dulles in Bermuda in March 1957 they were promised a number of medium range ballistic missiles as a testimony of the enduring vitality of the alliance. This improvement in Anglo-American relations was cemented by Queen Elizabeth's state visit to Washington in October 1957 and by the missile agreement which was signed in February 1958. Dulles's close friendship with the German Chancellor Konrad Adenauer continued to exercise considerable influence over German–American relations and their connection remained the pivot of the administration's European policy during the period when France was going through the series of governmental crises which resulted in the emergence of General De Gaulle as president of the new Fifth Republic. Relations with the Soviet Union continued to improve as Khrushchev consolidated his personal power. After the launching in October 1957 of the world's first man-made space satellite, Sputnik I, an achievement which demonstrated the Soviet lead over the United States in missile technology, Moscow made tentative overtures towards the calling of another summit conference. 1958 was, however, dominated by Middle Eastern questions and by the renewed Chinese bombardment of Quemoy and Matsu, and when the Russians once again demanded Western withdrawal from West Berlin, nothing more was heard of the summit proposal.

Although Dulles's last year in office was gravely troubled by recurrent crises around the perimeter of the 'free world' he could nevertheless look back upon an era in which his diplomacy had not been entirely unsuccessful. A global system of alliances had been constructed and American policy had matured beyond nuclear threats to recognition of the necessity of local defences and mobile tactical forces to conduct limited operations. Even the earlier policy of waving the nuclear deterrent had perhaps produced the desired result in that no direct challenge had been thrown to the west in the years since 1953. However, Dulles had also failed because the high aspirations which he brought to the practice of diplomacy had led him to hold out promises which were by their nature impossible to fulfil, and some of the discernible shifts in American policy, originating elsewhere, had only received his reluctant support. After he died, his fervent determination to withstand Communism and maintain the free world as a moral as well as a military and political force began to be seen in the context of his times and to be given greater recognition. But despite his efforts the United States was on the defensive and initiative had passed to the Communists.

EISENHOWER DIPLOMACY, 1959–1960

In his last months the secretary of State once again firmly resisted all pressures for a summit conference, but in the end yielded half-heartedly and without any hope of real achievement. The president supported the idea with enthusiasm; he continued to believe in the value of face-to face negotiation and was certain that the differences between East and West could be resolved if an occasion were created for men of good faith to meet together. He came to regard a new summit meeting as the great opportunity for ending his presidential years with glory and honour, and devoted his energies to the task of making it possible. His faith in personal diplomacy by heads of state was not, however, confined to one comprehensive summit meeting; nor was he naïve enough to imagine that such a meeting could profitably be convoked without extensive preparation. Consequently Anastas Mikoyan, first deputy premier of the Soviet Union, made an unofficial visit to the United States in January 1959 and his successor, Frol Kozlov, followed him in June. In July Vice-President Nixon returned the compliment by visiting Moscow, where he engaged in the famous 'kitchen' debate with Khrushchev which was to figure prominently in the presidential campaign of 1960. On 3 August Eisenhower announced that he would exchange official visits with Khrushchev and the Russian leader visited the United States in September. For Khrushchev to make the first visit was a significant sign of friendship and augured well for the future. Both before and after Khrushchev's visit a stream of European statesmen crossed the Atlantic, and President Eisenhower began the extensive travels which were to characterise his last eighteen months in office. He went to West Germany, France and Britain in August–September, and in December toured eleven countries in Europe, the Middle East and Africa, carrying with him the message of good will which he hoped would transform the tone of international politics in the 1960s. During the December tour, a formal proposal for a summit meeting in Paris was made by Britain, France and the United States.

Although the spring of 1960 was preoccupied with preparations for the summit, events in Latin America also claimed his attention. Since the formation of the Organisation of American States in 1948, United States policy had been largely confined to programmes of bilateral economic assistance which had achieved little success because of the instability of the military dictatorships which ruled in many of the states. There was, however, one exception that underlined the extent to which, despite the professions of the Good Neighbor policy, the United States was still prepared to wield the 'big stick'. In the new situation of cold war and ideological confrontation its use was covert rather than open but the State Department's disavowal of intervention was widely disbelieved. In 1954 the Central Intelligence Agency actively participated in a revolution against the Communist-dominated government of President Arbenz of Guatemala. Designed both to protect American economic interests in Guatemala and to preserve the integrity of the western hemisphere against communism this successful action partly explains the violent anti-American feeling encountered by Vice-President Nixon when he toured eight Latin American countries in 1958. In Caracas, Venezuela, he only narrowly escaped physical injury and such demonstrations stimulated moves towards a unified hemispheric economic programme —but progress was slow. Resentment of American power was widespread and when President Batista of Cuba was overthrown in 1959 by Fidel Castro, an idealistic young guerilla leader who wanted to give Cuba democratic government and economic independence of the United States, there was a strong possibility that his movement might have a wide appeal throughout Latin America. These developments led to new moves by the American administration to improve its image south of the Rio Grande, and in February 1960 Eisenhower extended his goodwill missions to Brazil, Argentine, Chile and Uruguay. His great popularity made the tour a great personal success, but although his idealistic speeches dispelled some of the suspicion of American motives which prevailed in the southern hemisphere, he offered no substantial programme to help ailing economies and, unlike Khrushchev on his foreign visits, made no announcements of specific financial assistance. The president's journey helped to draw attention to the problems of Latin America, but the most acute of these, the increasing drift of Cuba towards Communist China and the Soviet Union, was in no way resolved. By mid-summer Castro had expropriated American-owned companies in Cuba and the United States was about to embark upon a policy of economic sanctions against the island.

However, in May 1960, when Eisenhower flew to Paris for his meetings with Macmillan, De Gaulle and Khrushchev, these troubles seemed slight when compared with the benefits that were expected to flow from the summit. The president's optimism remained high, despite the appearance on the horizon of an ominous cloud which daily threatened to become blacker. On 5 May Khrushchev had accused the United States of trying to wreck the conference by committing acts of aggression against the Soviet Union, specifically through violating Russian air space by making unauthorised flights over the Soviet Union. Two days later he challenged an American statement that a U 2 plane was missing whilst engaged in high altitude weather research in the Middle East by claiming that the U 2 had been shot down over central Russia, that it contained espionage equipment, that the pilot had been captured alive and had admitted that his mission was photo-reconnaissance over the Soviet Union. On 9 May, Christian Herter, the new secretary of State, confirmed the general accuracy of his report and disclosed that such flights had been in progress for some years. On 11 May Eisenhower accepted full responsibility. He then flew to Paris and at the first session of the conference an enraged Khrushchev, who before the presidential statement had expressed his conviction that Eisenhower must have been personally unaware of what had been going on, made it quite clear that the summit was dead and that the president was no longer welcome to visit the Soviet Union in June as planned. So ended the great dream of a summit conference at which the future peace of the world would be assured so far as reasonable men could determine. Eisenhower's original mistake in allowing the U 2 flights to continue immediately prior to the conference was aggravated by his devastating error in admitting the facts and accepting responsibility instead of bluffing; his naïve honesty overcame him and he showed himself ill-equipped to deal in the hard world of power politics. The summit which was to have been the pinnacle of his achievement as a man of peace, had collapsed into disaster.

His final crucifixion was yet to come. He had planned to visit the Far East after his Russian tour and the itinerary included Japan, with whom a new Treaty of Mutual Co-operation and Security was being negotiated. Despite the debacle in Paris he decided to continue with the tour, and set off via Alaska to the Philippines. In Japan, however, violent popular demonstrations broke out against the United States; long-standing dislike of American bases within the country was strengthened by fears that they might be used for U 2 flights and hence involve Japan in difficulties with the Soviet Union and Communist China. The president's press secretary and the American ambassador had to be rescued by helicopter from a mob at Tokyo airport, and when rioting continued the Japanese prime minister withdrew Eisenhower's invitation. The fact that he refused to resign and insisted on ratification of the new treaty did not sweeten the bitter pill, and the enthusiastic reception that the president received in Chiang Kai-Shek's Formosa (Taiwan) and in South Korea did not mitigate the fact that he was unwelcome in a country with which, despite all past difficulties, the United States had enjoyed amicable relations since the end of the Second World War. Not until September did Eisenhower recover some of his lost prestige. When Khrushchev made a personal appearance before the United Nations General Assembly and indulged in a stormy tirade against the United States and its political leaders the president followed with another of his customary reasoned appeals for international co-operation and world peace. His tarnished image was somewhat restored, but it was now an image without substance.

The defeat of the Republican party in the 1960 elections completed the discomfiture of the Eisenhower administration. Unpopular in many foreign countries, faced in the Caribbean with an insurgent Cuba, and with no clear policy towards the new and emerging states of Africa, neither the diplomacy of secretary Dulles nor that of the president himself had succeeded in accomplishing the high aims with which they had taken office in 1953. On the fringes of the free world communism rather than Western democracy seemed to be in the ascendant, and the president's agonised cry 'What happened to all those fine young people with stars in their eyes who sailed balloons and rang doorbells for us in 1952?' was an apt epitaph for the disappointments suffered by the United States in international affairs as well as for the unfulfilled hopes of domestic policy.

7

DOMESTIC AFFAIRS, 1945–1961

The active international role adopted by the United States added a new note of tension to domestic affairs and helped to mould the course of domestic policy. Traditionally the American democratic experiment had been regarded in the Old World with fascinated disbelief, except by those millions of immigrants who responded to the lure of liberty, opportunity and free land; and the manners, customs and institutions of the Republic had always received critical examination, With the closing of the frontier which for almost three centuries had offered hope if nothing more to the poor immigrant, and then the passage of immigration restriction legislation, the 'melting pot' image began to be lost and to be replaced by a view of America that stressed its rampant capitalism rather than its democratic aspirations. Thereafter the image changed rapidly: in the 1930s the country seemed to have become once again a great laboratory of social experiment; during the war years it was an affluent land flowing with commodities that everyone else desired but few possessed; after the war it became the bastion of the 'free world', and unless the domestic history of the American people demonstrated beyond all reasonable doubt that its capitalist system was superior to the claims of its Communist rival there could be no hope of winning the cold war. Capitalism and free democracy were on trial and the traditional foreign examination, analysis and criticism of the United States ceased to be a casual pursuit and became a continuous study.

Having thus become the focus of attention the American, traditionally uncertain of his own identity, again sought to define his 'American-ness' and to establish a consensus of accepted belief and behaviour that could be held up before the eyes of the world, both as evidence of his own achievement and as a commodity exportable to less favoured nations. This double tension bore fruit in the rise of 'McCarthyism' in the early 1950s. 'Conservative' forces became dominant and individualism succumbed to the inherent pressures towards conformity that De Tocqueville had earlier seen to be the product of egalitarianism, and which were now strengthened by the demands of the cold war. However, in 1945 the most immediate question was whether the social and economic planning of the past twenty-two years would be consolidated and advanced, or whether it would be rejected in the attempt to find a new policy of 'normalcy'. The nature of America's post-war image hinged on the manner in which this question was answered.

TRUMAN ACCEPTS THE CHALLENGE

Few presidents can have been less obviously qualified for the presidency than Harry S. Truman, who succeeded on the death of Roosevelt from a massive cerebral haemorrhage on 12 April 1945. An obscure politician from Missouri he had been sent to the Senate in 1934 by the political machine of Pendergast, the local Democratic 'boss'. His record in Washington was completely undistinguished but he voted consistently for the New Deal and was re-elected in 1940. The following year, when the increasing volume of defence contracts opened the possibility of large-scale corruption in the placing of orders and fixing of prices, Truman displayed an initiative that was eventually to put him in the White House: he sponsored and became the first chairman of a senate investigating committee. This Truman Committee rapidly achieved an enviable reputation for efficiency, thoroughness, and complete integrity which made him compromise candidate for the second place on the Democratic presidential ticket in 1944. Choice of Truman was a political decision in which his own merits and claims on the nomination were more negative than positive, and as vice-president he did not enjoy the president's complete confidence, nor was he brought into the business of the executive branch in any meaningful way. He had no real power and it would have been surprising had he been given greater authority, for the vice-presidency was traditionally regarded as an honorific office of little substance, despite the fact that the incumbent is constitutionally first in line for the presidency itself should the president die in office or be rendered incapable of fulfilling his duties.

When Truman was sworn in he knew nothing of many of his predecessor's policies and was completely ignorant of the Manhattan Project for developing the atomic bomb, but his response to the burdens of the presidency was magnificent. He grew rapidly in stature and displayed above all the capacity to make decisions and to stand by them with determination, a quality symbolised by the card that stood upon his desk reading 'The buck stops here'. His strength in the field of foreign affairs has already been underlined. It was Truman who decided to drop the atomic bombs upon Japan; Truman who adopted the policies of containment and Marshall Aid; Truman who decided to intervene in Korea and to recall General MacArthur for insubordination. These events mark the measure of the man's achievements but he was also not without distinction in the realm of domestic affairs. He secured the continuance of the New Deal and ensured that the federal government would not revert to the *laissez faire* policies of the 1920s.

Truman's domestic programme evolved at a time of considerable dislocation. Although the coming of peace brought fears of unemployment and depression, pressure for rapid demobilisation of the wartime armies was inexorable. After the Potsdam conference the president had no illusions about the difficulties of establishing good working relations with the Soviet Union but his worries were not shared by the general public. Demobilisation began as soon as the war in Europe ended and continued with increasing speed after the collapse of Japan; by midsummer 1946 the fourteen million men under arms had been reduced to a little over two million. With some fluctuations this number decreased still further in the late 1940s. Despite its world role the United States was confronted with the normal difficulty in a democratic society of keeping large peacetime forces under arms; and the traditional dislike of a large standing army was strengthened by the American monopoly of atomic weapons which seemed to provide a security shield against attack. Reabsorption of the demobilised men was made easier by the passage of the Servicemen's Readjustment Act in July 1944, commonly called the G.I. Bill of Rights. This helped rehabilitation by extensive unemployment benefits and educational privileges including four free years of college training, a provision which reduced the economic impact of peace by temporarily removing thousands of men from the labour market. Serious economic difficulties were still expected to result from the substantial increase in the civilian labour force at a time when war industries were being run down and to meet them Truman sent to Congress, in September 1945, a twenty-one point programme embodying the liberal and progressive policies which were to be the keynote of his administration.

He not only sought to consolidate the New Deal but to carry it further in the direction set by Roosevelt. The programme called for the raising of the national minimum wage; passage of Fair Employment Practices and Full Employment Acts; large-scale federal planning for the conservation of natural resources; construction of public works for regional development on the model of the T.V.A.; the nationalisation of atomic energy, and a number of radical measures such as federal aid to education and national health insurance and medical care. Truman later christened this complex of policies his Fair Deal. Although he failed to secure passage of its more extreme components his limited success helped to pave the way for the emergence of a broad new consensus which, after the years of Eisenhower Republicanism in the 1950s, enabled later administrations to extend the influence of the federal government into hitherto inviolate areas of national life.

From the outset Truman's chances of securing ratification of his programme were limited. His political influence was necessarily weaker than that of a president who had been elected in his own right, and when the country moved into a period of prosperity instead of the expected slump inherent resistance to fundamental reform was strengthened. Within six months of the end of the war unemployment had dropped to the irreducible minimum and industrial expansion, stimulated by a $6,000 million tax reduction in November 1945 and by the speedy lifting of many wartime controls, had exceeded expectations. These buoyant conditions produced their own problems and mounting pressures towards inflation began to threaten domestic economic stability. As highly paid war-industry workers suffered wage reductions on their transfer to normal industrial processes a wave of strikes was felt in major basic industries. These were particularly acute in the steel and automobile plants. Employers refused to grant wage demands unless they were accompanied by a rise in prices, and rejected a compromise which would have allowed limited wage and price increases until it had been amended to ensure profits at the 1941 level. Throughout the spring of 1946 inflation continued and was accompanied by a rash of labour and industrial disputes. John L. Lewis's United Mine Workers struck and the railroad unions threatened to go out. The president reacted with characteristic energy by taking over the mines and threatening to assume control of the railroads. Under federal sponsorship labour won most of its demands, but in the process Lewis was alienated. Truman's political position might have been strengthened by more cautious action.

In this context the president's legislative programme ran into rough water. The Full Employment Bill, including provision for setting up a three-member Council of Economic Advisers which has since become the spearhead of federal planning, passed Congress in February 1946 but with amendments eliminating federal responsibility for maintaining full employment in time of depression by deficit spending. The Atomic Energy Act was passed in August but little further progress was made. Over every issue hung the shadow of conflict over price controls, with Truman attempting to hold the line and Congress wavering between keeping moderate controls and allowing a free market to meet existing demand. In October 1946 many of the remaining controls were lifted, but as this was followed by a swift inflation of prices Truman reaped both the dissatisfaction of business and agrarian interests which had resented the uncertainty of the earlier period and that of the consumer who was faced with a continuous rise in the cost of living. The president managed to project an image of ineptitude, and liberal faith in his determination and ability to secure enactment of his programme began to waver. Disillusionment increased when two heroes of the liberal-progressives, Harold Ickes and Henry Wallace, left the government; Ickes resigned over the appointment of a wealthy oil man as under-secretary of the Navy and Wallace was dismissed from the department of Commerce because of his opposition to Truman's foreign policy.

The result of these confusions was Republican victory in the congressional and state elections of 1946. The Grand Old Party won control of both Houses of Congress for the first time since 1930, and the Republican standard bearer of 1944, Thomas Dewey, was re-elected governor of New York with a majority of over a half million votes, thereby increasing his standing as titular leader of the Republicans and the leading potential challenger for the presidency in 1948.

The 80th Congress which assembled in January 1947 was dominated by the conservative wing of the Republican party and its dominant personality, Senator Robert Taft of Ohio, in his opposition to 'big government' and 'creeping socialism' presented the greatest threat to the success of the Fair Deal. Becoming popularly known as 'Mr Republican' he wanted to return, not to complete *laissez faire*, but to an undefined time when the federal government played a less active role in the affairs of the nation

and individual initiative was untrammelled by what he considered
to be excessive restriction and control. From the beginning of the
session relations between the new Congress and the executive
branch were stormy and the president completely failed to establish
a working relationship with the legislature. It rejected extension
of the social security programme and was opposed to federal aid
to education and to public housing projects. It reduced appropriations for conservation works and threw out a minimum wage bill.
After the president had vetoed two tax reduction bills on the
grounds that they discriminated against low incomes and would
stimulate inflation a third bill was passed over his veto.

The greatest victory of the 80th Congress was to pass the Taft–
Hartley Labor–Management Relations Act over the president's
veto in June 1947. In the eyes of its critics the act sought to
remove the protection given to labour by the Wagner Act of 1935,
but in the opinion of its supporters it merely redressed the balance
between labour and management by reducing the power of the
unions. It outlawed the 'closed shop', authorised the president to
issue injunctions to prevent strikes which might impair the
national safety, and provided for 'cooling off' periods of 90 days
before strike action could be engaged. 'Unfair' labour practices
such as the secondary boycott were prohibited, union officers had
to certify that they were not Communists and unions were
required to register with the department of Labour and submit
annual financial reports. Employers were henceforth to be
allowed to sue unions for breach of contract. Although some
restraints upon the unions were perhaps necessary the act went
beyond the righting of the balance of power between organised
labour and the employers and crippled many union activities. In
a number of states it was followed by passage of 'right to work'
laws which sought to dilute the collective bargaining power of the
unions by outlawing the 'closed shop'. One incidental consequence
had not been foreseen by its proponents: it turned the political
power of organised labour back to the support of President
Truman.

1948, YEAR OF POLITICAL CONFUSION

In the presidential election year of 1948 party politics were in
greater disarray than they had been for twenty years. Prospects
for a Republican victory seemed bright; their success in 1946 had
given them a new sense of confidence that was enhanced by

Truman's failure to conciliate Congress and by the visible rifts within the Democratic party. Their only embarrassment lay in the choice of presidential nominee, for there were a number of hopefuls in the field who each represented a section of the party and commanded considerable support.

The leading grass-roots candidate was Governor Harold E. Stassen of Minnesota, a moderate progressive with a widespread following throughout the Middle West and appreciable support among eastern Republicans because of his adherence to the established bipartisan foreign policy. However, many party leaders supported not Stassen but Senator Taft. His conservatism appealed to business groups throughout the country, and from his political stronghold in the hinge state of Ohio he could hope to capture the whole of the Middle West. His greatest weakness was that he had formerly been one of the most articulate of isolationists and only half-heartedly supported the dominant internationalism of the post-war period. The extent to which the recent revolution in American foreign policy had transformed the traditional patterns of political activity was underlined by the fact that Taft's views on foreign relations were regarded as a serious barrier to his nomination. In the search for a winning candidate approaches were made to General Eisenhower, hero of the crusade in Europe, and only when Eisenhower rejected these advances did the party turn again towards its titular leader Governor Dewey. Despite his great victory in 1946 Dewey was thought to be politically tarnished by defeat in 1944 and was also believed to be too closely identified with east coast liberal Republicanism, but he still enjoyed wide support and at the Philadelphia convention was nominated on the third ballot. The vice-presidential nominee, Governor Earl Warren of California, also represented the moderate-liberal wing of the party. The candidates were supported by a brief platform which endorsed the major achievements of the New Deal, including its welfare and public housing programmes, called for stronger guarantees for civil rights, approved the established bipartisan foreign policy and was reminiscent of traditional Republican philosophy only in its promise of further tax reductions and a plea for greater efficiency in government. The conservative wing of the party had been thwarted by cold political calculation. In repudiating its dominant congressional group the Republican party recognised that the New Deal had altered the political attitudes of the nation and created a moderate consensus to which even a re-invigorated conservatism could make little appeal.

This happy resolution of Republican differences was not echoed within the ranks of the Democrats. After his dismissal Henry Wallace had become editor of the *New Republic*, and losing the restraints of office tried to draw the Democratic party towards a policy of socialism and positive co-operation with the Soviet Union. In 1947 he organised a group called the Progressive Citizens of America, and in December announced that he would run for the presidency on a third party ticket. Observers predicted that he would poll more votes than La Follette in 1924, and that most of these would be taken from the Democratic party, thereby imperilling its electoral chances. Progressives within the Democratic party who had created their own inner organisation, the Americans for Democratic Action, were faced with a formidable dilemma; they had to decide whether to continue to support President Truman or to abandon him for Wallace. In order to avoid making the direct choice they tried in vain to find a compromise candidate and approached Justice William O. Douglas of the Supreme Court, one of the vice-presidential possibilities of 1944, and also General Eisenhower. The movement to oust Truman in favour of Eisenhower was supported by a number of urban political bosses but the general was no more receptive to Democratic overtures than he had been to those of the Republicans. The party had also to contend with the increasing restlessness of the southern conservatives who threatened to bolt the convention if a strong civil rights plank were adopted.

In these circumstances the Democratic convention, also meeting in Philadelphia, was rumbustious. The A.D.A. lobby, led by Mayor Hubert Humphrey of Minneapolis, secured the drafting and adoption of a vigorously liberal platform which contained a positive civil rights plank calling for the establishment of a Fair Employment Practices Commission and federal anti-lynching and poll tax bills. Endorsement of Truman's programme was followed by his renomination. Any other choice, even had a candidate been available, would have been regarded as a public repudiation of the past three years. Such tactics, however, did not succeed in reuniting the party. The Wallace radicals seceded, organised an independent Progressive party and wrote a platform advocating the gradual nationalisation of basic industry, an immediate end to segregation, and the re-orientation of foreign policy towards an immediate *entente* with the Soviet Union. This split was not as dangerous as it might have been for the Progressives failed to take with them the majority of progressive Democrats; it was widely feared that Wallace was being exploited by Communists and that his party was a Communist front organisation, fears that became accentuated as the campaign developed. But in addition to the alienation of the radicals the Democratic party was faced with the secession of the southern conservatives. They bolted in defiance of the civil rights plank and at a convention in Birmingham Alabama in July 1948 formed the States Rights, or Dixiecrat party, with Governor Strom Thurmond of South Carolina as their presidential candidate, thereby threatening the Democracy with the loss of 'the solid South' upon whose votes it had depended since the end of Reconstruction.

With the Democratic party divided the Republicans were justifiably confident of victory. Public opinion polls showed Dewey with a comfortable lead and he conducted a quiet campaign in the course of which, following his personal beliefs and the party's platform, he endorsed much of recent Democratic domestic and foreign policy. However, despite all the evidence to the contrary Truman continued to believe that he could be re-elected; his new self-confidence and pugnacity were roused and for the first time in his career he showed himself to be a master politician. The first move was to recall the 80th Congress into special session in the summer of 1948. It was thus placed in the embarrassing position of either ratifying the Republican platform and thereby approving much of his own programme or, by failing to do so, of seeming to be motivated by political animosities rather than legislative vigour. When it failed to act he labelled it 'the do nothing congress' and used the slogan effectively in his campaign. His second step was to undertake a strenuous 'whistle stop' tour of the country in the course of which he made hundreds of speeches and addressed millions of people; fighting hard both for his policies and his own political future his onslaught on the American electorate impressed many of the people but failed to convince political leaders that he could win. These doubts were shared by the press, most of which was Republican controlled, and on the morning after polling day the first edition of the Chicago *Tribune* carried a deep banner headline DEWEY DEFEATS TRUMAN. However, in the event Truman had confounded his critics; with a popular majority of over two million he gained 304 votes in the electoral college to

Dewey's 189. Thurmond and Wallace trailed behind with votes of between one and one and a half million. The Democratic revolt had fizzled out in the polling booths and the president had scored a great personal triumph over both Governor Dewey and the majority of informed political opinion. He had also helped his party to regain control of both Houses of Congress.

In 1948 psephology, or the analysis of voting patterns, was a relatively new science and the techniques of the social scientists working in this field were rudimentary and often intuitive. It will never be certain how Truman achieved the greatest political upset in American electoral history but a number of contributory factors can be listed. As the incumbent president he possessed the great advantage of being able to appeal to the country from the dignity of the White House, a not inconsiderable asset at a time of peace and relative prosperity. Moreover, the defection of the Dixiecrats, the administration's support of civil rights and its opposition to Taft–Hartley strengthened its appeal to the Negro vote, to labour and to the mass of moderate New Dealers, whilst the secession of the Wallace Progressives helped to weaken conservative fears of Communist penetration within the Democratic party. There was no fundamental disagreement over foreign policy, a factor which helped Truman considerably in some of the mid-western states. He was strengthened in the farm belt by the Agricultural Act of 1948 which, by adopting a more flexible system of price supports, frightened the farmer away from his emotional instinct towards the Republican party. Lastly, although the evidence is far from clear, it is probable that Truman's fighting personal campaign won him considerable support.

THE FAIR DEAL IN OPERATION

With this unexpected electoral mandate President Truman entered his second term with confidence and in the inaugural message of January 1949 presented his programme under the label of the Fair Deal, thereby emphasising its continuity with Theodore Roosevelt's Square Deal and the New Deal of Franklin Roosevelt. Progressivism was clearly in the saddle, and the country seemed to be firmly committed to the use of governmental controls in order to achieve fulfilment of the promise of American life that Herbert Croly had enunciated forty years earlier.

The Fair Deal represented no sudden change of direction; it

merely re-emphasised and extended the measures which Truman had placed before the 79th and 80th Congresses. The core of the programme was economic and social welfare under federal sponsorship, and although he did not achieve all that he had hoped he gained more than many expected. Amendments to the Fair Labor Standards Act in 1949 and 1950 raised the national minimum wage from 40 to 75 cents an hour. Extensions of the Social Security Act brought millions of additional workers under the scheme and increased some benefits by as much as 75 per cent. The federal Housing Act of 1949 provided substantial funds for slum clearance and the provision of low income housing. In 1951 rent controls were extended to cover previously exempted categories. New conservation projects were started, and although the president failed to win legislative support for the establishment of regional agencies on the model of the Tennessee Valley Authority, funds for the T.V.A. itself were substantially increased. The activities of the Rural Electrification Administration and the Farmers' Home Administration, which had replaced the New Deal's Farm Security Administration, were also extended. Truman's farm programme however, which sought to tackle the perennial problem of over-production, met with opposition both from farm groups and from Congress and was rejected. As proposed by secretary of Agriculture Charles Brannan it proposed a guaranteed 'farm standard income' based on the average of the previous ten years but contained conditions for production and price control that were unacceptable. The Agricultural Act of 1949 was a compromise that retained the parity principle but made provision for a more flexible operation of that principle in future years; it was not substantially different from the 1948 Act except that support prices were raised. Attempts to repeal the Taft–Hartley Act failed, as did the more radical components of the Fair Deal. The scheme for national health insurance ran up against the strenuous opposition of the powerful American Medical Association and was rejected. Attempts to provide federal aid for education enjoyed considerable bipartisan support but aroused the opposition of the Roman Catholic Church because of the failure to include aid to parochial schools. The recommendations of the Committee on Civil Rights, established in 1946, for the creation of a permanent Fair Employment Practices Commission and passage of federal anti-lynching and anti-poll tax laws were consistently struck down in Congress.

Despite these failures the first half of Truman's second term was enlivened by a sense of progress and achievement that might have paved the way for an even greater assumption by the federal government of responsibility for guiding the economic and social development of the nation. But in 1950 the rise of McCarthyism, assisted by the outbreak of the Korean war, revealed that the tensions brought about by the international rivalries of the cold war had produced domestic consequences which inhibited further experimentation. Seemingly threatened from within as well as from without the American people increasingly demanded of its members conformity to ancient myths, elevated the shibboleths of the past and tolerated the rise of a dangerous radical who abused the basic principles of the democracy which he claimed to defend.

LOYALTY, DISLOYALTY, AND JOSEPH MCCARTHY

Although McCarthyism suddenly flowered in 1950 the conditions which nurtured it had been developing for a number of years. One of the consequences of the cold war was the premium placed upon loyalty to 'American' ideals, customs and institutions. In order to stand firm against the Communist bloc it was felt that the country had to close its ranks and present a united front to the enemy. As the battle against Communism did not just spring from the realities of power politics but also represented the confrontation of opposing ideologies it had the logical concomitant that loyalty to the American ideology had to be preserved at whatever the cost. A state of war was in being and it was believed that, as had been the case during the two world wars, some of the traditional liberties of the individual had to be sacrificed for the common good.

Such beliefs were strengthened by the fact that fears of Communist infiltration were not unfounded. Before the end of the war the Office of Strategic Services discovered that numerous classified documents had found their way into the hands of Communist front organisations, and when a Communist spy ring was uncovered in Canada in 1946 there seemed every reason to believe that the United States government was also threatened. On 22 March 1947 President Truman launched a full-scale investigation of all federal employees as a result of which a number were dismissed. The wisdom of this inquiry is beyond doubt, and the number of persons dismissed was not large, but in the proceedings the unfortunate principle of guilt by association seemed to have been admitted. Fear of Communist subversion became general and emotionalised at the time of the trial of Alger Hiss in 1948 for perjury in connection with his political past, and the administration contributed to the scare by prosecuting eleven leading Communists under the Smith Act of 1940 on the grounds that they had conspired to *teach* the violent overthrow of the government of the United States. Their convictions were upheld by the Supreme Court in 1951 and another traditional freedom of the American citizen, the right of free speech, seemed to have been discarded. The trial in 1950 of Klaus Fuchs, a German-born British subject who had worked on the atomic bomb at Los Alamos, stimulated further congressional action and in the same year the McCarren Internal Security Act was passed over the president's veto. The act required all Communist organisations to register with the Justice Department, providing complete lists of members and financial statements, and excluded Communists from employment in defence agencies and from holding passports; but its recognition that membership of the Communist party or of a Communist front organisation was not in itself a crime, and its focus upon *acts* seeking to overthrow the government of the United States rather than *words*, reflected a continuing moderation that was soon to be lost. In August 1950 the heads of departments and agencies concerned with matters of national security were empowered to dismiss employees who were regarded as security risks although no specific charges had been levied against them. Such persons could demand a hearing but had no right of appeal, a denial that seemed to run counter to ingrained American traditions and basic human rights.

Growing fear of Communist infiltration and subversion which might ultimately lead to an attempt to take over the government revealed not only a healthy recognition of the nature of Communist tactics but an unhealthy lack of confidence in the virility of American institutions and beliefs. This psychosis, when coupled with the outbreak of the Korean war in June 1950, provided the background for the emergence on the national scene of Senator Joseph McCarthy of Wisconsin.

After a chequered career in Wisconsin state politics and in the marines McCarthy was elected to the Senate in 1946. Between then and 1950 he was an undistinguished and unremarkable junior senator until, in a speech at Wheeling West Virginia on

9 February 1950, he claimed that he knew the names of 205 Communists employed in the Department of State. This figure was later reduced to 57 and when challenged he was unwilling or unable to produce any names but asserted that the distinguished Far Eastern expert Owen Lattimore was the head of a spy ring. His choice of Lattimore was perhaps significant because of the belief strongly held in some quarters that Nationalist China had been betrayed to the Communists at the Yalta conference, a belief that made the attack on Lattimore more plausible. McCarthy always employed the technique of 'the big lie', taking evasive action whenever attempts were made to pin him down, and the volume of his accusations made it difficult to investigate their validity. The issue of Communist penetration in government was so inflammable that the Truman administration handled him carefully; the Democratic party had to be particularly cautious, for since the New Deal conservatives had charged it with having socialistic tendencies. No significant action was taken even in 1951 when McCarthy accused former secretary of State George Marshall and General Eisenhower of being Russian stooges. The negligible impact that the accusation had upon Eisenhower's fortunes in the 1952 presidential campaign should have made President Eisenhower confident enough to confront the senator, but such a move would have been alien to his concept of executive responsibility and the fall of McCarthy came about through his own self-exposure rather than through the efforts of responsible men in the White House. His attack on subversion in the army led to televised hearings in which his vicious, unpalatable and manic tactics were exposed before a nation-wide audience, and the senate gained sufficient courage to pass a motion of censure. He fell from grace into obscurity and died in 1957, almost forgotten except by the men, including J. Robert Oppenheimer, whose professional careers had been ruined by the hysteria which he had generated. However, at a time when the Republic seemed to be fighting for its life against the most insidious enemy it had ever faced, witch-hunting was merely an extreme manifestation of the tensions felt by American society. It was therefore perhaps inevitable that in its search for a president in 1952 the electorate should choose, not a great political leader, but a comfortable figure who might restore a sense of stability and security.

THE ELECTION OF 1952

As in 1868 the United States turned in its hour of need to a successful general renowned for his loyalty and devotion to the cause and to the country for which he had fought. The emergence of Eisenhower as a political idol did not, however, occur spontaneously, and the political in-fighting that accompanied his rise was indicative of the extent to which the lessons of the twentieth century had been absorbed.

The leading Republican candidate for the presidential nomination seemed to be Taft of Ohio. He had been re-elected to the Senate in 1950 and, as in 1948, was strongly supported by party organisations in the south and middle west and by conservative groups throughout the nation. He was the acknowledged leader of the devoted opponents of President Truman. Stassen was again eager for the nomination, but he was again rejected by the eastern wing of the party which was still nominally under the influence of former candidate Thomas Dewey. These eastern Republicans were moderate progressives who supported Truman's foreign policy, and did not wish to undo the New and Fair Deals, but wanted to contain further extensions of the role of the federal government and re-establish more of the traditional balance between federal, state and individual authority. They turned again to General Eisenhower and this time he agreed to stand, but only in order to prevent the neo-isolationist Taft from gaining the nomination. In the primaries the general showed strength in the north and east, the senator in the middle west, and when the convention opened the issue was still in doubt. Intra party manoeuvring then brought the nomination to Eisenhower, with Senator Richard Nixon of California, hero of the Hiss trial, as his running mate.

In the Democratic party President Truman, although technically eligible, did not wish to stand again. (Under the 22nd Amendment, ratified in 1951, no president may serve more than two terms.) Although in the primaries Senator Estes Kefauver of Tennessee, the 'Davy Crockett candidate', seemed to build up an impregnable lead the president and the party bosses inclined towards Governor Adlai Stevenson of Illinois. When Stevenson insisted that he did not wish to be a candidate they turned towards the vice-president, Alben Barkley but at the last minute labour leaders refused to accept Barkley and Stevenson was prevailed upon to stand. He was nominated on the third ballot together with Senator John Sparkman of Alabama. It was an excellent combination of northern liberal and southern moderate and the platform reiterated the unfinished business of the Fair Deal.

The campaign that followed was more than a clash of personalities; it was a clash of values. In a series of witty, brilliant and intelligent speeches Governor Stevenson offered what was probably the best analysis of the nation's problems that had ever before been heard on the stump, but this intellectualism and liberalism went beyond what the people wanted; despite his appeal to the 'eggheads' he failed to arouse popular enthusiasm. General Eisenhower on the other hand promised an end to frustration by ending the war in Korea, demanded lower taxes, a reduction of the bureaucracy of government, the elimination of Communists from positions of authority, and seemed to offer the stability that the people craved. He cast himself as the leader above politics who, as he had led the victorious armies in the Second World War, would guide the United States out of its difficulties into a new period of peace, prosperity and freedom. He won by a landslide. The great tide of Democratic successes had finally ebbed.

EISENHOWER REPUBLICANISM

Repudiation of the Democratic party meant the temporary repudiation of many of its aspirations but not the rejection of what had been accomplished. Although Eisenhower had few opinions about the details of government he subscribed to a general philosophy of moderation and believed that the future lay between the two extremes of unharnessed capitalism and uncontrolled government. He conceived his mission in the White House to be the creation of a form of liberal Republicanism that would appeal to the great consensus which he instinctively felt rather than intellectually understood to exist, hoping thereby to build within the Republican party a strong enough group to keep the conservatives in check.

He was, however, a political innocent, with a distrust for professional politicians and admiration for success in business and the professions. He had himself reached the top of his chosen career, the army, and this had brought him to the presidency of the United States; he applauded the captains of business and industry who had themselves in similar fashion mastered their own professions and reached positions of eminence. Such feelings partly explain the fact that his administration was packed with successful businessmen: Charles E. Wilson, president of General Motors, became secretary of Defence; George Humphrey, president of Mark Hanna and Co., became secretary of the Treasury; Sinclair Weeks, a New England manufacturer, became secretary of Commerce; Foster Dulles, one of the highest paid corporation lawyers in the country, was appointed secretary of State. Superficially it seemed a businessman's administration, but criticism of personnel without regard to policy is dangerous, for the work of the executive branch of the federal government in its twentieth-century role demands many of the qualities that bring success in the private sector. However, the president's self-appointed task of creating 'modern Republicanism' became more difficult because the cabinet projected an image more akin to that of the 1920s than to modern ideals of liberal policy. When Wilson made the unfortunate remark that what was good for the country was good for General Motors and vice versa he was widely believed to be more concerned with the fortunes of his former employer than with the general welfare. Moreover, this cabinet became of more than ordinary importance because Eisenhower carried with him into the White House the military concepts of organisation and command in which he had himself been trained, and instituted a staff system in which policy was filtered through to the president via an assistant to the president, Sherman Adams, who acted as general liason officer and assumed a role similar to that of adjutant and staff officer combined.

No administration, however, could completely ignore the lessons and experiences of the immediate past, and when confronted with the realities of office, particularly the problems attendant upon the end of the Korean war, the government showed itself fully aware of Keynesian theories. Although it did not go as far as its Democratic critics wanted there was no attempt made to put the clock back, except in the negative sense that whenever there was conflict between private interests and public initiative the private sector was encouraged at the expense of greater federal activity. On taking office the administration dropped many economic controls, and imposed restrictions on credit borrowing, but the decline in industrial production and farm income in the early months of 1954 saw the adoption of easy money policies accompanied by tax cuts and increases in social security benefits. These measures contributed to a new burst of prosperity but when this presented the renewed danger of inflation regulators were again applied. Continued wage increases in 1955 and 1956 minimised their effect, prices went spiralling upwards and productivity began to decline. In the winter of 1957–8 a serious recession set in which resulted in a substantial rise in the number of unemployed. Again Keynesian stabilisers were used and in general Republican policies seemed to work, at the price of a constant unemployment rate of about three million. But the Republicans were no more successful in solving the perpetual farm problem than their predecessors had been. Farm output continued to increase even though the farm population was declining; surpluses of primary products overflowed the warehouses and storage elevators; farm income fell whilst the retail prices of farm produce continued to rise because of ever-increasing processing and distribution costs. Eisenhower's secretary of Agriculture, Ezra Taft Benson, favoured a fairly free market in farm commodities and wanted to see a shift away from rigid price supports to a flexible system related to current prices. Such 'free enterprise' was unacceptable to the Democrats, who wanted to see a continuation of high support prices coupled with the withdrawal of land from cultivation, a policy that was partly adopted by Benson as the soil bank programme of 1956. The differences between the parties on the difficult and apparently insoluble farm problem became a difference of emphasis rather than of approach: some controls were clearly necessary; the argument lay over their degree.

There were other areas in which the distinction between the two major parties was more clearly drawn and visible. Corporation taxes were lowered, depreciation allowances increased, and easier provision made for charging business losses against taxes. Emphasis was placed upon balancing the budget, a feat eventually achieved, and the tax cut bill of 1954 was accompanied by a considerable reduction in government expenditure. The Reconstruction Finance Corporation was abolished, and a number of government-owned synthetic rubber factories were sold. Eisenhower was unsympathetic towards the T.V.A. and unwilling to allow it to expand its hydro-electric facilities; in 1954 the contract for a new power plant on the Mississippi was granted to a private syndicate, Dixon-Yates, although critics pointed out that the saving on construction costs would be more than balanced by the increased price that the federal government would have to pay for power. Eventually under pressure the contract was rescinded and given to the city of Memphis, but private power interests were allowed to tap the resources of the Snake River at Hell's Canyon; and the offshore oil fields, the 'tidelands', were transferred from the jurisdiction of the federal government to that of the states off which they lay. The president accepted the necessity of making federal funds available for highway and school construction but provided them in the form of federal underwriting of bond issues on a self-liquidating basis. Expenditure on public housing was small.

The difference between this programme and that advocated by the Democrats was considerable, but it was more moderate than the conservatives in his party wanted. The president's liberal Republicanism was beginning to take shape and it is significant that on a number of issues administration bills tended to gain congressional support from an alliance of liberal Democrats and liberal Republicans and to be opposed by conservatives of both parties. In Eisenhower's first Congress his own party held a small majority but his relations with the Senate majority leader, William Knowland of California, were at best stormy and in complete contrast to the *rapport* which he established with Senator Lyndon Johnson when the Democratic party regained control.

The president's general popularity with the majority of the people and his appeal to the middle of the road consensus virtually ensured his re-election in 1956. His political future, and indeed his life, were threatened in September 1955 when he had a heart attack whilst vacationing in Denver Colorado after the Geneva conference but he recovered completely, and Vice-President Nixon received general acclaim for his skilful handling of the delicate situation of being acting president in all but name whilst avoiding the appearance of assuming presidential prerogatives. Eisenhower's operation for ileitis in June 1965 aroused concern, but as he had recovered so well from the heart attack this new illness did not seriously weaken his electoral prospects. He was renominated by acclamation and defeated Stevenson, who was again the Democratic candidate, by an even bigger landslide than in 1952.

For the first year of his second term the president impressed the nation with a new-found political vigour. He fought for his programme against conservative opposition from within his own party, and his appeal to liberals was strengthened when his secretary of the Treasury resigned over the largest peacetime budget ever proposed in the history of the United States. He also took an active stand on civil rights. In 1953 he had appointed Earl Warren, the liberal Republican governor of California, chief justice of the United States Supreme Court, and the following year Warren handed down the historic opinion of *Brown v. the Board of Education of Topeka* which reversed the 1896 ruling of *Plessy v. Ferguson* that segregation of the Negro was constitutional if the separate facilities provided for him were equal in amenity to those serving whites. This landmark in constitutional interpretation was the starting-point for the great civil rights movement which has dominated the late 1950s and the 1960s. In 1957 President Eisenhower introduced a civil rights bill, with the dual purpose of strengthening the position of the federal courts through legislative action, and of winning back to Republican allegiance the Negro vote which had been lost during the New Deal. This time he could rely upon conservative Republicans to support him but it was only the masterly parliamentary tactics of Senator Johnson and liberal congressional Democrats which guided the bill successfully through the legislature against southern opposition. The Civil Rights Act of 1957 was the first such measure to be passed since the days of Reconstruction at the end of the civil war.

The Negro question also provided the occasion for a display of executive power that caused considerable criticism at the time but provided a significant precedent for later use. Following the 1954 Supreme Court decision the federal courts sought to enforce desegregation of the public schools in a number of districts throughout the south and the border states. In Little Rock, Arkansas, this policy met with strong local opposition and Negro students were refused admission to the Central High School in defiance of a court order. When Governor Orval Faubus refused to co-operate with the federal authorities Eisenhower took the Arkansas National Guard under federal control and compelled submission by force of arms. Politically his action was disastrous in the south, for it raised the spectre of military reconstruction, and even liberals were dismayed by this overt use of federal power against state authorities. But the incident unconsciously underlined the extent to which the fundamental bases of American society were being transformed: executive power was increasingly becoming the instrument of change, even under a president whose view of the independent role of the federal executive was as limited as that of President Eisenhower.

Beginning in 1958, however, his domestic political influence began to decline. He suffered from the knowledge that he could not run again in 1960 and a continuing series of foreign policy crises, together with the death of John Foster Dulles upon whom he had relied so much in recent years, caused him to spend proportionately more time on foreign relations than he had done in the past. His desire to leave office with solid achievement behind him as a man of peace dominated even the hope of creating 'modern Republicanism'. At times he displayed more vigorous leadership in domestic affairs than he had previously done, but it was in defence of the more conservative aspects of his programme. The enforced resignation of Sherman Adams shortly before the congressional elections of 1958 after revelations that he had accepted gifts from Bernard Goldfine, a New England manufacturer, which might have influenced some of his executive decisions laid both the White House staff and the president's command system open to partisan political attack. It was perhaps partly for this reason that Eisenhower personally intervened in the election campaign of 1958, charging the Democrats with dangerous radicalism, and allowed Vice-President Nixon to go on the stump with even greater aggressiveness.

In the event the Democrats gained a sweeping majority in both houses and the proceedings of the 86th Congress were characterised by conflict between an alliance of the executive branch, regular congressional Republicans and southern Democrats, against the liberal forces. Eisenhower refused to support the small but articulate group of senatorial 'modern Republicans' over the election of a minority leader to succeed Knowland who had resigned to run for the governorship of California. The 'modern Republican' candidate, John Sherman Cooper of Kentucky, was defeated by Everett Dirksen of Illinois. The president frequently used the power of the veto to kill farming, housing and public works measures and seemed to have turned back towards a more traditional type of Republicanism. In a legislative battle to revise the Taft–Hartley Act he secured the adoption of a compromise bill which only made small changes in favour of the unions. The Civil Rights Act of 1960, although hailed by liberals of all parties, was as much dictated by political considerations as anything else. Eisenhower's more positive and dynamic political leadership was no longer directed towards consolidating the new Republicanism, and without his encouragement and support it began to lose its momentum. The administration reassumed the image with which it had entered office: that of comfortable moderate-conservatism with reassuring obeisance to ancient myths.

In the last analysis President Eisenhower's achievement was that he placed his healing touch upon a nation suffering from the hysteria of the McCarthy era and gave time for the American people to assimilate the vast changes that had recently taken place in their domestic society and in their world role. He gave a new dignity to America's world commitment; and if he had played politics more, might have achieved within his own party the silent revolution which his warm-hearted human instincts realised had to be brought about if Republicanism were to be a major political force in the second half of the twentieth century.

THE AFFLUENT SOCIETY AND ITS TENSIONS

The years over which Eisenhower presided were generally good times for the American people. They enjoyed a higher standard of living than ever before; the average working week had declined to 40 hours; income was more evenly distributed and most families owned a car, refrigerator and television set. The average American could with some justification believe that he lived in an affluent society. But there also existed geographical, class and racial pockets of poverty that were only to receive the direct and urgent attention of government in the 1960s. Poor farmers, lower paid workers, old people living on retirement pensions and the Negro community as a whole suffered from a cost of living that by 1956 had risen 14 points since 1949 (1947–1949 = 100), and enjoyed few of the benefits of a rise in the gross national product from $250,000 million in 1949 to $397,000 million in the last quarter of 1955. There were also others from whom, although they were not economically poor except by choice, arose an articulate and increasingly vociferous protest at what seemed to be the direction taken by American society.

Much of American wealth was the product of business enterprise and the business world was dominated by the large corporations. These not only set standards of production and marketing techniques but demanded of their executives conformity to well defined standards of dress and behaviour, to such an extent that the title of Sloan Wilson's novel *The Man in the Gray Flannel Suit* (1955) gained wide currency as a generic descriptive term for the mid-century businessman. In addition to regulating the manners of its managerial workers the large corporation influenced popular taste and consumer habits throughout the nation. With a population that already exceeded 170 million the United States was a mass market for mass-produced commodities ranging from breakfast cereals and motor cars to television and radio programmes, films, plays and novels. A high standard of living meant high costs which themselves dictated large sales. Both commerce and the entertainment industry became the slaves of public opinion polls and consumer preference charts, and these combined with the pressures noted by De Tocqueville to create patterns of conformity that broke down regional and social differences. As more and more Americans moved into the suburbs, a move made possible by increased wealth and universal ownership of the motor car, the values of America seemed to become those of the middle-class suburb moulded by the demands of mass-production industry and the mass media of communication. Some of these values were admirable: the neighbourhood concept represented the resurrection of the community consciousness of earlier times; but 'togetherness' soon came to mean the narrowness of Gopher Prairie and Main Street and the suburb was increasingly indentified with acquisition, comfort and conformity. David Riesman analysed the modern American in *The Lonely Crowd* (1950) and argued that the 'inner-directed' man of the past, moulded by the traditions of his individual and family experience, had been replaced by the 'other-directed' man who so adapts himself to conform to his environment that he destroys his individual identity. The great middle class was examined by C. Wright Mills in *White Collar* (1951); the corporation moulded executive was called by William Whyte *The Organisation Man* (1956), and Lloyd Warner placed the suburb under his microscope in a series of sociological studies.

Such pressures towards conformity were intensified by the international role of the United States in the battle against Communism. The strains of the cold war gave rise to the ideological rejection of diversity that McCarthy exploited and placed a further premium upon identification with the norm. To a growing number of creative minds America seemed to have lost its promise and become an homogenised society in which individual liberty and self-expression were being sacrificed at the altars of orthodoxy and mammon. In the middle 1950s isolated protests fused into a movement similar in origins to the 'lost generation' of the 1920s but far more outspoken in its expression.

Whilst exploring the meaning and significance of the 'lost generation' in a conversation with John Clellon Holmes in 1948 the writer Jack Kerouac reportedly coined the phrase 'beat generation' to describe his own contemporaries. When his novel *On the Road* was published in 1957 it became one of the major texts of the new 'school'. Like the Angry Young Men in Britain the beats searched for the meaning of life in what they believed to be an alien world. They rejected the executive middle-class suburb and all that it stood for. They rejected its literature: two of the most successful novels of the decade were Herman Wouk's *Marjorie Morningstar* (1955) and James Gould Cozzens's *By Love Possessed* (1957) which provided verbose and not too uncomfortable titillation of perennial moral problems. They rejected Hollywood, which continued to produce happy ending romances and westerns such as *High Noon* (1952) and *Shane* (1953) portraying a simple moral universe in which good and evil met in classic confrontation. The movement represented the recurring American search for lost innocence, but instead of trying to reform America the beats opted out, finding a path towards personal salvation in the Zen Buddhist teaching that truth cannot be attained by reason. Their primitivism involved not only the rejection of middle-class life but the embracing and elevation of habits and activities that found no place in conventional society. They found 'holiness' in sexual deviation and drug addiction, and virtue in all forms of self-expression. They cultivated the Negro, whose plight symbolised the narrow hypocrisy of the dominant white economic and social groups; the cool beat of jazz musicians like Charlie Parker influenced their poetic and rhythmic forms.

For the world they lived in they wanted to substitute a vision of youth. The poet Gregory Corso proclaimed that:

Youth quarrels vexation American disappointment of cherished hope, an enlightment, a testimonial of honor and distinction.

The Beat Generation foretells that all youth America will leave their homes and sojourn among strangers.

The Beat Generation is a dream of youth, a dream that will live to a great age like a pair of scissors, or a knife, or any other pointed deathical instrument. (*Variations on a Generation*, 5)

When Lawrence Ferlinghetti, founder of the City Lights Book-shop in San Francisco, published Allen Ginsberg's *Howl* in 1959 the beat movement began to extend far beyond the small groups in New York City, in North Beach, San Francisco, and in Venice West, Los Angeles, where it had been originally nurtured. In *Howl* the influence of Walt Whitman is clear, but whereas Whit-man sought to 'report all heroism from an American point of view' and to sing:

How America is the continent of glories, and of the triumph of freedom
    and of the Democracies, and of the fruits of society,
    and of all that is begun...

Ginsberg had lost this pervading optimism and despaired of the future:

I saw the best minds of my generation destroyed by madness, starving
    hysterical naked,
dragging themselves through negro streets at dawn looking for an angry fix,
angelheaded hipsters burning for the ancient heavenly connection to the
    starry dynamo in the machinery of night...

Fear of the dynamo which had obsessed Henry Adams, and despair heightened by knowledge that with the splitting of the atom man-kind had reached the edge of self-destruction, made the search for personal identitity a matter of urgent necessity.

For the beats America was no longer a 'continent of glories' but:

with its ghost towns and empty Ellis Islands, and its surrealist landscape of
        mindless prairies
        supermarket suburbs
        steamheated cemeteries
        cinerama holy days
        and protesting cathedrals
a kissproof world of plastic toiletseats tampax and taxis
        drugged store cowboys and las vegas virgins
        disowned indians and cinemad matrons
        unroman senators and conscientious non-objectors
and all the other fatal shorn-up fragments of the immigrant's dream come
        too true and mislaid
            among the sunbathers!
    (LAWRENCE FERLINGHETTI, *A Coney Island of the Mind*, 3)

By the 1950s seven out of every ten Americans lived in the city or the suburbs and the beat movement was essentially an urban protest against contemporary urban-suburban society. But, faith-ful to the American tradition, they also yearned for direct contact with nature. The agrarian myth is particularly strong in the work of Kerouac: the theme of *The Dharma Bhums* (1958) is the healing mysticism of lonely mountains; the western farmer becomes an object of passing veneration in *On the Road*; part of the reason for admiration of the Indian and the Mexican peasant lies in the belief that they are still close to the land. At the root of the urban exoticism of the beats hides the ingrained American ideal of the simple life.

Although many of the leading writers associated with the movement were middle-aged young men they expressed the frustrations felt by the teenage and college generations. Youth was anxious and uncertain, neither knowing what it wanted nor where to look. Even the challenge of the space age, which began with the launching of the first successful Russian Sputnik in 1957, did not seem to fulfil the basic needs of young America. Partly, perhaps, this was because in addition to adding a new dimension to the human experience Sputnik stimulated the international rivalries of the cold war. National prestige was felt to be at stake and a space race developed. The United States intensified its own efforts and an American satellite was launched in January 1958. Thereafter the stages of man's exploration of space were marked by triumphs on both sides: in April 1961 a Russian, Yuri Gagarin, became the first man to be placed into orbit of the earth and successfully brought back; the American John Glenn equalled the feat in February 1962. In 1965 each country orbited two-man space craft and astronauts successfully took 'walks' in space. Such programmes were only made possible by great expenditure and organised effort, and despite the individual bravery and resourcefulness of the 'space-men' the flights represented the success of team work. This was perhaps also a reason why, despite the enthralling nature of the achievement, they failed to provide for many Americans the dramatic symbol the times seemed to demand.

Holden Caulfield in J. D. Salinger's *The Catcher in the Rye* (1951) became the Huckleberry Finn of his time. The hipster of the late 1940s, the amoral virility of Marlon Brando in films such as *The Wild One* (1953), the pathetic aggression of James Dean, whose death in an automobile crash seemed entirely appropriate, provided the anti-heroic qualities of popular adolescent culture. In a society which idolised youth, sought to disguise middle age, and beautify death the revolt against conformity began to permeate deeper and deeper and helped to make the country ready for change and prepared to accept new challenges. The presidential election of 1960 opportunely provided the occasion for a release of emotion, and the magnetic appeal of the Democratic candidate liberated many of the discontents which had been smouldering throughout the preceding decade.

THE ELECTION OF 1960

The presidential campaign fitted well into the stereotypes of the American imagination. After the tumult of the primaries was over the electorate was presented with a choice that threatened to expose many of its basic prejudices.

The Democratic party had a plethora of candidates, including not only those who had declared themselves openly but others who lurked in the wings hoping to emerge at a deadlocked convention. Leading the field in ambition and vitality if not certain prospect was the handsome young senator from Massachusetts John F. Kennedy. The son of Joseph P. Kennedy, who after making a fortune on the stock exchange had served as Roosevelt's first chairman of the Securities and Exchange Commission and then as ambassador to London, John Kennedy represented not the 'proper' Bostonians but the Irish Catholic immigrants. After three terms in the House of Representatives he had successfully challenged Henry Cabot Lodge for the Senate in 1952. Liberal, handsome, wealthy and energetic he was determined to become president but he had little support from party bosses outside his own state.

Another candidate was Hubert Humphrey of Minnesota, who first became noticed in politics as the crusading reform mayor of Minneapolis in 1945, was one of the charter members of the Americans for Democratic Action and in 1948 became the first Democratic senator ever to be elected from his state. A strong Stevenson supporter he was a possible vice-presidential candidate in both 1952 and 1956, became widely respected among professional politicians, and after extensive and well-publicised talks with Khrushchev in 1958 during a visit to Moscow acquired considerable popular prestige.

Former president Harry S. Truman's candidate was Stuart Symington, his secretary of the Air Force and senator from Missouri since 1952. Symington was a handsome middle-aged man of dignified presence and considerable executive experience; with the support of Truman's friends in the party he seemed to be the obvious compromise choice for a deadlocked convention. Lyndon Johnson of Texas and his sage, Sam Rayburn, also hoped for a deadlocked convention. Since his arrival in the Senate in 1948, and especially during his years as majority leader, Johnson had built up a strong following on Capitol Hill; despite his southern identification he had entered politics as a protégée of Franklin Roosevelt and inherited much New Deal support. A number of other minor candidates appeared on the scene and in the background was Adlai Stevenson, known to be unwilling to run but probably prepared to be drafted.

The strategy was clear from the start. The active candidates would be Kennedy and Humphrey; each would have to enter the state primaries for each had to show that he could turn out the vote. Humphrey had to demonstrate that a liberal of his persuasion, without a national organisation and with only small funds at his disposal, had an appeal outside his own region. Kennedy had to prove beyond all reasonable doubt that a Boston-born Irish Catholic who looked younger than his 43 years could break down the prejudices and traditions of rural and protestant America and lay the ghost of Al Smith's defeat in 1928.

Sixteen states held presidential primary elections and of these Kennedy chose to enter seven and Humphrey five. They first met in direct confrontation in Wisconsin, a strongly progressive state adjoining Humphrey's home territory of Minnesota. It was of mixed ethnic stock and mixed religion; contained rich manufacturing and farming areas but also depressed regions in the north where the mines and the soil were equally exhausted. After a hard campaign Kennedy won with 56 per cent of the vote, but the result was inconclusive for he carried the Catholic and predominately urban districts and lost the protestant farming areas to Humphrey. The whole thing had to be done again elsewhere and he decided to run in West Virginia.

The importance of West Virginia lay in its ethnic, religious and economic characteristics. A remote Appalachian state served by poor communications it had been largely peopled by immigrants of British stock and rigid protestant persuasion. The rich coal mines which had given it prosperity in the second half of the nineteenth century were now depleted, leaving it poor and backward. Humphrey made the disastrous mistake of deciding to oppose Kennedy: if he won he could hardly hope for the nomination after defeat in his own mid west and if he lost Kennedy would seem unbeatable. The only political reward of winning would be that he could exercise considerable influence in determining the choice of the convention if it became deadlocked and this possibility may have influenced his decision. However, for Kennedy, the election would be decisive and the choice of the Democratic convention might be determined among the West Virginia hills. The wealthy Kennedy organisation moved in by plane; Humphrey trailed in by bus. Whilst Humphrey struggled Kennedy blanketed the state and met the religious issue squarely, knowing that defeat in a state which contained only 5 per cent Catholics would irreparably damage his chances. Against all the odds he won handsomely; the road to Los Angeles and the convention seemed open and by the time the Democrats assembled in July he had some 600 votes committed and promises of the 761 needed to win.

Whilst the convention was publicly preoccupied with preliminary business he negotiated with the state caucuses and picked up another 100 votes; unless a well-organised 'stop Kennedy' movement developed he seemed likely to gain the nomination on the first ballot. Stevenson's name was placed in nomination, and he received tumultuous applause, but this was a sign of affection divorced from political reality and he presented no serious threat. Johnson's supporters fought hard, but could not overcome the Kennedy bandwagon which was now rolling smoothly and on the first ballot Kennedy was nominated. Party wounds were healed by Johnson's surprise acceptance of Kennedy's support for the vice-presidential nomination and the Democratic slate, combining northern and southern interests, presented a formidable challenge to the Republicans.

From the beginning the Republican party had an easier task in choosing its candidate. Vice-President Richard Nixon's ambitions were well known, and although he did not have the open support of President Eisenhower, who did not wish to dictate to the party, he was widely favoured by party leaders. His handling of the vice-presidency had done much to remove the old nickname of 'Tricky Dicky' earned during his hard-hitting campaigns for the House and the Senate in the 1940s, and memories of 1952 were growing dim. He had then been almost forced to withdraw from the ticket after revelations that a secret campaign fund had been set up by some of his supporters, and only a very emotional and successful television explanation, in which he invoked his wife Pat's 'respectable Republican cloth coat' had stilled doubts of his own integrity. Nixon's only possible opponent was Governor Nelson Rockefeller of New York, a leading liberal Republican who, despite his announcement in December 1959 that he was not a candidate, remained a potential threat throughout the early months of 1960. In many ways a genuine 'modern Republican' Rockefeller continually sought to exercise his influence on behalf of weakening the conservative elements of the party, and the clash between him and the 'regulars' erupted in the week before the convention opened. Threatening to carry the fight to the convention floor unless the civil rights and defence planks were modified he had to be appeased. Nixon flew to New York for a personal conference with the governor and approved the fourteen-point 'Compact of Fifth Avenue' in which he substantially accepted most of Rockefeller's views. To the Republican platform committee this seemed betrayal, and only after he had deployed all the political power at his command was the platform committee persuaded to accept the major points of the Compact. Once this had been accomplished, however, Nixon was nominated on the first ballot, with Henry Cabot Lodge of Massachusetts as vice-presidential candidate.

The battle between Democrats and Republicans in 1960 was, in the person of the candidates, a conflict between the two traditionally rival segments of American society. Nixon came from a modest small-town protestant background, had made his way in politics during years dominated by fear of Communism and had shown no aversion to exploiting such fear in his campaigns. He had the support of business and stood upon the Eisenhower record of prosperity and 'peace without surrender'. Kennedy's origins were in the city, he came from immigrant Irish Catholic stock and represented the new wealth of twentieth-century America, made not in productive industry but in stock speculation. Rockefeller and Cabot Lodge were both 'patricians' in politics; Kennedy symbolised the emergence of a new type. Although only three years younger than Nixon he seemed boyish by comparison and his style appealed to the youth of America.

Kennedy's campaign was run by young men. His general manager and closest associate was his 33-year-old brother Robert; Kenneth O'Donnell, 35, was his tactical genius and, with Lawrence O'Brien, 42, led Kennedy's Irish 'mafia'. Theodore

Sorensen, 31, was his 'intellectual blood bank'; brother-in-law Stephen Smith, 31, looked after the administration of the campaign; Pierre Salinger, 34, was responsible for press relations, and the public opinion expert Louis Harris, 38, was in charge of the continuous process of testing opinion and trends throughout the country. This inner group of young men were, together with the candidate, to be the architects of victory.

Kennedy began the campaign with his acceptance speech to the Democratic National Convention. Consciously echoing the phrases of Franklin D. Roosevelt he invoked the slogan of the New Frontier with a plea to get America moving again both in foreign and domestic affairs. He played with ideas, represented intellect, but unlike Stevenson in 1952 and 1956 avoided the label of intellectual. He gave youth the feeling that something would be done and instilled confidence by his own air of knowing what he was about. Part of his appeal was that he was undoubtedly photogenic in a way that Nixon, with his heavy black shadow of a beard and sunken eyes, was not. This fact was to be of considerable importance because the 1960 campaign was memorable for the resurrection of an old campaigning stunt in a new disguise. In the senatorial campaign of 1858 Lincoln and Stephen A. Douglas had engaged in a series of joint debates throughout the state of Illinois, and in 1960 four television debates were staged between the Democratic and Republican candidates. Nixon's participation was a tactical mistake, for issues were not as important to the campaign as image and impact. Although the debating honours were more or less even Kennedy got the national coverage that he needed, scored over Nixon on appearance and personality, and in an age of television established his 'star quality'. He was, however, also well aware that his religion was still potentially the most explosive electoral issue and one which might bring about his defeat. As in the primaries he took the first opportunity to try to stifle it and accepted an invitation from the Greater Houston Ministerial Conference to be questioned on the relationship between his personal faith and his public responsibilities. When he made the outright statement that he believed in an America 'where the separation of Church and State is absolute', and would regard as improper any attempt by his church to influence his public actions, he won the respect of his audience and appeased the fears of much of the electorate. Throughout the campaign the Kennedy organisation displayed this acutely developed political sense of when to confront inflammatory issues. Nixon had received warm ovations in the south and there was a strong possibility that he might make even deeper inroads into this area of traditional Democratic strength than Eisenhower had done in 1952 and 1956. Kennedy had to walk softly and the desegregation issue did not receive emphasis in his speeches. However, less than a month before the election he made a gesture which, whilst not positively alienating the white south, won him the Negro vote in the northern cities: he telephoned the wife of Martin Luther King, the civil rights leader who was in gaol in Georgia, expressing his sympathy and promising intervention if King were not released.

But despite his political skill and the impact of his personality not all of the electorate wanted liberalism, even of the restrained kind that Kennedy professed. Many Americans favoured Nixon's brand of moderate conservatism which had the added attraction of being supported by the still-popular President Eisenhower. The president was not asked to take an active part in the campaign until its final stages but some of his personal popularity passed over to Nixon and an earlier intervention might have tipped the balance. Many Americans were suspicious of Kennedy's youth and relative inexperience and many were concerned about his religion. Had Nixon, like his opponent, concentrated on the electorally important regions of the industrialised middle western and middle Atlantic states, instead of honouring a rash convention pledge that he would campaign in all fifty states (Hawaii and Alaska entered the Union in 1959), he might have overcome his personal disadvantages and been elected. As it was he was defeated by the narrow margin of 84 in the electoral college and by 112,000 in the popular vote. A Democrat was back in the White House and the New Frontier was open.

8

NEW FRONTIERS

In the early 1830s De Tocqueville wrote of the United States and Russia that each 'seems to be marked out by the will of Heaven to sway the destinies of half the globe'. His prophesy has come true. Despite the resurgence of Europe and changes in Africa and the Far East the two super powers dominate the cold war. The United States is the wealthiest nation in the world, matched in technological progress and power only by the Soviet Union, and the average American is better fed, better housed and better educated than his counterpart in any other country. Such achievements do not, however, represent complete fulfilment of the American dream. Despite its rich promise much of the reality of American life falls far short of the hopes that drew millions of emigrants to the land of opportunity.

It has been estimated that 50 million of the 190 million inhabitants of the United States live on inadequate incomes, and that 93 per cent of these are without any form of medical insurance. One-third of the farm population lives below the poverty line. Although only 10 per cent of the population is coloured, Negroes constitute 25 per cent of the poor. 22·9 per cent of all Negro marriages end in divorce or separation compared with 7·9 per cent of white marriages. Nearly 25 per cent of all Negro births are illegitimate compared with 3 per cent white. Crime rates rise yearly and one of the effects of Negro poverty is the high incidence of crime among the Negro community. Large areas in the major cities are depressed slums, and although clearance and renewal projects in cities such as Washington, St Louis, Chicago and Philadelphia have received wide acclaim they make little impact on the problem. Dispossessed families, largely Negro, find that rentals in the new buildings are beyond their means and the result of clearing one slum is usually the creation of another in adjoining districts. The transportation network, particularly from commuter suburbs into the cities, is grossly overcrowded. Although many schools are unequalled anywhere in their facilities and educational standards many more are utterly inadequate and badly staffed. The contemporary United States is a nation of extremes, of extreme wealth and dire poverty, beauty and ugliness, hope and despair.

The task of securing a wider distribution of wealth and removing the blots upon the landscape caused by an individualistic, acquisitive and unthinking people is made more difficult by the continuance of the strong tradition of localism and self-help. It is still widely accepted that the individual must realise his own potential, assisted by the community only on a voluntary basis, and that governmental power should be used only as a last resort. Locally elected school boards control the school system, and taxes for specific welfare projects are often sent for public referendum. The elective system for public office at the county as well as state level means that political and personal factors still have an immense influence on the quality of local government although the number of civil service appointments by merit is continually increasing. Some of the roots of this practice can be traced to the town meeting of colonial New England. Belief in local autonomy and the accompanying fear of over-centralised government helped to mould the framing of the constitution of 1787, and despite their keen sense of nationalism the democratic theories of Jefferson and Andrew Jackson helped to strengthen the tradition of local competence. As reserved powers were kept in the hands of the states, only interpretation of the general clauses of the constitution could give the federal government authority to act in areas other than those directly assigned to it.

The system had much to commend it, for it helped to restrain the development of an unwieldy federal bureaucracy which might have proved inefficient in a country the size of the United States. But from the beginning of the republic a contrary tradition also developed. Federal power was continually expanded into areas where the states were either unwilling or unable to act and it became a widely used instrument for checking abuses and eliminating neglect. Reformers sought federal action to abolish slavery, control working conditions, and regulate big business. The growth of industry in the second half of the nineteenth century and the rise of great corporations created units of private power which could easily dominate local legislatures. Bigness in industry dictated the use of big government and the policies of Theodore Roosevelt, Woodrow Wilson, Franklin Roosevelt and Harry Truman were characterised by a greater use of federal power to curb *laissez faire*. The older tradition was still alive; in March 1960 Eisenhower vetoed a bill which would have provided federal loans for the construction of sewage disposal plants on the grounds that such a use of federal money would stifle local initiative, but a domestic revolution was taking place. Increasingly men came to look to Washington for protection both at home and abroad; and none looked more intently than the Negro population.

CIVIL RIGHTS AND THE NEGRO

In *The Fire Next Time* the Negro writer James Baldwin wrote: 'Yes, it does indeed mean something—something unspeakable— to be born, in a white country, an Anglo-Teutonic, antisexual country, black'. Although a citizen the Negro lived in a white man's world.

After Reconstruction the freed Negro was quickly subjected not only to social discrimination born of prejudice but, in the southern states of the union, to economic and political discrimination supported by state legislation. He was effectively deprived of the franchise by poll taxes, literacy tests, and other devices which sought to keep him in a subordinate and depressed status. Acts of terrorism and violence were used in an attempt to break his will: between 1884 and 1900 almost 2,500 Negroes were lynched, to be followed in the first fourteen years of the twentieth century by another 1,100. Violence begat violence, the crime rate among Negroes was high and riots were common. After the First World War lynching gradually declined in frequency but the general condition of the Negro was little improved. Most were congregated in the states of the deep south but there were significant minorities in the northern industrial cities; some had gone there immediately after emancipation in search of work in a free society; many more moved during the world war and the migration continued during the 1920s. It was to these northern Negroes that Marcus Garvey's Universal Negro Improvement Association appealed. Garvey emphasised racial pride, asserted the superiority of the black race and proposed the mass emigration of American Negroes back to Africa where they might build a nation of their own. The idea of moving back to Africa was not a new one; it had been current before the Civil War, and even Lincoln at one time believed that it provided the real solution to the American race problem. But Garvey looked at the issue from the point of view of the Negro, whose own freedom and dignity, not white security, was at stake. At first he attracted wide support, but after his imprisonment for fraud the U.N.I.A. collapsed.

The traditional outlet for Negro protest was the National Association for the Advancement of Colored People which, from the date of its foundation in 1909, had enjoyed bi-racial support. The N.A.A.C.P. abandoned the teaching of the great Negro educator Booker T. Washington, who believed that the Negro could not immediately gain equality with whites and should first win their respect by learning simple trades and crafts, and demanded full civil rights and equality without the previous condition of tutelage. It advocated non-violent protest, tried to work through the courts, lobbied the legislatures and sought to educate public opinion. Its pace was necessarily slow, but significant, and it consistently rejected more direct action. The Negro sociologist W. E. B. Dubois was prominent among its early leaders but was forced to withdraw from the movement when he took a more radical stance.

Under the New Deal and during the Second World War the condition of the Negro gradually improved. New economic opportunities opened up and in 1946 President Truman's inter-racial committee on civil rights recommended legislation to break down the barriers of segregation. Although Congress failed to act voluntary local committees sought to educate the public away from racial prejudice, the armed forces began to integrate in 1949 and the process continued throughout the Korean war. Federal courts ordered a number of segregated institutions of higher learning to accept Negro students and the Supreme Court's ruling in the Brown case opened the way for integration of the public schools. Four years earlier it had ordered the desegregation of dining facilities on inter-state trains, and in 1955 the Interstate Commerce Commission demanded the desegregation of all inter-state terminal facilities. Labor unions began a registration drive among negro workers and when the A.F. of L. and the C.I.O. merged in 1955 two negroes became vice-presidents of the joint organisation. The quiet but persistent pressure from the N.A.A.C.P. in the early and middle 1950s achieved results but progress was slow; some southern states prohibited the association from operating within their borders and an increasing number of Negroes wanted more direct action to make the validity of their cause known.

In 1956 a Negro clergyman, Martin Luther King, organised a boycott of the city bus system in Montgomery, Alabama. The boycott cut the business of the company by 75 per cent and it abandoned its long-established practice of segregating passengers according to their colour. The first round had been won and King founded the Southern Christian Leadership Conference to organise an intensive civil rights drive. Southern whites met the new threat by forming White Citizens Councils throughout the southern states and carried the fight back to the Negro. Court decisions in favour of Negroes were resisted and in the case of Autherine Lucy, a coloured student who sought admission to the University of Alabama under a federal court order, the opposition was successful. She was suspended after riots had broken out. A growing wave of violence weakened the influence of the N.A.A.C.P. and that of the National Urban League, an organisation dedicated to combatting discrimination in large corporations and federal agencies, and strengthened the more radical groups. The Congress on Racial Equality, founded in 1941, became more active after Montgomery, and the Southern Christian Leadership Council gathered increasing momentum.

In 1960 the struggle entered a new phase. On a small scale volunteers had been trying to gain admittance to segregated places for a number of years. The customary tactic adopted was the 'sit-in' whereby demonstrators sat at segregated lunch counters or in segregated restaurants until they were either forcibly removed or served. In 1960 a student sit-in at a Woolworth lunch counter in Greensboro North Carolina caught the public imagination. Students throughout the south became active and a new organisation, the Student Nonviolent Co-ordinating Committee (Snick), was founded. Henceforth it provided the vanguard of protest. Sit-ins widened their objectives to include segregated beaches, churches, playgrounds and cinemas, and in 1961 a group of Freedom Riders went into the south to test the determination of the courts to enforce the growing number of injunctions against discrimination. Riots broke out, particularly in Alabama, and the emotional fervour they generated did much to draw attention to their crusade; but in practical terms little was achieved. Southern white resistance to change hardened and a number of devices were employed to preserve the *status quo*; in Prince Edward County, Virginia, for example, rather than obey a court order to desegregate the public schools they were closed down and the facilities rented to private associations of white citizens for the private education of their children. Although only three states, South Carolina, Alabama and Mississippi maintained completely segregated schools eleven other states had only token integration and the number of Negro pupils receiving education side by side with whites remained small.

The racial problem is a human problem that can not easily be solved by judicial fiat or legislative act. Negroes are socially, economically, politically and educationally deprived and as a result many live in slums where promiscuity, disease and crime are rife. The conditions in which they live breed characteristics that help to confirm the white belief that they are an inferior race. The pattern is true outside the south as well; in the north white resentment focuses on the problem of housing. There is bitter hostility to Negroes moving into white housing areas on the grounds that property values become depressed. The Negro question presents the greatest domestic challenge of the 1960s. It had to be faced if the New Frontier was to be advanced.

KENNEDY AND THE NEW FRONTIER

The inauguration of John F. Kennedy on 20 January 1961 marked not only the beginning of a new era in American politics but the re-awakening of youthful hope both at home and abroad. As had been the case in 1933 this was due almost entirely to the force of the president's personality.

When he took the oath of office his slim figure dominated the scene, overshadowing the benign presence of the retiring president and contrasting sharply with the white-haired dignity of the poet Robert Frost who had been asked to recite. Frost, overcome by emotion and defeated by the weather, could not read his lines and instead declaimed an old poem; but Kennedy spoke well. He roused the crowd with a renewed appeal for the New Frontier, stressed that 'the torch has been passed to a new generation of Americans—born in this century, tempered by war, disciplined by a hard and bitter peace', and called for sacrifice: 'ask not what your country can do for you—ask what you can do for your country'. He offered not ease but hard work; not complacency but self-examination; not casual acceptance of the ideals of the Declaration of Independence but continuous struggle towards fulfilment of the American dream for all citizens without distinction of colour, race, class or creed.

A little less than three years later he was assassinated. Few of the major parts of his legislative programme had been enacted but his aspirations and the manner of his death left an indelible impression upon the American people; he accomplished more by what he tried to do than by what he immediately achieved. His successor Lyndon Johnson succeeded where he had failed and then invoked the concept of the Great Society to symbolise acceptance of the challenges that remained. As the United States tried, however haltingly, to redefine and practise ideals of justice and democracy in face of the complex problems of the mid twentieth century, the country once again acquired a new image in the eyes of the outside world.

Kennedy's determination to get the United States moving again was symbolically underlined when his cabinet was announced. Its average age was 47, ten years younger than the Eisenhower cabinet, and whilst paying due regard to the principle of geographical balance was clearly left of centre in the political spectrum. Arthur Goldberg, legal counsel for the A.F. of L/C.I.O. became secretary of Labor; Abraham Ribicoff, a liberal Connecticut Democrat, became secretary of Health, Education and Welfare; Orville Freeman, former progressive governor of Minnesota, was given the department of Agriculture; the president's younger brother Robert entered the cabinet as attorney general. Two liberal Republicans, Douglas Dillon and Robert McNamara, took the departments of the Treasury and Defense. Dean Rusk of the Rockefeller Foundation was appointed secretary of State; Adlai Stevenson had been expected to be offered the post but his nomination as ambassador to the United Nations brought his great experience into the orbit of policy making. With the other nominees they were a distinguished group. The bright young men of Kennedy's campaign moved into the White House executive offices.

When he delivered his first state of the union message to Congress in January 1961 Kennedy, like Roosevelt before him, spoke of a time of national peril and national opportunity. He stressed economic problems: the fact that farm income had declined by 25 per cent since 1951; that unemployment had risen above five million; that economic growth was slack, prices were rising and there was a continuing deficit at home and in the overseas balance of payments. He drew attention to social problems: 25 million Americans lived in substandard homes; classrooms were overcrowded; many citizens, particularly among the aged, needed medical care and attention; water supplies were inadequate.

Abroad there were communist pressures around the perimeter of the free world; new states in Africa and the Far East were struggling to preserve their independence; civil war existed in the Congo and in Latin America the danger of subversion spreading from Cuba threatened the already precarious stability of the continent. He outlined weaknesses in existing defence machinery and strategic concepts. He recognised that America should use its economic strength to help less favoured nations and announced that he would ask congress for a more flexible system of foreign aid. A new Alliance for Progress would provide funds for investment in Latin America. He advocated the formation of a National Peace Corps whose members would devote their particular skills to the improvement of conditions in underdeveloped countries. He paid tribute to the work of the United Nations.

Political considerations partly dictated the tone of Kennedy's address for it is customary tactics to detract from the achievements of the opposition party, but his remarks were also shaped by an awareness that much needed to be done both at home and abroad. But on the most urgent domestic problem which was at the same time the most inflammatory political issue he said little. There was a passing reference to the Negro dilemma but nothing more. Caution prevailed and the president directly challenged neither widespread racial prejudice nor the particular fears of the southern wing of his own party.

In the weeks that followed legislation to implement the aims of the New Frontier was introduced, and a priority programme emerged to which the administration was committed. But commitment did not automatically ensure success, despite the influence of the White House, for the narrow margins of Kennedy's victory in 1960 meant that he could not claim an overwhelming popular mandate. The election had underlined the division of American society between those who wanted further innovation along the now traditional Democratic path and those who were content with their lot, had prospered during the years of Eisenhower Republicanism, and genuinely believed that the historic federal–state relationship should be preserved. This absence of a strong mandate made it difficult for Kennedy to control the conservative southern Democrats. Their position in the party at large had been weakened by secession in 1948 but in Congress they maintained their hold on the powerful committee chairmanships. The south had been a one party section for so long that the seniority rule, whereby chairmanships went to the members with most seniority on the committees, gave them a controlling influence over the passage of legislation to the floor. The president met this problem head-on and demonstrated that he would not quietly submit to southern dictation. At the beginning of the 87th Congress administration forces under the leadership of Sam Rayburn succeeded in enlarging the membership of the House Rules Committee and weakened the power of the conservatives. This was a significant tactical victory which helped to bring the party into line. Johnson's continuing influence on Capitol Hill also helped, for he could call in many political debts outstanding from his years as majority leader in the Senate.

The result was success on major but established Democratic policies. Social security benefits were extended, the minimum wage was raised to $1.25 an hour, a bill to provide relief for depressed areas was passed. But the crucial parts of Kennedy's programme, the bills embodying the spirit of the New Frontier, were rejected by Congress just as the most progressive parts of Truman's Fair Deal had been. He failed in the attempt to provide federal aid for the construction of school buildings and the improvement of teachers' salaries. He failed to secure acceptance of the plans for setting up community health centres and was soundly defeated on the proposals for medicare, or health insurance for the aged under the social security system. Such schemes conflicted with basic American traditions which had their roots both in prejudice and in well defined and long standing beliefs. Education had never been a concern of the federal government but had always been under state and local control: federal aid might mean federal administration and the bureaucratisation and regulation of teaching methods and the curricula. Aid to the public schools might be followed by aid to parochial schools and the tax payer saw no reason why his taxes should help to support minority groups. Fear that the traditional separation of Church and state might also be endangered was particularly compelling at a time when the president of the United States was himself a Roman Catholic. Medicare was opposed by the powerful American Medical Association and by the private insurance lobbies which saw it as a threat to their vested interests; it denied individual responsibility and was the symbol of creeping socialism. Increased federal spending on social welfare was generally obnoxious to conservatives as it seemed to previsage deficit financing.

Having encountered these rebuffs Kennedy acted with restraint when the second session of Congress met in January 1962. Two additional factors dictated caution. Rayburn had died in November and the speakership of the House of Representatives had passed to the conservative Democrat John McCormack of Massachusetts; 1962 was congressional election year and he did not want to endanger prospects by splitting the party over the priorities of his programme. Without brandishing his power he quietly used it to secure the election of liberal New Frontiersmen as floor leader and party whip in the House and tried to persuade Congress of the necessity of moving forward in the directions he had outlined. Again he had only limited success, securing passage of a bill creating a federal programme for retraining unemployed workers in the new skills demanded by improved technology, and the largest appropriation for public works in depressed areas since the New Deal. He failed to obtain approval of a plan for the development of mass transit systems to relieve urban traffic congestion. The medicare and education bills were again rejected.

The normal pattern in the off-year congressional elections was for the dominant party to lose ground but in 1962 the Democrats increased their majorities. This was the first reversal of the trend since 1934 and represented a major political victory. Although it was partly a result of the Cuban crisis of the autumn of 1962 the congressional liberals were strengthened by the replacement of a number of conservative Democrats by New Frontiersmen. The Republicans were in confusion: Nixon was defeated in his bid for the governorship of California and even in New York, where Governor Rockefeller was re-elected with increased majorities, the success of Mayor Wagner of New York in breaking the power of Tammany Hall opened the way for a resurgence of Democratic appeal throughout the state.

In the 88th Congress, however, Kennedy was again faced with the entrenched power of the southern conservatives. Once again the New Frontier programme was re-submitted, including medicare, bills for providing increased educational and employment opportunities for young people, measures for the development of recreational facilities, for the creation of a domestic peace corps and for the reduction of taxes. The tax bill finally passed but of the educational programmes only a bill giving federal aid to medical schools was approved. Medicare again failed.

Whilst these battles were being waged Kennedy also had to

contend with the country's economic problems. Economic policy was directed towards trying to stimulate employment, halt inflation and reduce the deficit in overseas trade and expenditure without creating a loss of confidence in the basic stability of the economy. The country was prosperous but there were threatening storm signals. Apart from the particular problems of depressed areas and the Negro community unemployment during the years of Kennedy's presidency ranged from 6·9 to 5·3 per cent of the work force, representing between five and six million people out of work. Although five million new jobs had been created since 1961 the increase in automation and a continually growing population meant that the unemployment situation was at best contained. Average weekly earnings of factory workers had risen to almost $100 and the gross national product expanded by approximately 3·6 per cent a year but the consumer price index also climbed steadily. The fiscal years 1961 and 1962 each closed with a budget deficit of about $3,000 million. The deficit in the American balance of payments caused a continued drain on gold reserves which by the middle of 1963 had dropped to $15,500 million, the lowest holding since April 1939.

Kennedy attacked the complex economic problem on a number of fronts. To check the outflow of gold and dollars he ordered economy at overseas bases and closed many down altogether, including a number of U.S.A.F. bases in England. The value of duty-free merchandise that returning tourists were allowed to bring into the United States was cut to $100 and a 'See the U.S.A.' campaign was launched to encourage Americans to take their holidays at home. A Trade Expansion Act giving the president authority to cut tariffs by as much as 50 per cent passed Congress in 1962 after a political battle lasting nine months; Kennedy believed that it would not only improve the image of the United States abroad but would act as an incentive to domestic industry to cut costs. In April 1962 his determination to stop inflation was dramatically illustrated. United States Steel raised its prices by 10 per cent and other producers followed suit. Roger Blough, president of United States Steel, was called to the White House and accused of acting irresponsibly in defiance of the national interest; and it was announced that defence contracts would only be awarded to the smaller companies which had not raised prices. The president's decisive intervention had the desired result, the increase was rescinded and his action appeared to be justified by later reports that United States Steel's profits in 1962 were running at double the rate of the comparable period the previous year. However, Kennedy's stand may also have helped to disturb the stock market. On 28 May 1962 it suffered the biggest fall since 1929. Although the losses were quickly recovered trading remained sluggish and the Federal Reserve Board cut margin requirements for stock purchase from 70 to 50 per cent in an attempt to stimulate investment. The expanding social welfare programmes acted as economic 'pump primers' and defence costs, which amounted to over 50 per cent of an annual budget that approached $100,000 million, also poured money into the economy.

In 1963 the situation remained much the same. Unemployment remained steady, prices continued to keep pace with the rise in earnings and the drain on gold was not checked. New measures were tried, including a higher rediscount rate and taxes on the purchase of long-term foreign securities, but the administration placed most emphasis on a bill to reduce the general level of personal taxation by 20 per cent in the hope of stimulating domestic consumption and investment. It failed to pass Congress.

The one area in which the president was not prepared to compromise was the mutual security and foreign aid programmes over which there had been much congressional heart-searching in recent years. Kennedy believed that foreign aid was an essential part of the foreign policy of the United States, for by demonstrating that the country was prepared to share its wealth with less favoured nations it was a major weapon in the cold war. When he entered office he tried to secure authorisation for a long-term programme which would relieve the administration from the uncertainty of annual appropriations but he was defeated in Congress. At the same time his request for almost $5,000 million for foreign aid in 1961–2 was cut by $500,000,000. In each of the following two years Congress appropriated $1,000 million less than he asked for. To many congressmen expenditure on foreign aid in return for uncertain advantage seemed foolish at a time when there was already a drain on gold reserves and holdings of foreign currencies.

Despite his criticisms of Eisenhower during the election campaign Kennedy's foreign policy in general bore a marked resemblance to that of his predecessor. He stood firm on the established policy of defending the perimeter of the free world. He supported intervention by the United Nations in the Congo. One of Dean Rusk's first official acts was to attend the meeting of SEATO in Bangkok and military forces in the western Pacific area were strengthened following the outbreak of tensions in Laos. Although during the campaign there had been suggestions that the United States should no longer oppose the entry of Communist China into the United Nations the new administration quickly indicated its continued support of Chiang Kai-Shek.

The first major crisis in foreign affairs came over Cuba. Agencies of the federal government had for some time been giving undercover support to Cuban exiles who opposed the Castro régime; in the spring of 1961 a series of air attacks on the island were widely believed to have been launched from bases in Florida controlled by the Central Intelligence Agency. These raids were followed by an abortive invasion attempt at the Bay of Pigs. It was a disastrous failure partly because, as later revelations indicated, the administration had at the last minute refused to provide the promised air cover. After this debacle relations between the United States and the Cuban government continued to deteriorate; the C.I.A. admitted that it had provided funds and training facilities for the exiles; sanctions against Cuba were suggested, and Castro for his part threatened to expropriate the American naval base at Guantanamo Bay. Kennedy's role in the first Cuban crisis was an indecisive one that dismayed his admirers and enchanted his critics but the following year he took a stronger, if not entirely defensible, position.

Early in 1962 much of the remaining American trade with the island was banned and he warned that the United States would neither tolerate Cuban subversion in the rest of Latin America nor allow the Monroe Doctrine to be broken by foreign interference in the western hemisphere. This overt challenge to the Communist world was countered by the Soviet Union with a warning of equal gravity that an attack on Cuba would not be disregarded. Shortly before the congressional elections air photographs revealed the existence on the island of Russian built missile sites. Tension mounted and the world seemed to have arrived again at the brink of war. Kennedy acted coolly but stood his ground. He ordered a blockade to prevent further arms shipments reaching Cuba and declared that if the missiles already in position were kept in place the United States would not stop short of military action to safeguard its security. When the Soviet

Union challenged the legality of the blockade he ordered the interception of twenty five Russian ships bound for Cuba. This action was reinforced by a resolution adopted by the Organisation of American States authorising the use of force. Khrushchev backed down, recalled the ships and agreed to remove the missiles. Kennedy had employed the quarantine strategy advocated by Franklin Roosevelt, had gone closer to the brink than Dulles had ever found necessary, and had won. His domestic popularity soared, the crisis had been surmounted, but the problem of Cuba remained. Castro was a continuing threat, not so much to the United States itself but to the rest of Latin America. Stable government in the southern republics was still a dream and their political, social and economic conditions offered a fertile field for socialist agitation which the United States, despite the Good Neighbor policy, could not easily combat. Kennedy's Alliance for Progress only slowly came into being; problems were so large that the offer of investment capital could only produce results in the long term, and time was quickly running out.

In the wider world Kennedy's foreign policy was conditioned by the same domestic and external forces as that of his predecessor. Although he had stated his dislike of personal diplomacy he soon went on the world circuit to meet foreign leaders. Macmillan visited Washington in the spring of 1961 and the president made a European tour in which he met Western statesmen and held talks with Khrushchev in Vienna. There was no relaxation of East–West tension, and the building of the Berlin Wall in the summer of 1961 seemed to symbolise a hardening of feelings between the two worlds. The banning of atomic tests was widely discussed but little progress was made. The following year there was a change in the climate of opinion. At Chapel Hill in North Carolina President Kennedy spoke of the dangerous illusion of total victory and total defeat, and after the Cuban crisis, during the course of which he and Khrushchev had taken each other's measure, Russian–American relations improved. A new bond of mutual respect was established which finally enabled the long-projected test ban treaty to be concluded in July 1963. Important though this achievement was, however, it was overshadowed by the domestic problem revolving around the Negro, a problem with which, until 1963, Kennedy tried to avoid becoming publicly engaged.

It was not, however, one that could be pushed aside for long.

The Negro was restless and increasingly articulate and active. Although his condition had improved in recent years he was also more aware of his deprivations. Token integration paid obeisance to the Brown decision but in Louisiana in 1961 for example only 4 out of 278,000 Negro pupils were receiving education in desegregated schools. Kennedy was well aware of the facts but although he supported a proposed constitutional amendment banning poll taxes he did not seek new legislation to safeguard civil rights. This was partly due to a political calculation of its effects on southern congressmen, but his reluctance was also based on the belief that only a change of heart by white citizens would allow real progress to be made, and that existing legislation was sufficient provided that it were enforced. On 15 January 1962 he stated that he would seek to advance Negro rights but only 'in a way that will maintain a consensus of national opinion'.

The method he employed at first was quiet but persistent pressure from the federal government through the federal courts. Under Robert Kennedy the Department of Justice did what it could and a number of small but significant victories were recorded. Severe crisis came, however, in September 1962 when a Negro student, James Meredith, was denied admission to the University of Mississippi in defiance of a court order. President Kennedy employed in modified form Eisenhower's Little Rock tactics. Federal marshals were sent to the university to enforce compliance and although rioting broke out in which two men died Governor Ross Barnett capitulated. Success in Mississippi was followed by the admission of Negro students to colleges in South Carolina and Louisiana. Only Alabama was left with a completely segregated educational system. This last citadel fell in the summer of 1963 after protracted resistance by Governor George Wallace, who carried out his threat to stand personally 'in the school house door' to keep Negroes out but finally moved aside. Increasing tension throughout the nation over the civil rights question gave publicity to a militant Negro organisation, the Black Muslims, which wanted complete segregation of the white and black races and the creation of Negro states within the union. Their leading spokesman, Malcolm X, articulately voiced these radical demands and although the Muslims remained a minority group they drew attention to the danger of society splitting into two distinct racial segments.

Kennedy finally decided that the time was ripe for the introduction of new civil rights legislation. In February 1963 he outlined his proposals and in June laid his bill before Congress. It contained five titles, designed to ensure equal access to all facilities engaged in interstate commerce, to enable the attorney-general to institute court action for desegregating schools, to create a Community Relations Service, to stop discrimination in businesses receiving federal funds, and to make clear that the federal government had no obligation to provide money for any activity in which discrimination occurred. The bill was debated against a background of increasing violence. S.C.L.C., C.O.R.E. and Snick were concentrating on getting Negroes put on the voting registers and throughout the summer months the southern states witnessed a series of riots which started in Greenwood, Mississippi, and reached their climax in Birmingham, Alabama. Martin Luther King was arrested several times and his supporters were attacked with police dogs, electric cattle goads and other 'law enforcement devices' by the Birmingham police under the command of 'Bull' O'Connor. In Mississippi an N.A.A.C.P. official, Medgar Evers, was murdered. There were also serious riots in northern cities such as Baltimore, Philadelphia, Rochester and New York. The disturbances received attention in the world press as well as at home and the Negro cause found general support; conversely the image of white America suffered and the promise of the New Frontier curdled. In August 1963 200,000 Negroes and white supporters marched on Washington to present their grievances to the administration. The march was impressively organised and passed of quietly without incident; the inherent dignity of the Negro protest and the validity of their claim of equality was dramatically demonstrated. But, despite the haunting appeal of their theme song, '*We shall overcome*', when schools opened again after Labor Day violence continued and Kennedy's civil rights bill was still held up in Congress.

ASSASSINATION

In the third week of November 1963 President Kennedy flew to Texas on a political tour designed to heal internal rivalries within the state Democratic party which threatened to open the way for Republican victory in the 1964 campaigns. He was accompanied by his wife Jacqueline Kennedy for whom it was a rare experience; she usually avoided political engagements outside Washington.

The president spoke in San Antonio, Houston and Fort Worth. On Friday 22 November he flew to Dallas, a brash, wealthy and conservative town in which the New Frontier was hated by the dominant business interests and where Adlai Stevenson had recently been assaulted by a picket. There were fears that the president's reception might be chilly but he was warmly welcomed and the visit turned into a triumphal procession. At 12.30 p.m. as the motorcade was travelling to a luncheon engagement he was shot in the head; his death was announced shortly afterwards.

American and world opinion was shocked by the tragedy in a wave of emotion without parallel in recent times. The pointlessness of the crime was then made more unbelievable by the bizarre events that followed. Eye-witnesses claimed that the shots had been fired from the sixth floor of the Texas Book Depository and Lee Harvey Oswald, an employee of the warehouse who had been allowed to leave the premises shortly after the shooting, was later stopped in the street for questioning. He killed a policeman before being captured. The following morning Oswald was being transferred from police headquarters to the county gaol when he was himself shot dead by a nightclub proprietor, Jack Ruby. An incredulous world watched this latest development on television and the lack of adequate police protection for Oswald, together with the fact that his removal time had been widely publicised, immediately aroused rumours of a conspiracy to silence the suspected assassin. Such suspicions were intensified when it later became known that Oswald had lived in Russia after being dishonourably discharged from the marines, that he had a Russian wife, and in July 1963 had tried to secure a visa for Cuba. Whilst many believed Oswald to be a Communist others saw him as an agent of right-wing groups; few believed that he had acted alone, although he had a history of psychiatric disorder. Even the publication a year later of the Warren Commission's report failed to satisfy many observers at home and abroad. The cold war breeds an atmosphere of suspicion among the credulous.

With Kennedy's death the initial period of the New Frontier was over but the vision of a better America that he had projected gained strength by the way in which he died. His successor Lyndon Baines Johnson accepted the challenge and made fulfilment of the polities he had inherited the first task of his own administration.

THE NEW FRONTIER—SECOND PHASE

The tragic circumstances of Johnson's accession to the presidency did not leave him much freedom of action. Political and popular emotion at the death of John Kennedy meant that Johnson had to subscribe to the principles of the New Frontier at least until after the presidential election of 1964. But if there had ever been doubt about the extent of his own personal commitment it was immediately removed by the vigour and determination with which he accepted the duty of getting Kennedy's bills through the legislature. The fact that within two years Congress had passed all of the major legislation that Kennedy had tried unsuccessfully to get accepted was a tribute not only to affectionate memory of the late president but to the triumphant political skill of the new.

Johnson gave first priority to the Civil Rights bill. The task was not easy. It had to survive a southern filibuster which lasted for 75 days and was only stopped by the successful adoption of the closure rule to shut off debate. When Johnson and Senator Hubert Humphrey, who was in charge of the bill in the Senate, secured closure it was the first time in the history of Congress that the rule had been successfully invoked over civil rights and with this victory opposition began to dissipate. Indirect pressure came from the people at large, for the frequent riots in northern as well as southern cities underlined the fact that the Negro problem was a national problem and not just a matter of local concern to the south. The fear of responsible Negro leaders that violence might create a 'white backlash' of reaction against the Negro was dispelled by Johnson himself; he emphasised that he would not tolerate violence from whatever quarter it came. The murder of three young civil rights workers in Georgia in June 1964 re-emphasised the necessity of changing the environment in which such crimes were possible and came at an opportune time for the Civil Rights Bill. In July it passed both Houses of Congress and received the president's signature.

Many of its clauses reiterated and clarified existing legislation but one of its provisions directly confronted one of the major barriers to the improvement of the Negro's lot in the south. Even in states like Louisiana and Mississippi, where the Negro population almost equalled that of the whites, they were effectively disenfranchised. Ratification of the 24th amendment in January 1964 had done little to improve their condition, for poll taxes were now hardly used. There were better means of keeping the Negro out of the polling booth. The 1964 act was much more important. It made the completion of six years of public school presumptive proof of literacy for the purpose of the franchise. If this provision were applied large numbers of the Negroes would be able to vote, and with the vote would come a greater measure of control over their own destiny.

Johnson was equally successful, although not without a considerable degree of political controversy, on the other outstanding measures of the New Frontier. The tax reduction bill was passed, as were bills providing federal grants to colleges and universities and an authorisation to spend more than $1,500 million on vocational training schemes for redundant workers. Medicare had passed the Senate before adjournment of the 88th Congress and in July 1965 it passed both Houses. By providing hospital and other services for persons over 65 it marked the conclusion of an effort launched by President Truman almost twenty years earlier and Johnson, with an appropriate sense of history, signed the act at the Truman Memorial Library in Independence Missouri in the presence of the former president.

The successful completion of the priority programme of the New Frontier wrote the final epitaph for John F. Kennedy. Had he not, with vision, vitality and sound political insight, sought to get the country moving again towards an acceptance of federal responsibility for helping to solve the complex problems of contemporary America the United States might still be uncertain of the meaning of its own ideals.

LYNDON JOHNSON AND THE GREAT SOCIETY

President Johnson is too great a political genius and too anxious to establish the reputation of his own administration to be content to stay for long under the inherited mantle of the New Frontier. Although he devoted his first months in office to the policies of his predecessor he also sought to coin slogans that were identified with himself. The first of these emerged in the message to congress in January 1964 advocating a 'war on poverty'. It projected policies that Kennedy had been formulating but Johnson made the programme peculiarly his own.

Kennedy had first directly encountered the problem of unemployment in depressed areas in the primary campaign in

Minnesota. His vocational training schemes were designed to relieve some of the distress of such communities. He also set up a study group to investigate the particular problems of Appalachia. This mountainous region embracing West Virginia and parts of ten other states remained a backwater outside the affluence of the mid twentieth century. After civil rights the greatest domestic challenge was that presented by the uneven distribution of wealth. There were regional pockets of serious unemployment among white workers and most Negroes were poor. Although Galbraith had drawn attention to the problem in *The Affluent Society* widespread concern was not aroused until the publication in 1962 of *The Other America* by Michael Harrington. This study of poverty in the United States buttressed its passionate sympathy with impressive statistics. Harrington agreed that the definition of poverty varied according to the level chosen to represent an acceptable standard of living; the Bureau of Labor statistics assessed it at between $5,000 and $6,000 a year for a family of four. Adjusting these figures to what he considered to be a more realistic standard of living Harrington erected $3,000 to $3,500 as the absolute acceptable minimum. On this basis there were 50,000,000 poor in the United States. Poor whites formed a significant percentage of this total but the statistics were dominated by the Negro population. In 1958 non-white workers earned on average only 58 per cent of white wages. Harrington's figures together with his descriptions of distress shocked the nation and provided some of the impulse for Kennedy's depressed areas programme. They also stimulated the 'war on poverty'.

In 1964 the gross national product had risen to over $600,000 million for the first time. Unemployment had dropped to below 5 per cent of the working force but one out of every four Negro teenagers was out of work and there was little prospect of them ever finding jobs. The problem of poverty was intimately related to that of discrimination, for the condition of the Negro made him unprepared and untrained for the skilled jobs characteristic of advanced technology. In a message to Congress in January 1964 Johnson referred to the 'forgotten fifth' of the nation. Over nine million families had incomes falling below the $3,000 level and 50 per cent of the non-white population lived in abject poverty. The Negroes themselves were fully aware of their dilemma: the march on Washington in August 1963 had focused its demands on equal job opportunity, for without better education and higher incomes Negroes could not hope to rise out of the slums. Johnson secured passage of a $970 million appropriation to initiate a broad range of activities, including a domestic Job Corps patterned on the Peace Corps, and for the expansion of the retraining programmes launched by his predecessor but in 1964 his specific Appalachia bill failed. It did not pass until the summer of 1965 and then provided an initial $1,100 million for the construction of roads and other facilities designed to open up the region to new industries. By that time the 'war on poverty' had been subsumed into the larger concept of the 'Great Society'.

This began to take shape in the spring of 1964 and received its first eloquent and expanded formulation in the president's speech at the University of Michigan on 22 May. Johnson said that whereas the first half of the century had seen the use of invention and industrial processes to create an economy of plenty, the challenge of the next fifty years was whether the United States had the wisdom to deploy its wealth and enrich its civilisation. The cities had to be rebuilt to provide a harmonious and satisfying urban environment. Pollution had to be checked, water supplies expanded, and overcrowded recreational areas reorganised and enlarged. Schools were overstrained and poverty should not be a barrier to education. The transformation of America could not be solely the responsibility of Washington but neither could it be left to inadequate local resources. He asked for co-operation in a new form of 'creative federalism' and promised to try to move towards the 'Great Society..., towards a destiny where the meaning of our lives matches the marvellous products of our labor'. He underlined the theme later in the month and in June spoke of a great society 'where no man is a victim of fear or poverty or hatred, where every man has a chance for fulfilment and prosperity and hope'.

In the months that followed a battery of committees and task forces strove to formulate policies designed to realise this ideal.

The presidential election of 1964 was dominated by the economic, social and political implications of the Great Society concept. Johnson projected the new attitudes of contemporary America whilst his Republican opponent, Barry Goldwater of Arizona, reasserted older tenets of small government, freedom for the individual, and an aggressive anti-Communist 'big stick' foreign policy. The keynote of Goldwater's acceptance speech to the Republican national convention was 'Extremism in the cause of liberty is no vice. Moderation in the pursuit of justice is no virtue'. Stating on one occasion: 'I refuse on go around this country discussing complicated twisted issues' he invoked simple solutions for what he thought were essentially simple problems. Johnson on the other hand, understanding that the problems of the mid twentieth century are by their very nature complex and that only patient, intelligent analysis and persistent action can provide the right answers, made an intelligent rather than emotional appeal to the people. The extent to which he embodied the new consensus of national opinion was demonstrated by the electoral result He polled 61·2 per cent of the popular vote and topped even Roosevelt's massive majorities of 1936. This landslide victory paved the way for the formal debut of the Great Society in the president's state of the union message of 4 January 1965, and heralded the legislative successes that followed.

The Democratic party had substantial majorities in both Houses of Congress and the Republicans, shaken by their defeat and by the continuing intra-party dissensions between the Goldwater conservatives and liberal elements led by Governors Nelson Rockefeller of New York, Scranton of Pennsylvania, and Romney of Michigan were surprisingly quiescent. Their opposition focused upon details of method rather than basic objectives. With a display of political skill that was oiled by emphasis upon his own cultural regionalism, President Johnson even managed to restrain southern conservatives of his own party. Before midsummer he had achieved an astounding record of success. The 89th Congress accepted medicare and the Appalachia bill and provided the first federal assistance to elementary and secondary schools. It reduced excise taxes, ratified an omnibus programme for public housing and urban renewal and passed an important voting registration bill designed to remove technical restrictions upon the Negro's exercise of the franchise. Other measures passed one or other of the two Houses and prospects for their future ratification seemed bright.

Walter Lippmann has written that 'the Johnson conception of the Great Society rests on the two pillars of controlled affluence and of political consensus'. All of the president's political skill might have been used to no avail but for his belief in himself as the president of all the people and his repeated appeal to the middle of the road consensus. From the time of his accession he tried to heal the wounds of the business community caused by

Kennedy's handling of the steel crisis of 1962 and offered friendship and co-operation to industry. His understanding of the
necessity of compromise in political action, which had led some
liberal critics to doubt the sincerity of his commitment to mid-
century ideals, has proved singularly effective. In January 1965 he
opposed an attempted 5 per cent rise in the price of structural
steel but then softened the harshness of his opposition by applaud-
ing the public spirit of the manufacturers when they reduced the
size of the increase almost to the level of his 3·2 per cent guide-
line. The episode underlined a significant difference in political
touch between Johnson and Kennedy, and a sign of Johnson's
stature is that he managed to win and largely keep the confidence
of business without alienating labour. His political text of asking
all men to reason together, his often homely discourse and unsophisticated manners have produced the desired results. Despite
the problems that remain the Fair Deal and the New Frontier
appear to be coming to fruition under the aegis of the Great
Society.

But in the field of foreign relations the promise of the future
remains blurred and uncertain. The rigidity of the post-war containment theory reflected prevailing beliefs that the United States
had a vested interest not only in containing the power of the
Soviet Union, and more recently that of China, but also in
willing the overthrow of all types of local Communist régimes.
The corollary to this policy was support of all types of non-
Communist government. Although in Europe the political and
economic structure obscured the clarity of America's ideological
crusade it was seen in full light in underdeveloped areas. Intervention in Guatemala and opposition to Castro's Cuba reflected the
combined strength of traditional hemispheric policy and the new
sense of mission. Despite the rhetoric of the Alliance for Progress
the sending of troops to Santo Domingo in the summer of 1965
demonstrated that there had been no change of attitude.

This fusion of material with ideological interest can also be
seen in South-east Asia. Although not a signatory of the 1954
Geneva Treaty the United States exercised its influence on behalf
of right wing governments in South Vietnam. It voluntarily undertook to support South Vietnam against pressure from the Communist North, and when nationalist Viet Cong, assisted by the
Ho Chi Minh régime, threatened to overthrow President Diem
the United States sent military 'advisers' to help buttress his

waning authority. American economic and military aid to South Vietnam was increased after a domestic struggle for power in which Diem was assassinated, tactical fighting units joined the 'advisers' and by 1964 the United States was fighting an undeclared war. This war entered a new phase when, following Viet Cong attacks on American bases, President Johnson ordered air strikes upon military targets in North Vietnam. So far the Chinese have not openly intervened, and the Soviet Union has urged restraint, but the successful Chinese explosion of a nuclear device in October 1964 raises the spectre of more decisive Chinese action if they develop the capacity to threaten the United States with nuclear warfare.

Whether or not the Viet Cong represent a spontaneous democratic' uprising, or were from the beginning agents of an aggressive North Vietnam, the confused situation in South-east Asia underlines the difficulty of projecting established Anglo-Saxon traditions into underdeveloped areas with radically different cultural backgrounds. It heightens the dilemma of contemporary American foreign policy which, whilst vigorously protesting the inherent right of all peoples to self-determination, frequently appears in the posture of a reactionary counter-revolutionary force. The honest purpose of the United States in its post-war acceptance of the responsibilities of power remains open to misinterpretation in the countries most at stake in the cold war, even though to the Western world the sincerity of its commitment may be clear.

EPILOGUE

The lonely continent that received the first European immigrants is now a teeming land at the centre of world power. Gertrude Stein once wrote that 'After all anybody is as their land and air is ...It is that which makes them and the arts they make and the work they do and the way they eat and the way they drink and the way they learn and everything'. The immensity of the land and the rich resources that it bore constituted the primary environment of the immigrant, conditioned his response to the New World and transmuted his inherited traditions into new forms.

The themes of the colonial and nineteenth-century experience, and their twentieth-century development, produced contemporary America. Size is still a visible characteristic but it is the impact of man upon space that impresses a particular quality upon American life. The empty expanse of prairie has been turned into a wheat field stretching as far as the eye can see. Concrete roads reach to the horizons. Multiple crossings lie like petrified snakes. Grid street patterns defy natural contours. The visitor can still lose himself among forests but the city is dominant and he is more likely to wander on pavements through canyons of steel. Skyscrapers reflect the scale of the land and try to reduce it by a counter-assertion of strength and pride. Man's conquest is everywhere to be seen; even the desert has been partially tamed by air conditioning and irrigation, and plastic-lined lakes which offer the ulitmate mockery to nature are to be found in eastern California.

The urbanisation of America and its transformation into a technological society enabled the American to impose his will upon the landscape but in the process he alienated himself from it. Although remaining in the background of his consciousness it is no longer an integral part of his existence and has been relegated to the status of a business proposition or a recreational facility to be tentatively enjoyed and occasionally feared. Intellectual revolt against machine living takes many forms, and preoccupation with the spatial context of life has been one of the dominant themes of American writing and painting since the colonial period. In the 1940s artists like Jackson Pollock experimented with new forms in an attempt, as one critic stated,

to create a synthesis between this fresh insight into man and his environment in America, which was unlike anything else on earth, and the new vision had to be integrated with an equally new understanding of the land with all its physical and spiritual connotations. The integration had to be total and complete...Man's imprint on the land, or his presence in a new realization of interior or exterior space, at a certain moment in time, had also to show some traces of the fragility, the waywardness, the vulnerability, and the arbitrarily precise inflections of human impulse.

(BRYAN ROBERTSON, *Jackson Pollock*)

The present popularity of the open air life, for holidays, is an unsophisticated variant on the same yearning for re-integration with the natural world. Its classic suburban expression is the back-yard barbecue.

Although urbanisation has transformed the physical environment it has not changed one of the earliest observable American characteristics: mobility. In addition to social mobility the American has always been on the move geographically. This has been partly due to optimism: 'Go West young man and grow up with the country'; Thar's gold in them thar hills.' Things always look better over the hill and in the twentieth century things in the city always look better from the hill. The moving frontier still exists; the average American changes his home, his city, his state many times in a lifetime. In contemporary America California is once again the promised land and one thousand people move into the state each day. The history of the United States could be written in terms of its evolving transportation system; natural waterways, turnpikes, canals, railroads, motor roads and air routes have each captured the spirit of America at successive stages of development. The battered empty beer can by the side of the highway can be regarded as a symbol of the present day odyssey of the transient American in an industrialised age. (cf. John Kouwenhoven, *The Beer Can by the Highway*). 'The road', wrote Kerouac, 'is life.'

On the Road is an epic to the modern American.

We all realized we were leaving confusion and nonsense behind and per-forming our one and noble function of the time, *move*. And we moved! We flashed past the mysterious white signs in the night somewhere in New Jersey that say SOUTH (with an arrow) and WEST (with an arrow) and took the south one. New Orleans! It burned in our brains...What is that feeling when you're driving away from people and they recede on the plain till you see their specks dispersing?—it's the too-huge world vaulting us, and it's good-by. But we lean forward to the next crazy venture beneath the skies...We sat tight and bent our minds to the goal. We went over Ber-

thoud Pass, down to the great plateau, Tabernash, Troublesome, Kremm-
ling; down Rabbit Ears Pass to Steamboat Springs, and out; fifty miles of
dusty detour; then Craig and the Great American Desert. As we crossed
the Colorado-Utah border I saw God in the sky in the form of huge
gold sunburning clouds above the desert that seemed to point a finger at
me and say, 'Pass here and go on, you're on the road to heaven.' Ah well,
alackaday, I was more interested in some old rotted covered wagons and
pool tables sitting in the Nevada desert near a Coca-Cola stand and where
there were huts with the weatherbeaten signs still flapping in the haunted
shrouded desert wind, saying, 'Rattlesnake Bill lived here' or 'Broken-
mouthed Annie holed up here for years.' Yes, zoom!

The mobility of the American has contributed to his deeply
rooted egalitarianism. This has been further strengthened by the
demands of mass-production society. The sense of equality bred
conformity and in the twentieth century the mass media have
produced a mass culture. Dwight MacDonald has called its
contemporary manifestation 'Midcult', a middlebrow suburban
culture that, like genuine mass culture, believes in pleasing the
crowd but pretends to respect the values of 'High' culture whilst
watering them down to a common vulgarity. Midcult exists, but
thousands of Americans visit the Metropolitan Museum in New
York each week-end, throughout the nation over a thousand
symphony orchestras are supported by the public, and open-air
music festivals like that at Tanglewood in Massachusetts provide
examples of a degree of cultural recognition in society at large
that is far removed from the pessimistic analysis of Henry Adams's
successors. American culture embraces both the comic strip and
the highest form of cultural activity; it is a pluralistic society
which tries to reconcile the demands of mass consumption with the
ideals of its people.

David Potter has called the Americans a *People of Plenty*
but their bounty has been dearly won. Goods and possessions
matter as symbols of success but they are also positively enjoyed
for their own sake. People are both acquisitive and wasteful; mass
production and mass consumption are made possible by inventive
ingenuity and hard work and they are a reason for pride and not
a cause of shame. Sensual delight in the apparatus of living is,
however, accompanied by great generosity. The frontier tradition of helping strangers is still strong and extends to peoples in
foreign lands. Although the motives behind plans like Marshall
Aid have not been entirely altruistic the American tradition of

sharing wealth has set examples of generosity unparalleled in the history of Western civilisation.

Basic American faith in their democratic capitalist system, coupled with an acceptance of fundamental Christian teaching, ('in God We Trust' is engraved upon the coinage) produced a belief in 'the mission of America'. Confined within continental limits during the first hundred and fifty years of the Republic, and always in tune with the realities of the national interest, the mission now embraces most of the free world. This extension can be partly explained in terms of changes in the balance of world power, but an essential ingredient of the American opposition to Communism is that it is thought to represent an unpalatable and unacceptable affront to the dignity of man and the majesty of God. President Eisenhower summarised the view of his countrymen in his farewell message of January 1961 when he declared: 'We face a hostile ideology—global in scope, atheistic in character, ruthless in purpose, and insidious in method.' The strength of such beliefs explains why the country accepts the basic necessity of fighting the war in South Vietnam, although the size of the American commitment is a matter of widespread concern.

Adulation of individual achievement resulted in *laissez faire* capitalism but the twin tenets of capitalism and democracy have now intermingled in a realisation that true democracy cannot prevail in a system where capitalism is unrestrained. Through enlargement of the role of the federal government a mixed economy has therefore been created which resembles that of the European liberal tradition. Re-interpretation of the constitution has been the method employed to change the balance of authority between the individual, the state and the national government whilst enabling the people to retain the sense of security engendered by their historic institutions and traditional political system. The changing tempo of this quiet revolution has provided the dominant theme of domestic history in the twentieth century. Realisation of the Great Society depends upon the continuing vitality of the new relationship between federal and local authority through which the nation's resources can be fully mobilised to meet the challenges of the mid twentieth century. Despite the many problems that remain, the American dream of equal opportunity in a just society is perhaps now closer to fulfilment than ever before. Economic planning within the context of a free enterprise system has, over the past five years, been shown to work. Prejudice has been shown to be capable of erosion by sustained effort. Educational opportunities have been extended to such an extent that enrollment in institutions of higher education almost doubled between 1955 and 1964 to reach a figure of approximately five million.

Much of the progress of the past decade can be attributed to the innate strength of the American democratic tradition, but a significant contribution has been made by the external demands of the cold war, for rivalry with Communism heightened the necessity for the United States to be able to present a defensible image to the outside world. One example was the impetus given by Sputnik I to passage of the National Defence Education Act of 1958, designed 'to strengthen the national defence and to encourage and assist in the expansion and improvement of educational programs to meet critical national needs'. There have been many others. So long as the internal ramifications of foreign policy coincide with the genuine domestic aspirations of the American people there is hope for a continued improvement in the quality of American civilisation. But there is also need for care lest reaction to foreign pressures again turn consensus into a conformity that seeks to stifle intellectual liberty and deny freedom to dissent.

APPENDIX 1

THE CONSTITUTION OF THE UNITED STATES OF AMERICA

We, The People of the United States, in Order to form a more perfect Union, establish Justice, insure domestic Tranquility, provide for the common defence, promote the general Welfare, and secure the Blessings of Liberty to ourselves and our Posterity, do ordain and establish this Constitution for the United States of America.

ARTICLE I
SECTION I

All legislative Powers herein granted shall be vested in a Congress of the United States, which shall consist of a Senate and a House of Representatives.

SECTION 2

The House of Representatives shall be composed of Members chosen every second Year by the People of the several States, and the Electors in each State shall have the Qualifications requisite for Electors of the most numerous Branch of the State Legislature.

No Person shall be a Representative who shall not have attained to the Age of twenty-five Years, and been seven Years a Citizen of the United States, and who shall not, when elected, be an Inhabitant of that State in which he shall be chosen.

Representatives and direct Taxes shall be apportioned among the several States which may be included within this Union, according to their respective Numbers, which shall be determined by adding to the whole Number of free Persons, including those bound to Service for a Term of Years, and excluding Indians not taxed, three fifths of all other Persons. The actual Enumeration shall be made within three Years after the first Meeting of the Congress of the United States, and within every subsequent Term of ten Years, in such Manner as they shall by Law direct. The Number of Representatives shall not exceed one for every thirty Thousand, but each State shall have at Least one Representative; and until such enumeration shall be made, the State of New Hampshire shall be entitled to chuse three, Massachusetts eight, Rhode-Island and Providence Plantations one, Connecticut five, New-York six, New Jersey four, Pennsylvania eight, Delaware one, Maryland six, Virginia ten, North Carolina five, South Carolina five, and Georgia three.

When vacancies happen in the Representation from any State, the

Executive Authority thereof shall issue Writs of Election to fill such Vacancies.

The House of Representatives shall chuse their Speaker and other Officers; and shall have the sole Power of Impeachment.

SECTION 3

The Senate of the United States shall be composed of two Senators from each State, chosen by the Legislature thereof, for six Years; and each Senator shall have one Vote.

Immediately after they shall be assembled in Consequence of the first Election, they shall be divided as equally as may be into three Classes. The Seats of the Senators of the first Class shall be vacated at the Expiration of the second Year, of the second Class at the Expiration of the fourth Year, and of the third Class at the Expiration of the sixth Year, so that one-third may be chosen every second Year; and if Vacancies happen by Resignation, or otherwise, during the Recess of the Legislature of any State, the Executive thereof may make temporary Appointments until the next Meeting of the Legislature, which shall then fill such Vacancies.

No Person shall be a Senator who shall not have attained to the Age of thirty Years, and been nine Years a Citizen of the United States, and who shall not when elected, be an Inhabitant of that State for which he shall be chosen.

The Vice President of the United States shall be President of the Senate, but shall have no Vote, unless they be equally divided.

The Senate shall chuse their other Officers, and also a President pro tempore, in the Absence of the Vice President, or when he shall exercise the Office of President of the United States.

The Senate shall have the sole Power to try all Impeachments. When sitting for that Purpose, they shall be on Oath or Affirmation. When the President of the United States is tried, the Chief Justice shall preside; And no Person shall be convicted without the Concurrence of two-thirds of the Members present.

Judgment in Cases of Impeachment shall not extend further than to removal from Office, and disqualification to hold and enjoy any Office of honor, Trust, or Profit under the United States; but the Party convicted shall nevertheless be liable and subject to Indictment, Trial, Judgment and Punishment, according to Law.

SECTION 4

The Times, Places and Manner of holding Elections for Senators and Representatives, shall be prescribed in each State by the Legislature thereof; but the Congress may at any time by Law make or alter such Regulations, except as to the Places of chusing Senators.

The Congress shall assemble at least once in every Year, and such Meeting shall be on the first Monday in December, unless they shall by Law appoint a different Day.

SECTION 5

Each House shall be the Judge of the Elections, Returns and Qualifications of its own Members, and a Majority of each shall constitute a Quorum to do Business; but a smaller Number may adjourn from day to day, and may be authorized to compel the Attendance of absent Members, in such Manner, and under such Penalties as each House may provide.

Each House may determine the Rules of its Proceedings, punish its Members for disorderly Behavior, and, with the Concurrence of two-thirds, expel a Member.

Each House shall keep a Journal of its Proceedings, and from time to time publish the same, excepting such Parts as may in their Judgment require Secrecy; and the Yeas and Nays of the Members of either House on any question shall, at the Desire of one-fifth of those present, be entered on the Journal.

Neither House, during the Session of Congress, shall, without the Consent of the other, adjourn for more than three days, nor to any other Place than that in which the two Houses shall be sitting.

SECTION 6

The Senators and Representatives shall receive a Compensation for their Services, to be ascertained by Law, and paid out of the Treasury of the United States. They shall in all Cases, except Treason, Felony and Breach of the Peace, be privileged from Arrest during their Attendance at the Session of their respective Houses, and in going to and returning from the same; and for any Speech or Debate in either House, they shall not be questioned in any other Place.

No Senator or Representative shall, during the Time for which he was elected, be appointed to any civil Office under the Authority of the United States, which shall have been created, or the Emoluments whereof shall have been encreased during such time; and no Person holding any Office under the United States, shall be a Member of either House during his Continuance in Office.

SECTION 7

All Bills for raising Revenue shall originate in the House of Representatives; but the Senate may propose or concur with Amendments as on other Bills.

Every Bill, which shall have passed the House of Representatives and the Senate, shall, before it become a Law, be presented to the President of the United States; If he approve he shall sign it, but if not he shall return it, with his Objections to that House in which it shall have originated, who shall enter the Objections at large on their Journal, and proceed to reconsider it. If after such Reconsideration two-thirds of that House shall agree to pass the Bill, it shall be sent, together with the Objections, to the other House, by which it shall likewise be reconsidered, and if approved by two-thirds of that House, it shall become a Law. But in all such cases the Votes of both Houses shall be determined by Yeas and Nays, and the Names of the Persons voting for and against the Bill shall be entered on the Journal of each House respectively. If any Bill shall not be returned by the President within ten Days (Sundays excepted) after it shall have been presented to him, the Same shall be a Law, in like Manner as if he had signed it, unless the Congress by their Adjournment prevent its Return, in which Case it shall not be a Law.

Every Order, Resolution, or Vote to which the Concurrence of the Senate and House of Representatives may be necessary (except on a question of Adjournment) shall be presented to the President of the United States; and before the Same shall take Effect, shall be approved by him, or being disapproved by him, shall be repassed by two-thirds of the Senate and House of Representatives, according to the Rules and Limitations prescribed in the Case of a Bill.

SECTION 8

The Congress shall have Power to lay and collect Taxes, Duties, Imposts and Excises, to pay the Debts and provide for the common Defence and general Welfare of the United States; but all Duties, Imposts and Excises shall be uniform throughout the United States;

To borrow Money on the credit of the United States:

To regulate Commerce with foreign Nations, and among the several States, and with the Indian Tribes;

To establish an uniform Rule of Naturalization, and uniform Laws on the subject of Bankruptcies throughout the United States;

To coin Money, regulate the Value thereof, and of foreign Coin; and fix the Standard of Weights and Measures;

To provide for the Punishment of counterfeiting the Securities and current Coin of the United States;

To establish Post Offices and post Roads;

To promote the Progress of Science and useful Arts, by securing for limited Times to Authors and Inventors the exclusive Right to their respective Writings and Discoveries;

To constitute Tribunals inferior to the supreme Court;

To define and punish Piracies and Felonies committed on the high Seas, and Offences against the Law of Nations;

To declare War, grant Letters of Marque and Reprisal, and make Rules concerning Captures on Land and Water;

To raise and support Armies, but no Appropriation of Money to that Use shall be for a longer Term than two Years;

To provide and maintain a Navy;

To make Rules for the Government and Regulation of the land and naval Forces;

To provide for calling forth the Militia to execute the Laws of the Union, suppress Insurrections and repel Invasions;

To provide for organizing, arming, and disciplining the Militia, and for governing such Part of them as may be employed in the Service of the United States, reserving to the States respectively, the Appointment of the Officers, and the Authority of training the Militia according to the discipline prescribed by Congress;

To exercise exclusive Legislation in all Cases whatsoever, over such District (not exceeding ten Miles square) as may, by Cession of particular States, and the Acceptance of Congress, become the Seat of the Government of the United States, and to exercise like Authority over all Places purchased by the Consent of the Legislature of the State in which the Same shall be, for the Erection of Forts, Magazines, Arsenals, dock-Yards, and other needful Buildings;—And

To make all Laws which shall be necessary and proper for carrying into Execution the foregoing Powers, and all other Powers vested by this Constitution in the Government of the United States, or in any Department or Officer thereof.

SECTION 9

The Migration or Importation of such Persons as any of the States now existing shall think proper to admit, shall not be prohibited by the Congress prior to the Year one thousand eight hundred and eight, but a Tax or duty may be imposed on such Importation, not exceeding ten dollars for each Person.

The Privilege of the Writ of Habeas Corpus shall not be suspended, unless when in Cases of Rebellion or Invasion the public Safety may require it.

No Bill of Attainder or ex post facto Law shall be passed.

No Capitation, or other direct, tax shall be laid, unless in Proportion to the Census or Enumeration herein before directed to be taken.

No Tax or Duty shall be laid on Articles exported from any State.

No Preference shall be given by any Regulation of Commerce or Revenue to the Ports of one State over those of another: nor shall Vessels bound to, or from, one State, be obliged to enter, clear, or pay Duties in another.

No Money shall be drawn from the Treasury, but in Consequence of Appropriations made by Law; and a regular Statement and Account of the Receipts and Expenditures of all public Money shall be published from time to time.

No Title of Nobility shall be granted by the United States: And no Person holding any Office of Profit or Trust under them, shall, without the Consent of the Congress, accept of any present, Emolument, Office, or Title, of any kind whatever, from any King, Prince, or foreign State.

SECTION 10

No State shall enter into any Treaty, Alliance, or Confederation; grant Letters of Marque and Reprisal; coin Money; emit Bills of Credit; make any Thing but gold and silver Coin a Tender in Payment of Debts; pass any Bill of Attainder, ex post facto Law, or Law impairing the Obligation of Contracts, or grant any Title of Nobility.

No State shall, without the Consent of the Congress, lay any Imposts or Duties on Imports or Exports, except what may be absolutely necessary for executing its inspection Laws: and the net Produce of all Duties and Imposts, laid by any State on Imports or Exports, shall be for the Use of the Treasury of the United States; and all such Laws shall be subject to the Revision and Control of the Congress.

No State shall, without the Consent of Congress, lay any Duty of Tonnage, keep Troops, or Ships of War in time of Peace, enter into any Agreement of Compact with another State, or with a foreign Power, or engage in War, unless actually invaded, or in such imminent Danger as will not admit of delay.

ARTICLE II

SECTION I

The executive Power shall be vested in a President of the United States of America. He shall hold his Office during the Term of four Years, and, together with the Vice President, chosen for the same Term, be elected, as follows.

Each State shall appoint, in such Manner as the Legislature thereof may direct, a Number of Electors, equal to the whole Number of Senators and Representatives to which the State may be entitled in the Congress: but no Senator or Representative, or Person holding an Office of Trust or Profit under the United States, shall be appointed an Elector.

The electors shall meet in their respective States, and vote by ballot for two Persons, of whom one at least shall not be an Inhabitant of the same State with themselves. And they shall make a List of all the Persons voted for, and of the Number of Votes for each; which List they shall sign and certify, and transmit sealed to the Seat of the Government of the United States, directed to the President of the Senate. The President of the Senate shall, in the Presence of the Senate and House of Representatives, open all the Certificates, and the Votes shall then be counted. The Person having the greatest Number of Votes shall be the President, if such Number be a

Majority of the whole Number of Electors appointed; and if there be more than one who have such Majority, and have an equal Number of Votes, then the House of Representatives shall immediately chuse by Ballot one of them for President; and if no Person have a Majority, then from the five highest on the List the said House shall in like Manner chuse the President. But in chusing the President, the Votes shall be taken by States, the Representation from each State having one Vote; a Quorum for this Purpose shall consist of a Member or Members from two-thirds of the States, and a Majority of all the States shall be necessary to a Choice. In every Case, after the Choice of the President, the Person having the greatest Number of Votes of the Electors shall be the Vice President. But if there should remain two or more who have equal Votes, the Senate shall chuse from them by Ballot the Vice President.

The Congress may determine the Time of chusing the Electors, and the Day on which they shall give their Votes; which Day shall be the same throughout the United States.

No Person except a natural born Citizen, or a Citizen of the United States, at the time of the Adoption of this Constitution, shall be eligible to the Office of President; neither shall any Person be eligible to that Office who shall not have attained to the Age of thirty five Years, and been fourteen Years a Resident within the United States.

In Case of the Removal of the President from Office, or of his Death, Resignation or Inability to discharge the Powers and Duties of the said Office, the same shall devolve on the Vice President, and the Congress may by Law provide for the Case of Removal, Death, Resignation or Inability, both of the President and Vice President, declaring what Officer shall then act as President, and such Officer shall act accordingly, until the Disability be removed, or a President shall be elected.

The President shall, at stated Times, receive for his Services, a Compensation, which shall neither be encreased nor diminished during the Period for which he shall have been elected, and he shall not receive within that Period any other Emolument from the United States, or any of them.

Before he enter on the Execution of his Office, he shall take the following Oath or Affirmation:— 'I do solemnly swear (or affirm) that I will faithfully execute the Office of President of the United States, and will to the best of my Ability, preserve, protect and defend the Constitution of the United States.'

SECTION 2

The President shall be Commander in Chief of the Army and Navy of the United States, and of the Militia of the several States, when called into the actual Service of the United States; he may require the Opinion, in writing, of the principal Officer in each of the executive Departments, upon any Subject relating to the Duties of their respective Offices, and he shall have Power to grant Reprieves and Pardons for Offences against the United States, except in Cases of Impeachment.

He shall have Power, by and with the Advice and Consent of the Senate, to make Treaties, provided two thirds of the Senators present concur; and he shall nominate, and by and with the Advice and Consent of the Senate, shall appoint Ambassadors, other public Ministers and Consuls, Judges of the supreme Court, and all other Officers of the United States, whose Appointments are not herein otherwise provided for, and which shall be established by Law: but the Congress may by Law vest the Appointment of such inferior Officers, as they think proper, in the President alone, in the Courts of Law, or in the Heads of Departments.

The President shall have Power to fill up all Vacancies that may happen during the Recess of the Senate, by granting Commissions which shall expire at the End of their next Session.

SECTION 3

He shall from time to time give to the Congress Information of the State of the Union, and recommend to their Consideration such Measures as he shall judge necessary and expedient; he may, on extraordinary Occasions, convene both Houses, or either of them, and, in Case of Disagreement between them, with Respect to the Time of Adjournment, he may adjourn them to such Time as he shall think proper; he shall receive Ambassadors and other public Ministers; he shall take Care that the Laws be faithfully executed, and shall Commission all the Officers of the United States.

SECTION 4

The President, Vice President and all civil Officers of the United States, shall be removed from Office on Impeachment for, and Conviction of, Treason, Bribery, or other high Crimes and Misdemeanors.

ARTICLE III
SECTION 1

The judicial Power of the United States, shall be vested in one supreme Court, and in such inferior Courts as the Congress may from time to time ordain and establish. The Judges, both of the supreme and inferior Courts, shall hold their Offices during good Behaviour, and shall, at stated Times, receive for their Services, a Compensation, which shall not be diminished during their Continuance in Office.

SECTION 2

The judicial Power shall extend to all Cases, in Law and Equity, arising under this Constitution, the Laws of the United States, and Treaties made, or which shall be made, under their Authority;—to all Cases affecting

Ambassadors, other public Ministers and Consuls;—to all Cases of admiralty and maritime Jurisdiction;—to Controversies to which the United States shall be a Party;—to Controversies between two or more States;—between a State and Citizens of another State;—between Citizens of different States,—between Citizens of the same State claiming Lands under Grants of different States, and between a State, or the Citizens thereof, and foreign States, Citizens or Subjects.

In all Cases affecting Ambassadors, other public Ministers and Consuls, and those in which a State shall be Party, the supreme Court shall have original Jurisdiction. In all the other Cases before mentioned, the supreme Court shall have appellate Jurisdiction, both as to Law and Fact, with such Exceptions, and under such Regulations as the Congress shall make.

The Trial of all Crimes, except in Cases of Impeachment, shall be by Jury; and such Trial shall be held in the State where the said Crimes shall have been committed; but when not committed within any State, the Trial shall be at such Place or Places as the Congress may by Law have directed.

Section 3

Treason against the United States, shall consist only in levying War against them, or in adhering to their Enemies, giving them Aid and Comfort. No Person shall be convicted of Treason unless on the Testimony of two Witnesses to the same overt Act, or on Confession in open Court.

The Congress shall have Power to declare the Punishment of Treason, but no Attainder of Treason shall work Corruption of Blood, or Forfeiture except during the life of the Person attainted.

ARTICLE IV

Section I

Full Faith and Credit shall be given in each State to the public Acts, Records, and judicial Proceedings of every other State. And the Congress may by general Laws prescribe the Manner in which such Acts, Records and Proceedings shall be proved, and the Effect thereof.

Section 2

The Citizens of each State shall be entitled to all Privileges and Immunities of Citizens in the several States.

A person charged in any State with Treason, Felony, or other Crime, who shall flee from Justice, and be found in another State, shall on Demand of the executive Authority of the State from which he fled, be delivered up, to be removed to the State having Jurisdiction of the Crime.

No Person held to Service or Labour in one State, under the Laws thereof, escaping into another, shall, in Consequence of any Law or Regulation therein, be discharged from such Service or Labour, but shall be delivered up on Claim of the Party to whom such Service or Labour may be due.

SECTION 3

New States may be admitted by the Congress into this Union; but no new State shall be formed or erected within the Jurisdiction of any other State; nor any State be formed by the Junction of two or more States, or Parts of States, without the Consent of the Legislatures of the States concerned as well as of the Congress.

The Congress shall have Power to dispose of and make all needful Rules and Regulations respecting the Territory or other Property belonging to the United States; and nothing in this Constitution shall be so construed as to Prejudice any Claims of the United States, or of any particular State.

SECTION 4

The United States shall guarantee to every State in this Union a Republican Form of Government, and shall protect each of them against Invasion; and on Application of the Legislature, or of the Executive (when the Legislature cannot be convened) against domestic Violence.

ARTICLE V

The Congress, whenever two thirds of both Houses shall deem it necessary, shall propose Amendments to this Constitution, or, on the Application of the Legislatures of two thirds of the several States, shall call a Convention for proposing Amendments, which, in either Case, shall be valid to all Intents and Purposes, as Part of this Constitution, when ratified by the Legislatures of three fourths of the several States, or by Conventions in three fourths thereof, as the one or the other Mode of Ratification may be proposed by the Congress; Provided that no Amendment which may be made prior to the Year One thousand eight hundred and eight shall in any Manner affect the first and fourth Clauses in the Ninth Section of the first Article; and that no State, without its Consent, shall be deprived of its equal Suffrage in the Senate.

ARTICLE VI

All Debts contracted and Engagements entered into, before the Adoption of this Constitution, shall be as valid against the United States under this Constitution, as under the Confederation.

This Constitution, and the Laws of the United States which shall be made in Pursuance thereof; and all Treaties made, or which shall be made, under the Authority of the United States, shall be the supreme Law of the Land; and the Judges in every State shall be bound thereby, any Thing in the Constitution or Laws of any State to the Contrary notwithstanding.

The Senators and Representatives before mentioned, and the Members of the several State Legislatures, and all executive and judicial Officers, both of the United States and of the several States, shall be bound by Oath or Affirmation, to support this Constitution; but no religious Test shall ever be required as a Qualification to any Office or public Trust under the United States.

ARTICLE VII

The Ratification of the Conventions of nine States, shall be sufficient for the Establishment of this Constitution between the States so ratifying the Same.

DONE in Convention by the Unanimous Consent of the States present the Seventeenth Day of September in the Year of our Lord one thousand seven hundred and Eighty seven and of the Independence of the United States of America the Twelfth.

AMENDMENTS

[The first Ten Articles which were proposed in September 1789 and came into force in December 1791 are known as the Bill of Rights].

ARTICLE I

Congress shall make no law respecting an establishment of religion, or prohibiting the free exercise thereof; or abridging the freedom of speech, or of the press; or the right of the people peaceably to assemble, and to petition the Government for a redress of grievances.

ARTICLE II

A well regulated Militia, being necessary to the security of a free State, the right of the people to keep and bear Arms, shall not be infringed.

ARTICLE III

No Soldier shall, in time of peace, be quartered in any house, without the consent of the Owner, nor in time of war, but in a manner to be prescribed by law.

ARTICLE IV

The right of the people to be secure in their persons, houses, papers, and effects, against unreasonable searches and seizures, shall not be violated, and no Warrants shall issue, but upon probable cause, supported by Oath or affirmation, and particularly describing the place to be searched, and the persons or things to be seized.

ARTICLE V

No person shall be held to answer for a capital, or otherwise infamous crime, unless on a presentment or indictment of a Grand Jury, except in cases arising in the land or naval forces, or in the Militia, when in actual service in time of War or public danger; nor shall any person be subject for the same offence to be twice put in jeopardy of life or limb; nor shall be compelled in any Criminal Case to be a witness against himself, nor be deprived of life, liberty, or property, without due process of law; nor shall private property be taken for public use, without just compensation.

ARTICLE VI

In all criminal prosecutions, the accused shall enjoy the right to a speedy and public trial, by an impartial jury of the State and district wherein the crime shall have been committed, which district shall have been previously ascertained by law, and to be informed of the nature and cause of the accusation; to be confronted with the witnesses against him; to have compulsory process for obtaining Witnesses in his favor, and to have the Assistance of Counsel for his defence.

ARTICLE VII

In suits at common law, where the value in controversy shall exceed twenty dollars, the right of trial by jury shall be preserved, and no fact tried by a jury shall be otherwise re-examined in any Court of the United States, than according to the rules of the common law.

ARTICLE VIII

Excessive bail shall not be required, nor excessive fines imposed, nor cruel and unusual punishments inflicted.

ARTICLE IX

The enumeration in the Constitution, of certain rights, shall not be construed to deny or disparage others retained by the people.

ARTICLE X

The powers not delegated to the United States by the Constitution, nor prohibited by it to the States, are reserved to the States respectively, or to the people.

ARTICLE XI
[Proposed March 1794; Adopted January 1798]

The Judicial power of the United States shall not be construed to extend to any suit in law or equity, commenced or prosecuted against one of the United States by Citizens of another State, or by Citizens or Subjects of any Foreign State.

ARTICLE XII

[Proposed December 1803; Adopted September 1804]

The Electors shall meet in their respective states, and vote by ballot for President and Vice President, one of whom, at least, shall not be an inhabitant of the same state with themselves; they shall name in their ballots the person voted for as President, and in distinct ballots the person voted for as Vice President, and they shall make distinct lists of all persons voted for as President, and of all persons voted for as Vice-President, and of the number of votes for each, which lists they shall sign and certify, and transmit sealed to the seat of the Government of the United States, directed to the President of the Senate;—The President of the Senate shall, in the presence of the Senate and House of Representatives, open all the certificates and the votes shall then be counted;—The person having the greatest number of votes for President, shall be the President, if such number be a majority of the whole number of Electors appointed; and if no person have such majority, then from the persons having the highest numbers not exceeding three on the list of those voted for as President, the House of Representatives shall choose immediately, by ballot, the President. But in choosing the President, the votes shall be taken by states, the representation from each state having one vote; a quorum for this purpose shall consist of a member or members from two thirds of the states, and a majority of all the states shall be necessary to a choice. And if the House of Representatives shall not choose a President whenever the right of choice shall devolve upon them, before the fourth day of March next following, then the Vice President shall act as President, as in the case of the death or other constitutional disability of the President. The person having the greatest number of votes as Vice President, shall be the Vice President, if such number be a majority of the whole number of Electors appointed, and if no person have a majority, then from the two highest numbers on the list, the Senate shall choose the Vice President; a quorum for the purpose shall consist of two-thirds of the whole number of Senators, and a majority of the whole number shall be necessary to a choice. But no person constitutionally ineligible to the office of President shall be eligible to that of Vice President of the United States.

ARTICLE XIII

[Proposed February 1865; Adopted December 1865]

SECTION I

Neither slavery nor involuntary servitude, except as a punishment for crime whereof the party shall have been duly convicted, shall exist within the United States, or any place subject to their jurisdiction.

SECTION 2

Congress shall have power to enforce this article by appropriate legislation.

ARTICLE XIV

[Proposed June 1866; Adopted July 1868]

SECTION I

All persons born or naturalized in the United States, and subject to the jurisdiction thereof, are citizens of the United States and of the State wherein they reside. No State shall make or enforce any law which shall abridge the privileges or immunities of citizens of the United States; nor shall any State deprive any person of life, liberty, or property, without due process of law; nor deny to any person within its jurisdiction the equal protection of the laws.

SECTION 2

Representatives shall be apportioned among the several States according to their respective numbers, counting the whole number of persons in each State, excluding Indians not taxed. But when the right to vote at any elect on for the choice of electors for President and Vice President of the United States, Representatives in Congress, the Executive and Judicial officers of a State, or the members of the Legislature thereof, is denied to any of the male inhabitants of such State, being twenty-one years of age, and citizens of the United States, or in any way abridged, except for participation in rebellion, or other crime, the basis of representation therein shall be reduced in the proportion which the number of such male citizens shall bear to the whole number of male citizens twenty-one years of age in such State.

SECTION 3

No person shall be a Senator or Representative in Congress, or elector of President and Vice President, or hold any office, civil, or military, under the United States, or under any State, who, having previously taken an oath, as a member of Congress, or as an officer of the United States, or as a member of any State legislature, or as an executive or judicial officer of any State, to support the Constitution of the United States, shall have engaged in insurrection or rebellion against the same, or given aid or comfort to the enemies thereof. But Congress may by a vote of two thirds of each House, remove such disability.

SECTION 4

The validity of the public debt of the United States, authorized by law, including debts incurred for payment of pensions and bounties for services in sup essing insurrection or rebellion, shall not be questioned. But neither the United States nor any State shall assume or pay any debt or obligation incurred in aid of insurrection or rebellion against the United States, or any claim for the loss or emancipation of any slave; but all such debts, obligations and claims shall be held illegal and void.

SECTION 5

The Congress shall have power to enforce, by appropriate legislation, the provisions of this article.

ARTICLE XV
[Proposed February 1869; Adopted March 1870]

SECTION 1

The right of citizens of the United States to vote shall not be denied or abridged by the United States or by any State on account of race, color, or previous condition of servitude.

SECTION 2

The Congress shall have power to enforce this article by appropriate legislation.

ARTICLE XVI
[Proposed July 1910; Adopted February 1913]

The Congress shall have power to lay and collect taxes on incomes, from whatever source derived, without apportionment among the several States, and without regard to any census or enumeration.

ARTICLE XVII
[Proposed May 1912; Adopted May 1913]

The Senate of the United States shall be composed of two senators from each State, elected by the people thereof, for six years; and each Senator shall have one vote. The electors in each State shall have the qualifications requisite for electors of the most numerous branch of the State legislature.

When vacancies happen in the representation of any State in the Senate, the executive authority of such State shall issue writs of election to fill such vacancies: PROVIDED, That the legislature of any State may empower the executive thereof to make temporary appointments until the people fill the vacancies by election as the legislature may direct.

This amendment shall not be so construed as to affect the election or term of any senator chosen before it becomes valid as part of the Constitution.

ARTICLE XVIII
[Proposed December 1917; Adopted January 1919]

After one year from the ratification of this article, the manufacture, sale, or transportation of intoxicating liquors within, the importation thereof into, or the exportation thereof from the United States and all territory subject to the jurisdiction thereof for beverage purposes is hereby prohibited.

The Congress and the several States shall have concurrent power to enforce this article by appropriate legislation.

This article shall be inoperative unless it shall have been ratified as an amendment to the Constitution by the legislatures of the several States, as provided in the Constitution, within seven years from the date of the submission hereof to the States by the Congress.

ARTICLE XIX
[Proposed June 1919; Adopted August 1920]

The right of citizens of the United States to vote shall not be denied or abridged by the United States or by any States on account of sex.

The Congress shall have power, by appropriate legislation, to enforce the provisions of this article.

ARTICLE XX
[Proposed March 1932; Adopted February 1933]

SECTION I

The terms of the President and Vice President shall end at noon on the twentieth day of January, and the terms of Senators and Representatives at noon on the third day of January, of the years in which such terms would have ended if this article had not been ratified; and the terms of their successors shall then begin.

SECTION 2

The Congress shall assemble at least once in every year, and such meeting shall begin at noon on the third day of January, unless they shall by law appoint a different day.

SECTION 3

If, at the time fixed for the beginning of the term of the President, the President elect shall have died, the Vice President elect shall become President. If a President shall not have been chosen before the time fixed for the beginning of his term, or if the President elect shall have failed to qualify, then the Vice President elect shall act as President until a President shall have qualified; and the Congress may by law provide for the case wherein neither a President elect nor a Vice President elect shall have qualified, declaring who shall then act as President, or the manner in which one who is to act shall be selected, and such person shall act accordingly until a President or Vice President shall have qualified.

SECTION 4

The Congress may by law provide for the case of the death of any of the persons from whom the House of Representatives may choose a President whenever the right of choice shall have devolved upon them, and for the case of the death of any of the persons from whom the Senate may choose a Vice President whenever the right of choice shall have devolved upon them.

SECTION 5

Sections 1 and 2 shall take effect on the 15th day of October following the ratification of this article.

SECTION 6

This article shall be inoperative unless it shall have been ratified as an amendment to the Constitution by the legislatures of three fourths of the several States within seven years from the date of its submission.

ARTICLE XXI

[Proposed February 1933; Adopted December 1933]

SECTION 1

The eighteenth article of amendment to the Constitution of the United States is hereby repealed.

SECTION 2

The transportation or importation into any State, Territory or possession of the United States for delivery or use therein of intoxicating liquors, in violation of the laws thereof, is hereby prohibited.

SECTION 3

This article shall be inoperative unless it shall have been ratified as an amendment to the Constitution by convention in the several States, as provided in the Constitution, within seven years from the date of the submisson hereof to the States by the Congress.

ARTICLE XXII

[Proposed March 1947; Adopted February 1951]

No person shall be elected to the office of the President more than twice, and no person who has held the office of President, or acted as President, for more than two years of a term to which some other person was elected President shall be elected to the office of the President more than once.

But this article shall not apply to any person holding the office of President when this article was proposed by the Congress, and shall not prevent any person who may be holding the office of President, or acting as President, during the term within which this article becomes operative from holding the office of President or acting as President during the remainder of such term.

This article shall be inoperative unless it shall have been ratified as an amendment to the Constitution by the legislatures of three-fourths of the several States within seven years from the date of its submission to the States by the Congress.

ARTICLE XXIII
[Proposed June 1960; Adopted March 1961]

SECTION 1
The District constituting the seat of Government of the United States shall appoint in such manner as the Congress may direct:

A number of Electors of President and Vice President equal to the whole number of Senators and Representatives in Congress to which the District would be entitled if it were a State, but in no event more than the least populous State; they shall be in addition to those appointed by the States, but they shall be considered, for the purposes of the election of President and Vice President, to be Electors appointed by a State; and they shall meet in the District and perform such duties as provided by the Twelfth Article of amendment.

SECTION 2
The Congress shall have power to enforce this article by appropriate legislation.

ARTICLE XXIV
[Proposed September 1962; Adopted January 1964]

SECTION 1
The right of citizens of the United States to vote in any primary or other election for President or Vice President, for Electors for President or Vice President, or for Senator or Representative in Congress, shall not be denied or abridged by the United States or any State by reason of failure to pay any poll tax or other tax.

SECTION 2
The Congress shall have the power to enforce this article by appropriate legislation.

APPENDIX 2

STATISTICAL INFORMATION

TABLE I. POPULATION OF THE CONTINENTAL UNITED STATES

(Sources: *Historical statistics of the United States; Statistical abstract of the United States, 1965*)

1790	3,929,214	1880	50,155,783
1800	5,308,483	1890	62,947,714
1810	7,239,881	1900	75,994,575
1820	9,638,453	1910	91,972,266
1830	12,866,020	1920	105,710,620
1840	17,069,453	1930	122,775,046
1850	23,191,876	1940	131,669,275
1860	31,443,321	1950	150,697,361
1870	39,818,449	1960	179,323,175*

* 1960 total includes Alaska and Hawaii

TABLE 2. NON-WHITE POPULATION OF THE CONTINENTAL UNITED STATES

(Sources: *Historical statistics of the United States; Statistical abstract of the United States, 1965*)

1790	757,000	1880	6,753,000
1800	1,002,000	1890	7,846,000
1810	1,378,000	1900	9,185,000
1820	1,772,000	1910	10,240,000
1830	2,329,000	1920	10,890,000
1840	2,874,000	1930	12,488,000
1850	3,639,000	1940	13,454,000
1860	4,521,000	1950	15,755,000
1870	4,969,000	1960	20,492,000*

* 1960 total includes Alaska and Hawaii

TABLE 3. GROSS NATIONAL PRODUCT 1919–1964

(Sources: *Historical statistics of the United States; Statistical abstract of the United States, 1965*)

	Thousand million dollars		Thousand million dollars
1919	78.9	1942	159·1
1920	88·9	1943	192·5
1921	74·0	1944	211·4
1922	74·0	1945	213·6
1923	86·1	1946	210·7
1924	87·6	1947	234·3
1925	91·3	1948	259·4
1926	97·7	1949	258·1
1927	96·3	1950	284·6
1928	98·2	1951	329·0
1929	104·4	1952	347·0
1930	91·1	1953	365·4
1931	76·3	1954	363·1
1932	58·5	1955	397·5
1933	56·0	1956	419·2
1934	65·0	1957	442·8
1935	72·5	1958	444·5
1936	82·7	1959	482·7
1937	90·8	1960*	502·6
1938	85·2	1961	518·2
1939	91·1	1962	554·9
1940	100·6	1963	583·9
1941	125·8	1964 (prel.)	622·6

* Beginning 1960 includes Alaska and Hawaii.

TABLE 4. UNEMPLOYMENT IN THE UNITED STATES 1918–1964

(Sources: *Historical statistics of the United States; Statistical abstract of the United States, 1955–1965*)

	Total civilian unemployment	Percent-age		Total civilian unemployment	Percent-age
1918	560,000	1·4	1942	2,660,000	4·7
1919	950,000	2·3	1943	1,070,000	1·9
1920	1,670,000	4·0	1944	670,000	1·2
1921	5,010,000	11·9	1945	1,040,000	1·9
1922	3,220,000	7·6	1946	2,270,000	3·9
1923	1,380,000	3·2	1947	2,142,000	3·6
1924	2,440,000	5·5	1948	2,064,000	3·4
1925	1,800,000	4·0	1949	3,395,000	5·5
1926	880,000	1·9	1950	3,142,000	5·0
1927	1,890,000	4·1	1951	1,879,000	3·0
1928	2,080,000	4·4	1952	1,673,000	2·7
1929	1,550,000	3·2	1953	1,602,000	2·5
1930	4,340,000	8·7	1954	3,230,000	5·0
1931	8,020,000	15·9	1955	2,654,000	4·0
1932	12,060,000	23·6	1956	2,551,000	3·8
1933	12,830,000	24·9	1957*	2,936,000	4·3
1934	11,340,000	21·7	1958	4,681,000	6·8
1935	10,610,000	20·1	1959	3,813,000	5·5
1936	9,030,000	16·9	1960†	3,931,000	5·6
1937	7,700,000	14·3	1961	4,806,000	6·7
1938	10,390,000	19·0	1962	4,007,000	5·6
1939	9,480,000	17·2	1963	4,166,000	5·7
1940	8,120,000	14·6	1964	3,876,000	5·2
1941	5,560,000	9·9			

* Modified definitions of unemployment adopted in January 1957.
† Beginning 1960 includes Alaska and Hawaii.

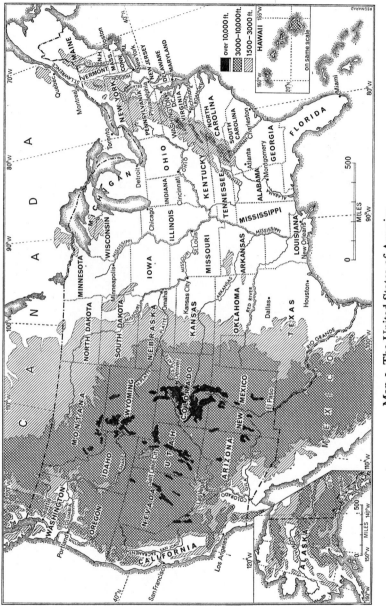

Map 1. The United States of America.

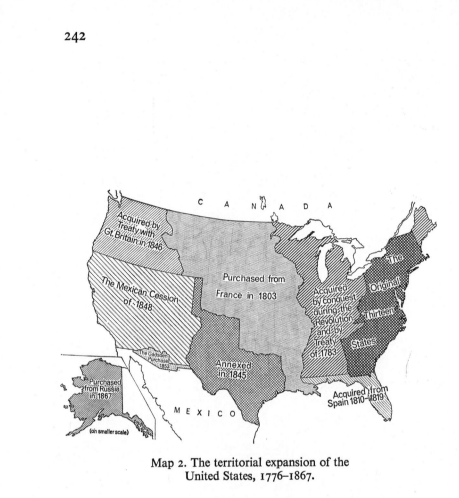

Map 2. The territorial expansion of the
United States, 1776–1867.

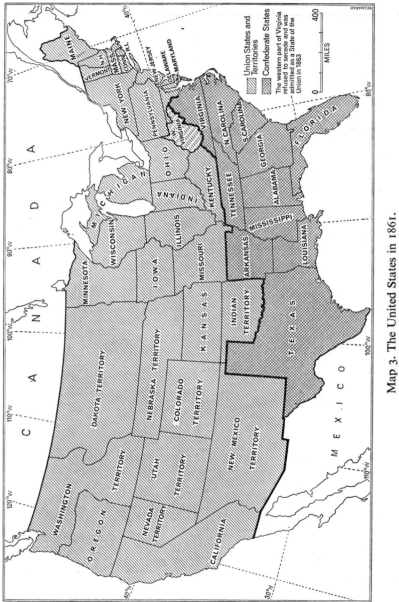

Map 3. The United States in 1861.

Union States and Territories

Confederate States

The western part of Virginia refused to secede and was admitted as a State of the Union in 1863

MILES

0   400

REGMARAD

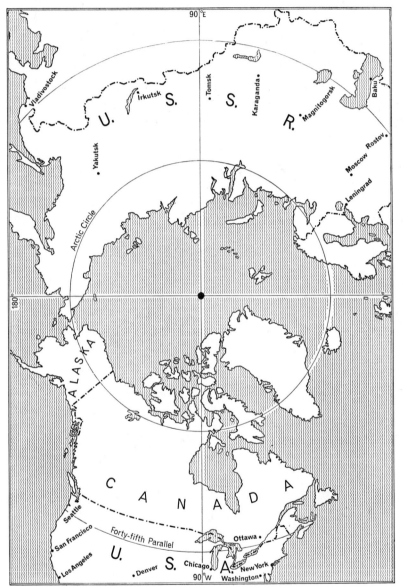

Map 4. The confrontation of the North American continent and the U.S.S.R.

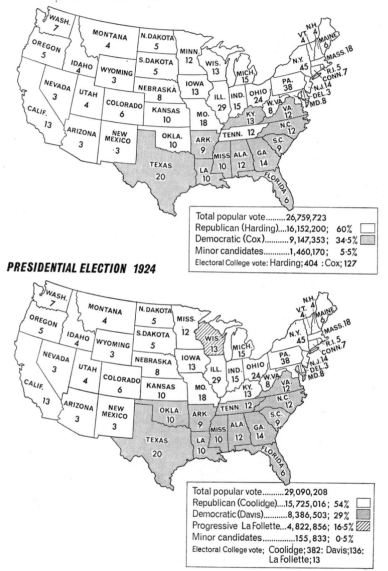

PRESIDENTIAL ELECTION 1920

Total popular vote.........26,759,723	
Republican (Harding)....16,152,200; 60%	□
Democratic (Cox)...........9,147,353; 34·5%	▨
Minor candidates............1,460,170; 5·5%	
Electoral College vote: Harding; 404 : Cox; 127	

PRESIDENTIAL ELECTION 1924

Total popular vote..........29,090,208	
Republican (Coolidge)....15,725,016; 54%	□
Democratic (Davis)...........8,386,503; 29%	▨
Progressive La Follette...4,822,856; 16·5%	▨
Minor candidates...............155,833; 0·5%	
Electoral College vote; Coolidge; 382: Davis;136: La Follette;13	

Map. 5. State voting patterns in presidential elections, 1920, 1924.

PRESIDENTIAL ELECTION 1928

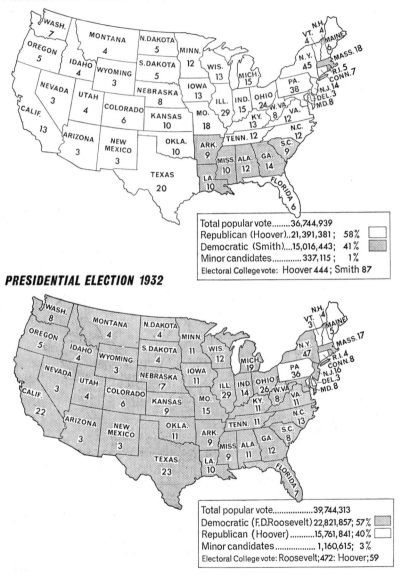

Total popular vote........36,744,939	
Republican (Hoover)..21,391,381 ;	58%
Democratic (Smith)....15,016,443 ;	41%
Minor candidates............337,115 ;	1%

Electoral College vote: Hoover 444; Smith 87

PRESIDENTIAL ELECTION 1932

Total popular vote.................39,744,313	
Democratic (F.D.Roosevelt) 22,821,857;	57%
Republican (Hoover)...........15,761,841;	40%
Minor candidates.................1,160,615;	3%

Electoral College vote: Roosevelt;472: Hoover;59

Map 6. State voting patterns in presidential elections, 1928, 1932.

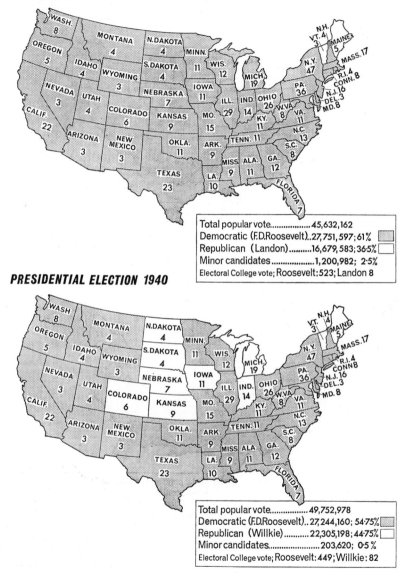

PRESIDENTIAL ELECTION 1936

Total popular vote	45,632,162	
Democratic (F.D.Roosevelt)	27,751,597; 61%	
Republican (Landon)	16,679,583; 36·5%	
Minor candidates	1,200,982; 2·5%	
Electoral College vote; Roosevelt: 523; Landon 8		

PRESIDENTIAL ELECTION 1940

Total popular vote	49,752,978	
Democratic (F.D.Roosevelt)	27,244,160; 54·75%	
Republican (Willkie)	22,305,198; 44·75%	
Minor candidates	203,620; 0·5%	
Electoral College vote; Roosevelt: 449; Willkie: 82		

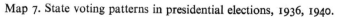

Map 7. State voting patterns in presidential elections, 1936, 1940.

248

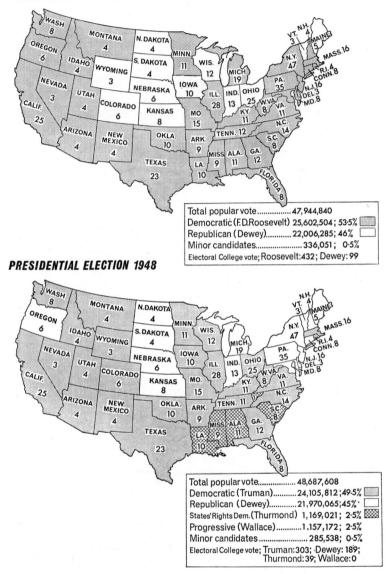

Map 8. State voting patterns in presidential elections, 1944, 1948.

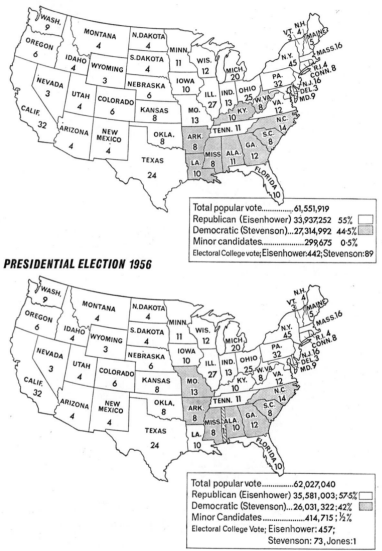

Map 9. State voting patterns in presidential elections, 1952, 1956.

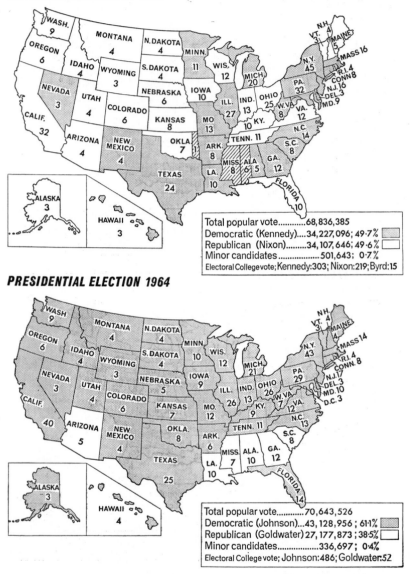

PRESIDENTIAL ELECTION 1960

Total popular vote............68,836,385	
Democratic (Kennedy)....34,227,096; 49·7%	
Republican (Nixon)..........34,107,646; 49·6%	
Minor candidates..................501,643; 0·7%	
Electoral College vote; Kennedy:303; Nixon:219; Byrd:15	

PRESIDENTIAL ELECTION 1964

Total popular vote............70,643,526	
Democratic (Johnson)...43,128,956 ; 61·1%	
Republican (Goldwater) 27,177,873 ; 38·5%	
Minor candidates..................336,697 ; 0·4%	
Electoral College vote; Johnson:486; Goldwater:52	

Map 10. State voting patterns in presidential elections, 1960, 1964.

GUIDE TO FURTHER READING

The literature dealing with American studies is so vast that only a short selection of books can be given here. Choice has been restricted to works which offer perceptive insight into the themes of twentieth century America. Except where later editions are specified the date of the first edition is given in each case, but many of the books are now available in paper-back. Each book is listed once only, although its contents may relate to the scope of several chapters.

The most elegantly written textbook, suitable both for the beginner and the advanced student, is Samuel E. Morison and Henry S. Commager, *The Growth of the American Republic* (5th edn, rev. and enl., 2 vols. 1962). A lively one-volume text is Morison's *Oxford History of the American People* (1965). Indispensable works of reference from which studies in depth should be pursued are: *Guide to the Study of the United States of America* (Library of Congress, 1960); Oscar Handlin and others, *Harvard Guide to American History* (1954); Henry S. Commager, *Documents of American History* (7th edn 1963); Robert E. Spiller and others, *Literary History of the United States* (3rd edn, rev. 1963). School readers in particular will find helpful the bibliographical pamphlets, *Books on America*, edited by Howard Temperley for the British Association for American Studies.

CHAPTER 1

Charles A. and Mary R. Beard, *The Rise of American Civilization* (2 vols. 1927–31); Ray A. Billington, *Westward Expansion* (2nd edn 1960); Nelson M. Blake, *A History of American Life and Thought* (1963); James Bryce, *The American Commonwealth* (rev. edn, 2 vols. 1914–15), Henry S. Commager, *The American Mind* (1950); Hector St John de Crèvecœur, *Letters from an American Farmer* (London edn 1912); Ralph H. Gabriel, *The Course of American Democratic Thought* (2nd edn 1956); Richard Hofstadter, *Anti-Intellectualism in American Life* (1963); Richard Hofstadter, *The Age of Reform* (1955); Richard Hofstadter, *The American Political Tradition* (1948); Max Lerner, *America as a Civilization* (1957); Robert E. Osgood, *Ideals and Self-Interest* (1953); Henry N. Smith, *Virgin Land* (1950); Alexis de Tocqueville, *Democracy in America* (1964 edn); Frederick J. Turner, *Frontier and Section* (R. A. Billington (ed.), 1961); Albert K. Weinberg, *Manifest Destiny* (1935).

CHAPTER 2

Frederick L. Allen, *Only Yesterday* (1931); Charles A. and Mary R. Beard, *America in Midpassage* (1939); Malcolm Cowley, *Exile's Return* (1951); Frederick J. Hoffman, *The Twenties* (1955); Herbert C. Hoover, *The Ordeal of Woodrow Wilson* (1958); Alfred Kazin, *On Native Grounds* (1942);

William E. Leuchtenburg, *The Perils of Prosperity 1914–1932* (1958); Robert S. Lynd, *Middletown* (1929); Arthur Mann, *La Guardia, a Fighter Against his Times* (1959); Henry L. Mencken, *A Carnival of Buncombe* (Malcolm Moos (sel. and ed.), 1956); Arthur M. Schlesinger, Jr., *The Crisis of the Old Order* (1957); Karl Schriftgiesser, *This Was Normalcy* (1948); Andrew Sinclair, *Prohibition, the Era of Excess* (1962); George H. Soule, *Prosperity Decade* (1947); William A. White, *A Puritan in Babylon* (1938).

CHAPTER 3

Selig Adler, *The Isolationist Impulse* (1957); Harry E. Barnes (ed.), *Perpetual War for Perpetual Peace* (1953); Charles A. Beard, *The Idea of National Interest* (1934); Alexander De Conde (ed.), *Isolation and Security* (1957); Robert H. Ferrell, *Peace in their Time* (1952); Robert H. Ferrell, *American Diplomacy in the Great Depression* (1957); A. Whitney Griswold, *The Far Eastern Policy of the United States* (1938); Cordell Hull, *Memoirs* (2 vols. 1948); William L. Langer and S. Everett Gleason, *The Challenge to Isolation, 1937–1940* (1952); William A. Williams, *The Tragedy of American Diplomacy* (rev. edn 1962); Bryce Wood, *The Making of the Good Neighbor Policy* (1961).

CHAPTER 4

Bureau of the Budget, *The United States at War* (1946); E. S. Corwin, *Total War and the Constitution* (1947); Frank B. Freidel (ed.), *The New Deal and the American People* (1964); John K. Galbraith, *The Great Crash* (1955); Eric F. Goldman, *Rendezvous with Destiny* (1952); Leslie R. Groves, *Now It Can Be Told* (1962); Herbert C. Hoover, *Memoirs* (3 vols. 1951–2); Walter Johnson, *1600 Pennsylvania Avenue* (1960); Alfred Kazin, *Starting Out in the Thirties* (1965); William E. Leuchtenburg, *Franklin D. Roosevelt and the New Deal 1932–1940* (1963); Broadus Mitchell, *Depression Decade* (1947); Frances Perkins, *The Roosevelt I Knew* (1946); Arthur M. Schlesinger, Jr., *The Coming of the New Deal* (1958); Arthur M. Schlesinger, Jr., *The Politics of Upheaval* (1960); David A. Shannon (ed.), *The Great Depression* (1960); Philip Taft, *Organized Labor in American History* (1964); Rexford G. Tugwell, *The Democratic Roosevelt* (1957); Edmund Wilson, *The Shores of Light* (1952); Edmund Wilson, *The American Earthquake* (1958).

CHAPTER 5

P. M. S. Blackett, *Military and Political Consequences of Atomic Weapons* (1948); Winston S. Churchill, *The Second World War* (6 vols. 1948–53); Wayne S. Cole, *America First* (1953); Walter P. Davison, *The Berlin Blockade* (1958); Herbert Feis, *The Road to Pearl Harbor* (1950); Herbert Feis, *The China Tangle* (1953); Herbert Feis, *Churchill, Roosevelt, Stalin* (1957); Herbert Feis, *Between War and Peace* (1960); Herbert Feis, *Japan Subdued* (1961); Denna F. Fleming, *The Cold War and Its Origins 1917–1960* (2 vols. 1961); Walter Johnson, *The Battle Against Isolation* (1944); Joseph M. Jones,

The Fifteen Weeks (1955); George F. Kennan, *American Diplomacy 1900–1950* (1951); William L. Langer and S. Everett Gleason, *The Undeclared War 1940–1941* (1953); Douglas MacArthur, *Reminiscences* (1964); Edwin O. Reischauer, *The United States and Japan* (rev. edn 1957); Paul W. Schroeder, *The Axis Alliance and Japanese–American Relations 1941* (1958); John L. Snell (ed.), *The Meaning of Yalta* (1956); John W. Spanier, *American Foreign Policy Since World War II* (rev. edn 1962); Harry S. Truman, *Memoirs* (2 vols. 1955); H. Bradford Westerfield, *Foreign Policy and Party Politics* (1955).

CHAPTER 6

Sherman Adams, *Firsthand Report* (1961); John R. Beal, *John Foster Dulles* (1959); Max Beloff, *The United States and the Unity of Europe* (1963); Theodore Draper, *Castro's Revolution, Myths and Realities* (1962); Dwight D. Eisenhower, *The White House Years* (2 vols. 1963–5); Russell H. Fifield, *The Diplomacy of Southeast Asia 1945–1958* (1958); Herman Finer, *Dulles Over Suez* (1964); Norman A. Graebner, *The New Isolationism* (1956); Emmet J. Hughes, *The Ordeal of Power* (1963); Henry A. Kissinger, *Nuclear Weapons and Foreign Policy* (1957); Robert D. Murphy, *Diplomat among Warriors* (1964); Robert E. Osgood, *NATO, The Entangling Alliance* (1962); Walt W. Rostow, *The United States in the World Arena* (1960); John W. Spanier, *The Truman–MacArthur Controversy and the Korean War* (1959); Maxwell D. Taylor, *The Uncertain Trumpet* (1960); William A. Williams, *The U.S., Cuba and Castro* (1962); David Wise and Thomas Ross, *The Invisible Government* (1964).

CHAPTER 7

James B. Conant, *The American High School Today* (1959); Whittaker Chambers, *Witness* (1952); Alistair Cooke, *A Generation on Trial* (1950); John K. Galbraith, *American Capitalism* (1952); John K. Galbraith, *The Affluent Society* (1958); Eric F. Goldman, *The Crucial Decade—and After* (1961); Harold M. Hyman, *To Try Men's Souls: Loyalty Tests in American History* (1959); Samuel Lubell, *The Future of American Politics* (rev. edn 1956); Samuel Lubell, *The Revolt of the Moderates* (1956); Thomas F. Parkinson (ed.), *A Casebook on the Beat* (1961); The President's Committee on Civil Rights, *To Secure These Rights* (1947); Charles H. Pritchett, *Civil Liberties and the Vinson Court* (1954); Richard H. Rovere, *Senator Joe McCarthy* (1959); Karl M. Schmidt, *Henry A. Wallace, Quixotic Crusader, 1948* (1960); David A. Shannon, *The Decline of American Communism* (1959); George A. Steiner, *Government's Role in Economic Life* (1953); Lewis L. Strauss, *Men and Decisions* (1962); W. Lloyd Warner, *American Life: Dream and Reality* (rev. edn 1962); Theodore H. White, *The Making of the President 1960* (1961); Robert C. Wood, *Suburbia, Its People and their Politics* (1959).

CHAPTER 8 AND EPILOGUE

Wayne Andrews, *Architecture, Ambition and Americans* (1964 edn); Ralph Ellison, *Invisible Man* (1952); John H. Franklin, *From Slavery to Freedom*, (rev. edn 1956); J. William Fulbright, *Old Myths and New Realities* (1964); Barry M. Goldwater, *The Conscience of a Conservative* (1960); Jean Gottmann, *Megalopolis* (1961); Michael Harrington, *The Other America* (1962); Jane Jacobs, *The Death and Life of Great American Cities* (1961); C. Eric Lincoln, *The Black Muslims in America* (1961); Seymour M. Lipset and Sheldon W. Walin, *The Berkeley Student Revolt* (1965); Alpheus T. Mason, *The Supreme Court* (1962); Robert G. McCloskey, *The American Supreme Court* (1960); John M. McCoubrey, *The American Tradition in Painting* (1963); Gunnar Myrdal, *An American Dilemma* (2 vols. 1944); Bernard Schwartz, *The Supreme Court* (1957); Arthur M. Schlesinger, Jr., *A Thousand Days* (1965); Theodore C. Sorensen, *Kennedy* (1965); Robert E. Spiller and Eric Larrabee (eds.), *American Perspectives* (1961); Alan F. Westin (ed.), *Freedom Now* (1964); Theodore H. White, *The Making of the President 1964* (1965); William S. White, *The Professional: Lyndon B. Johnson* (1964).

INDEX

Acheson, Dean, 133–4
Adams, Henry, 33–4, 183
Adams, John, 12
Adams, Sherman, 175, 179
Adenauer, Konrad, 148, 154
Admiralty courts, 10–11
Agricultural Act (1948), 168
Agricultural Act (1949), 169
Agricultural Adjustment Act (1933), 96–7
Agricultural Adjustment Act (1938), 97
Agricultural Marketing Act (1929), 88
agriculture, in colonies, 2, 4, 5–6; factor in westward movement, 16–17; influence on sectionalism, 18–19; mechanization of, 21–2, 24; base for political protest, 25; in First World War, 35–6; in 1920s, 51; and the depression, 83, 86, 88; in New Deal, 96 ff.; in Second World War, 107–8; in Fair Deal, 169; in 1950s, 175–6, 180, 192
Alliance for Progress, 198, 204, 213
America First Committee, 117
American Federation of Labor, 26, 49, 95–6, 194, 197
American Medical Association, 169, 199
American Mercury, 57
American Socialist party, 43
Americans for Democratic Action, 166, 185
Anacostia Flats, 89
Anderson, Sherwood, 57
Anglo-Japanese alliance (1902), 65–6
Anti-Saloon League, 42
Appomattox, 19
Arbenz, Guzmán, President, 156
Argentia, Newfoundland, 116
Argentina, 156
Articles of Confederation, 13–14
Ashwander v. T.V.A. (1936), 99
Atlantic Charter, 116, 124, 126
atomic bomb, 111, 123, 127, 130, 131, 142
Atomic Energy Act (1946), 163
Atoms for Peace, 149
Australia, 122, 139, 146
Austria, 61, 75, 81, 128, 149, 204

Badoglio, Pietro, 123
Baghdad Pact (1955), 150–1, 153
Baldwin, James, *The Fire Next Time*, 193
Barkley, Alben, 173
Barnett, Ross, 205
Baruch, Bernard, 35
Batista, Fulgencio, 156
Bay of Pigs, 203
Beach, Sylvia, '*Shakespeare and Company*', 57
beat generation, 182–4
Belgium, 61, 66–8
Benson, Ezra Taft, 176
Berle, Adolf A., Jr., 91
Berlin airlift, 130–1
Berlin Wall, 204
Black Muslims, 205
Blough, Roger, 201–2
Blue Eagle, 94
Bonus Expeditionary Force, 89
bootleggers, 53
Borah, William, A., 65, 113
Boston Massacre, 11
Boston Police Strike, 42, 45
Boston Tea Party, 11
Boulder Dam, 87
Bow, Clara, 54
Bradford, William, 3
Bradley, Omar, 138
Braintrust, 91–2
Brandeis, Louis, D., 92
Brando, Marlon, 184
Brannan, Charles, 169
Brazil, 156
Bretton Woods, 127
Briand, Aristide, 62–3
brinkmanship, 142
Brown v. the Board of Education of Topeka (1954), 178, 194, 205
Brussels conference (1937), 80
Brussels conference (1954), 148–9
Brussels Pact (1948), 149
Bryan, William Jennings, 25, 54–5, 66
Buenos Aires conference (1936), 70
Bulganin, Nicolai A., 149
Bulgaria, 128
Bunker's Hill, 12
Burma, 145
Byrnes, James, M., 107

Cairo conference (1943), 124
Calhoun, John C., 18
Cambodia, 144–5, 147
Canada, 6, 7, 8, 66
Capital Loans Committee, 35
Capone, Al, 53
Carnegie, Andrew, 24
Casablanca conference (1943), 124
cash and carry, 79, 113–14
Castro, Fidel, 156–7, 203–4, 213
Cather, Willa, *My Antonia*, 20; *O Pioneers*, 20
Central Intelligence Agency, 156, 203
Central Treaty Organisation, 153
Chamoun, Camille, 153
Chiang Kai-Shek, 120, 126, 132–3, 146–7, 158, 203
Chicago Symphony Orchestra, 37
Chicago *Tribune*, 167
Chile, 156
China, 39; and Washington conference, 65–8; and Manchurian crisis, 70–2; and Marco Polo Bridge incident, 80; *Panay* incident, 119; Open Door policy in, 119; Sino-Japanese War, 119–21; and Yalta, 126; collapse of Kuomintang, 132–3; creation of Chinese People's Republic, 133; Communist China and the Korean War, 136–40; 143, 144, 146–7, 154, 158, 203, 213–14
China lobby, 133
Church of Christ of the Latter Day Saints, 17
Churchill, Winston S., 124, 125, 128, 144
city machines, 20
Civil Rights Act (1957), 178
Civil Rights Act (1960), 179–80
Civil Rights Act (1964), 208–9
Civil War, 19, 20, 21, 22, 23–4, 37, 193
Civil Works Administration, 97
Civilian Conservation Corps, 97
Clark, J. Reuben, 69
Clayton Anti-Trust Act (1914), 28
Clemenceau, Georges, 39
Coercive Acts (1774), 11
Colombia, 30
Columbus, Christopher, 1–2, 6, 7
Committee for Industrial Organisation, 95
Committee of European Economic Co-operation, 129
Committee on Civil Rights, 169
Committee on Public Information, 110

Committee to Defend America by Aiding the Allies, 117–18
Commonwealth Club of San Fransicso, 91
Communist Labor party, 43
Communist party of America, 44
Compact of Fifth Avenue, 188
Concord, Massachusetts, 12
Conestoga wagon, 16
Conference for Progressive Political Action, 49
conformity, in First World War, 36–7; post-war, 42; in 1920s, 54–8; 159; McCarthy and, 170–2; in Eisenhower period, 173, 174; and reaction of beats, 180–5; 219
Congo, 198, 203
Congress of Industrial Organisations, 96, 194, 197
Congress on Racial Equality, 195, 206
Connally Act (1935), 95
conservation, 27, 87, 98–9, 162, 169, 211
Constitution of 1789, 14–15
containment, 129 ff., 141
Continental Congress, First, 11–12; Second, 12–13
Coolidge, Calvin, vice-presidential candidate, 45–6; as president, 48, 50; domestic policies, 50–2, and World Court, 64
Cooper, John Sherman, 179
Coral Sea, 122
Cornwallis, Lord, 13
Corso, Gregory, 182
Costello, Frank, 53
Coughlin, Father Charles, 78, 100–1
Council of Economic Advisers, 163
Council of National Defence, 34
Cox, James M., 44, 45, 60
Cozzens, James Gould, *By Love Possessed*, 182
Crane, Stephen, *Maggie, a Girl of the Streets*, 26
Credit Anstalt, 75
Creel, George, 110
Crèvecœur, Hector St John de, 1, 13
Crissinger, Daniel R., 47
Croly, Herbert, 168
Cuba, 29, 157–8, 198, 200; and 1962 missile crisis, 203–4; 207, 213
Czechoslovakia, 81, 129–30, 151

Darrow, Clarence, 54–5
Darwin, Charles, 24

Daugherty, Harry, 46–7
Davis, John, W., 49
Davis, Norman H., 72–3
Dawes Plan (1924), 75
Dean, James, 184
Debs, Eugene, 49
Declaration of Independence (1776), 12, 196
Defence Plant and Defence Supplies Corporation, 106
De Gaulle, Charles, 154, 157
Denmark 118
destroyer deal, 115
De Tocqueville, Alexis, 23, 159, 181, 191
Dewey, Thomas, 104, 163, 165–8, 173
Diem, Ngo Dinh, 213–14
Dienbienphu, 144–5
Dillon, Douglas, 197
Dirksen, Everett, 179
Dixiecrat party, 167–8
Dixon–Yates contract, 176
Doheney, Henry L., 47
Dos Passos, John, 33; *U.S.A.*, 56
Douglas, Stephen, A., 189
Douglas, William O., 105, 166
Drayton, Michael, *Ode to the Virginia Voyage*, 2
Dubois, W. E. B., 194
Dulles, John Foster, background of, 141; as secretary of State, 141 ff.; and Suez crisis, 151 ff., 175, 204
Dumbarton Oaks, 127

East German revolt, 148
Economic Co-operation Administration, 130
Eden, Anthony, 144, 149, 154
Egypt, 151–2, 153
Eisenhower, Dwight D., 123; and NATO, 131, 141; and Korea, 139; foreign policy of, 141 ff.; atoms for peace, 149; open skies proposal, 150; Eisenhower Doctrine, 152–3; world tour, 155–6; and Summit conference, 156–7; and Far East, 158; 165–6; 172; election of 1952, 173–4; domestic policies, 174 ff.; heart attack, 177; ileitis, 177; and civil rights, 178–9; 187, 192, 205, 218
Elk Hills, 47
Elkins Act (1903), 26
Elizabeth II, Queen, 154
Emergency Farm Mortgage Act (1933), 96
Emergency Fleet Corporation, 35

Espionage Act (1917), 36
Ethiopia crisis, 79–80
European Defence Community, 144, 148–9
European Economic Community, 153–4
European Economic Co-operation, 129
'ever normal granary', 97, 107
Evers, Medgar, 206

Fair Deal, 162–3, 168–70, 173, 174, 199, 213
Fair Employment Practices Bill, 162
Fair Employment Practices Commission, 169
Fair Employment Practices Committee, 109
Fair Labour Standards Act (1938), 95, 169
Fall, Albert B., 47–8
Far Eastern Commission, 132
Farley, James A., 90
Farm Board, 88
Farm Bureau, 107–8
Farm Credit Act, 96
Farm Security Administration, 169
Farmer-Labor party, 49
Farmers' Alliance, 25
Farmers' Home Administration, 169
Faubus, Orval, 178
Federal Bureau of Investigation, 44
Federal Reserve System, 27, 84, 93, 202
Federal Trade Commission, 28, 50
Federalists, 17–18
Ferlinghetti, Lawrence, 183
film industry, 50; *Married Flirts*, 54; *Women Who Give*, 54; *The Queen of Sin*, 54; *High Noon*, 182; *Shane*, 182; *The Wild One*, 184
Finland 128
Fitzgerald, F. Scott, 33; *This Side of Paradise*, 54; *The Beautiful and the Damned*, 54; *The Great Gatsby*, 54
Five-Power Treaty (1922), 66–7
flappers, 53
Florida land boom, 84
Food Administration, 35, 37, 107–8
Forbes, Charles B., 47
Fordney–McCumber tariff (1922), 51, 74
Foreign Affairs, 129
Formosa, 133–4, 136, 143, 146–7, 158
Forrestal, James V., 108
Fort Sumter, 19
Founding Fathers, the, 14–15, 17

Four Power Treaty (1922), 66–7
Fourteen Points, 38–40
France, Empire in North America, 6–8, 9; and First World War, 36; and the Peace conference, 39–40; search for security, 61 ff.; and Washington conference, 66–8; and Manchurian crisis, 70–2; and disarmament, 72–3; and gold standard, 76; and Second World War, 113–14, 119, 123, 127; post-war relations with, 128, 130; and Indo-China, 144–5; and E.D.C., 148–9; and Suez, 151; 154, 157
franchise, in colonies, 5; pre-Civil War, 23–4; extension to women, 53
Frankfurter, Felix, 91
Freedom Riders, 195
Freeman, Orville, 197
French Alliance (1778), 13
frontier, the, in colonial period, 3–6; in nineteenth century, 16–19; closing of, 28; 159
Frost, Robert, 196
Fuchs, Klaus, 171
Fuel Administration, 35
Fulbright–Connally Resolution (1947), 126–7
Full Employment Bill, 162–3

Gagarin, Yuri, 184
Galbraith, John Kenneth, *The Affluent Society*, 210
Garland, Hamlin, 57
Garner, John Nance, 90
Garvey, Marcus, 193
Gaspee, 11
General Motors, 175
Geneva conference (1954), 144–5, 213
Geneva conference (1955), 150
Geneva Disarmament conference (1933–4), 72–3, 77
Geneva Protocol, 61
Germany, emigration from, 20; and First World War, 30–2, 36–7; and the Treaty of Versailles, 38–40; relations with in the 1920s, 61–2, 64; and disarmament, 72–3; Anchluss, 81; Munich agreements, 81; and Second World War, 113–16, 118; and Tripartite Pact, 119; Nazi–Soviet Pact, 120, 121, 122–3, 128; West German Federal Republic, 130; Dulles and, 148–9, 154, 155; Kennedy and, 204

G.I. Bill of Rights, *see* Servicemen's Readjustment Act
Gilded Age, the, 24, 33
Ginsberg, Allen, *Howl*, 183
Glass-Steagall Act (1933), 93
Glenn, John, 184
Gold Reserve Act (1934), 93–4
Gold Rush (1849), 17
Goldberg, Arthur, 197
Goldfine, Bernard, 179
Goldwater, Barry, 211–12
'good neighbor' policy, 69–70, 156
Grange, the, 24–5
Grant, Madison, 55
Grant, Ulysses S., 19
Great Britain, and the North American colonies, 2–15, 16; nineteenth-century emigration from, 20; and First World War, 31, 35; and the Treaty of Versailles, 39–40; relations with between the wars, 61 ff.; relations with in Second World War, 113–18, 122–3, 124–5; Truman's policies towards, 127–31; and Korean War, 136; and Indo China, 144–5; and SEATO 145–6; Eisenhower's policies toward, 148 ff.; Kennedy and, 204
Great Society, 197, 209 ff., 218
Greater East Asia Co-Prosperity Sphere, 119, 121
Greater Houston Ministerial conference, 189
Greece, 128
Greenland, 116
Guadalcanal, 122
Guantanamo Bay, 203
Guatemala, 156, 213
Guffey–Snyder Act (1935), 95
Guffey–Vinson Act (1937), 95

Haiti, 69
Hamaguchi, Yuko, 70
Harding, Warren G., presidential candidate, 45–6; domestic policies, 46–8, 50–2; foreign policies, 60 ff.
Harrington, Michael, *The Other America*, 210
Harris, Louis, 189
Havana, 29
Hawaii, 28, 29
Hawley–Smoot tariff (1930), 75, 88
Hearst, William Randolph, 78, 90
Hemingway, Ernest, *The Sun Also Rises*, 57

Hepburn Act (1906), 26
Herter, Christian, 157
Hiroshima, 111
Hiss, Alger, 171
Hitler, Adolf, 73, 123
Ho Chi Minh, 213
Holmes, John Clellon, 182
Homestead Strike (1892), 26
Hoover, Herbert 35; as secretary of Commerce, 47, 50; and World Court, 64; and Latin America, 69, 72; as president, 85-9, 90
Hoovervilles, 86, 89
Hopkins, Harry, 97-8
House, Edward M., 38-9
Housing Act (1949), 169
Howells, William Dean, 33
Hudson, Henry, 6
Hughes, Charles Evans, 47, 66, 68-9
Hull, Cordell, policies as secretary of State, 75 ff.; 92, 121
Humphrey, George, 175
Humphrey, Hubert, 166, 185-90, 208
Hungary, 61, 128
Hussein, King ibn Talal, 153
hydrogen bomb, 142, 149

Iceland, 116
Ickes, Harold, 92, 97, 163
immigration, in colonial period, 2-5, 8; in nineteenth century, 15, 19-21; restriction of, 55-6, 65, 110, 159
Inchon, 137
India, 145
Indians, 2, 6, 7, 9, 10, 16
Indo-China, 119-20, 144-5
Indonesia, 145
Industrial Workers of the World, 43
industry, 15, 21-2, 23; corporation and trust, 26-8; extent of in 1890s, 28; in First World War, 34-6, 37; in 1920s, 50-2; and the depression, 83-5, 86, 88; in the New Deal, 94-6, 98, 103; in Second World War, 105, 111; in post-war period, 162-3; in 1950s, 175-7, 180-1, 192; in 1960s, 201-2, 213
International Atomic Energy Commission, 149
International Bank for Reconstruction and Development, 127
International Monetary Fund, 127
internationalism, 59 ff.
Inter-State Commerce Commission, 26, 194

Iraq, 150, 153
Iran, 128, 150, 153
Ireland, emigration from, 19-20
Iron Curtain, 112, 128
isolationism, 59 ff.
Israel, 150-1
Italy, 20, 39, 66-8, 79-80, 81, 122-3
Iwo Jima, 122

Jackson, Andrew, 18, 192
James, Henry, 33, 58
Jamestown, 2
Japan, 30, 39, 56; and Washington conference, 65-8; and Manchurian crisis, 70-2; and Sino-Japanese War, 80, 119; relations with 1940-1, 119-21; and Second World War, 111, 121-4; post-war reconstruction, 132, 158
Japanese-American Treaty of Commerce and Navigation (1911), 119
Jefferson, Thomas, 16, 18, 30, 192
Jeffersonian Republicans, 17-18
Jewett, Sarah Orne, *The Country of the Pointed Firs*, 4
Job Corps, 211
Johnson, Hiram, 113
Johnson, Hugh, 94, 117
Johnson, Lyndon B., Senate majority leader, 177-8, 186-7, 197, 207; presidency, 208 ff.
Jordan, 153

Kaiser, Henry, 106
Kassim, Abdel Karim, 153
Kefauver, Estes, 173
Kellogg, Frank B., 62-3, 69
Kellogg-Briand Pact (1928), 62-3
Kennan, George, 129
Kennedy, Jacqueline, 206-7
Kennedy, John F., 85, 91; political background, 185; election of 1960, 185-90; and the New Frontier, 196 ff.; assassination, 206-7, 209-10, 213
Kennedy, Joseph P., 185
Kennedy, Robert F., 188, 197, 205
Kerouac, Jack, *On the Road*, 182, 184, 216-17; *The Dharma Bhums*, 184
Keynes, John Maynard, 39
Khrushchev, Nikita, S. 149, 154; and Nixon, 155; visits U.S., 155; 157-8, 185, 204
King, Martin Luther, 190, 194-5, 206
Knowland, William, 144, 177

Knox, Frank, 104
Korea, 112, 134–40, 161
Kouwenhoven, John, *The Beer Can by the Highway*, 216
Kozlov, Frol, 155
Ku Klux Klan, 42, 43, 55

Labor, Bureau of, 26
labour, in colonial period, 4; role of immigrants, 20–2; and Square Deal, 26; and New Freedom, 28; in First World War, 35; after First World War, 42–3; and the 'red scare', 43–4; in New Deal, 95–6, 103; in Second World War, 105–6, 108, 109; in post-war period, 162, 164, 168
La Follette, Robert M., 49, 166
La Mare, Chester, 53
Landon, Alfred, 100
Laos, 144–5, 147, 203
Lattimore, Owen, 172
League of Nations, 39–41, 45, 59 ff.; and Manchuria, 71–2, 77, 79
Lebanon, 153
Lee, Robert E., 19
Lend Lease, 107, 115–16
Leopold and Loeb Case, 54–5
Lever Act (1917), 43
Lewis, John L., 95, 162
Lewis, Sinclair, *Main Street*, 56–7
Lexington, Massachusetts, 12
Liberty League, 100
Liberty ship, 105–6
Lilienthal, David, 99
Lima conference (1938), 70
Lincoln, Abraham, 18–19, 23, 37, 189, 193
Lindbergh, Charles A., 117
Lippmann, Walter, 212
Little Rock, Arkansas, 178, 205
Lloyd George, David, 39
Lloyd, Henry Demarest, *Wealth against Commonwealth*, 26
Lloyd, Selwyn, 154
Locarno treaties (1925), 61, 63
Lodge, Henry Cabot II, 185, 188
London Economic conference, *see* World Economic conference
London, Jack, *The Valley of the Moon*, 34
London Naval conference (1930), 72–3
London Naval conference (1935), 73
Long, Huey, 100
lost generation, 57–8
Lowden, Frank O., 45

Lucy, Antherine, 195
Lytton, Victor A., 71

MacArthur, Douglas, 89, 122, 132, 136–9, 161
MacDonald, Dwight, 217
MacLeish, Archibald, *American Letter*, 1; *Voyage West*, 2
Macmillan, Harold, 154, 157, 204
Mahan, Alfred Thayer, 29
Maine, U.S.S., 29
Malcolm X, 205
Malenkov, Georgi, 149
Malik, Jacob, 139
Manchukuo, 71
Manchurian crisis, 68, 70–2
Manhattan Project, 111, 160
'manifest destiny', 16, 32
Marco Polo Bridge, 80
Marshall, George, 129, 133, 172
Marshall, John, 18
Marshall Plan, 129, 131, 161, 217
Martin, Joseph W., 138
Matsu, 146–7, 154
Maximilian of Austria, 68
Mayflower, 2, 5
Mayflower Compact, 5
McAdoo, William Gibbs, 35, 45, 48
McCarren Internal Security Act (1950), 171
McCarthy, Joseph, 171 ff., 181
McCarthyism, 159, 170–2
McClure's Magazine, 26
McCormack, John, 200
McKinley, William, 26, 29
McNamara, Robert, 197
medicare, 162, 199–200, 209
Mellon, Andrew, 47, 50, 88
Mencken, H. L., 57
Meredith, James, 205
Metals Reserve Corporation, 106
Metropolitan Museum, 217
Mexico, 6, 16, 31, 68–9
Midway, 122
Mikoyen, Anastas, 155
Miller–Tydings Act (1937), 95
Mills, C. Wright, *White Collar*, 181
Missouri, U.S.S., 132
Moley, Raymond, 91
Monroe Doctrine, 30, 68–9, 203
Montevideo conference (1933), 69
Montgomery Alabama bus boycott, 194–5
Montgomery, Bernard L., 123
More, Thomas, 2

Morgan, J. Pierrepont, 44
Mormons, *see* Church of Christ of the Latter Day Saints
Morocco, 30
Morrow, Dwight, 69
Moscow conference (1943), 124
muckrakers, 26
Mukden, 70
Munich, 81
Munitions Standards Board, 34
muscle shoals, 98
Mussolini, Benito, 123

Nagasaki, 111
Nasser, Gamel Abdel, 151–2
Nathan, George Jean, 57
Nation, the, 49
National Association for the Advancement of Colored People, 194–5, 206
National Defense Act (1940), 120
National Defense Education Act (1958), 219
National Defense Mediation Board, 109
National Industrial Recovery Act (1933), 94 ff.
National Recovery Administration, 100, 117
National Urban League, 195
National War Labor Board, 35, 109
Nazi–Soviet Pact, (1939), 120
Negro, introduction as slaves 4; pre-Civil War, 23; emancipation, 23–4; in First World War, 37; in New Deal, 96; in Second World War, 109; in 1948 election, 168; in 1950s, 178–9, 182; in 1960s, 191; discrimination against, 193; numbers lynched, 193; civil rights movement, 193–6, 201, 205–6; march on Washington, 206; and civil rights, 208–9; and poverty, 210–11
Nelson, Donald M., 106
Netherlands, 6–7, 66–8, 145
Neutrality Acts, 77 ff., 113–14
New Deal, origins of, 90–1; in operation, 92 ff., 161, 165, 168, 169, 172, 173, 178, 186, 194, 200
new economic era, 50–2
New Freedom, 27, 49
New Frontier programme, 189, 190, 196 ff., 208 ff., 213
New Republic, 49, 166
New York Stock Exchange, 75, 84–5
New Zealand, 139, 146
Nicaragua, 69

Nine Power Treaty (1922), 66–7, 70–1, 80
Nixon, Richard, 155, 173, 177, 179, 187–90, 200
Non-Partisan Committee for Peace through Revision of the Neutrality Laws, 118
Non-Partisan League, 49
normalcy, 33 ff., 160
Norris, George, 99
Norsemen, 1
North Atlantic Treaty Organisation, 131, 145, 153
Norway, 118
Nye committee, 78–9, 113

O'Brien, Lawrence, 188
O'Connor, 'Bull', 206
O'Donnell, Kenneth, 188
Office for Emergency Management, 106
Office of Censorship, 109
Office of Defense Transportation, 107
Office of Facts and Figures, 110
Office of Price Administration, 106
Office of Production Management, 106
Office of Strategic Services, 170
Office of War Mobilization, 107
Okinawa, 122
old colonial system, 9
Olive Branch Petition (1775), 12
open door policy, 66, 119
open skies proposal, 150
Operation Torch, 122–3
Oppenheimer J. Robert, 111, 172
Oregon Trail, 16
Organisation of American States, 156, 204
Orlando, Vittorio E., 39
Oswald, Lee Harvey, 207
Ottawa Agreements (1932), 75

Paine, Thomas, *Common Sense*, 12
Pakistan, 146, 150, 153
Palmer, A. Mitchell, 44
Panama Canal, 29–30
Panay incident, 119
Paris, Pact of, (1928), 62–3
Paris, Treaty of, (1763), 8–9
Paris, Treaty of, (1873), 13
Parker, Charlie, 182
Pathet, Lao, 147
Patrons of Husbandry, *see* Grange, the
Peace Corps, 198, 211
peaceful co-existence, 149
Pearl Harbor, 104, 110, 118, 121–2

Pendergast, Tom, 160
Perkins, Frances, 92, 98
Permanent Court of International Justice, 63–4, 81
Pershing, John J., 36
Philadelphia Convention (1787), 14–15
Philippines, 29, 65, 139, 146, 158
Pilgrim Fathers, the, 3
Plessy v. Ferguson (1896), 178
Plymouth colony, 2–3
Point Four programme, 130
Poland, 126
Pollock, Jackson, 215–16
Pontiac, 10
Populist party, 25
Portugal, 66–8
Potsdam conference (1945), 127, 161
Potter, David, *People of Plenty*, 217
poverty, war on, 191, 209–11
proclamation of 1763, 10
Progressive Citizens of America, 166
Progressive party, of 1912, 27; of 1924, 49
prohibition, 42–3, 52–4
Public Utility Holding Company Act (1935), 101
Public Works Administration, 97
Puerto Rico, 29
Pullman Strike (1894), 26
Pure Food and Drug Act (1906), 26
Puritans, 3–4, 57
Pusan, 137

quarantine speech, 81
Quebec Act (1774), 11
Quebec conference (1943), 124
Quemoy, 146–7, 154

Radford, Arthur W., 144
Railroad Administration, 35
Raleigh, Walter, 2
Raskob, John J., 90
Rayburn, Sam, 186, 199, 200
Reciprocal Trade Agreements Act (1934), 76
Reconstruction Finance Corporation, 87–8, 93, 176
red scare, 43
Resettlement Administration, 97
Revenue Act (1934), 101
Revenue Act (1935), 101
Revenue Act (1942), 108
Rhee, Syngman, 135–40
Ribicoff, Abraham, 197
Ridgway, Matthew B., 138–9

Riesman, David, *The Lonely Crowd*, 181
Riis, Jacob, *How the Other Half Lives*, 26
Rio de Janeiro Treaty (1947), 131
Roanoke, 2
Robinson–Patman Act (1936), 95
Rockefeller, John D., 24
Rockefeller, Nelson, 150, 188, 200, 212
Rogers, Will, 48
Rome, Treaty of (1957), 153
Rommel, Erwin, 123
Romney, George, 212
Roosevelt, Franklin D., vice-presidential candidate, 44–6, 49, 60; and Latin America, 69–70; and disarmament, 72–3, and World Economic conference, 73–6; and internationalism, 77; and neutrality, 77–80; and isolationism, 78–82; as governor of New York, 87–9; presidential campaign, 90–1; domestic policies of the New Deal, 92 ff.; and third term, 103–4; and fourth term, 104–5; foreign policies in 'preparedness' period, 112 ff.; war policies of, 121–3; wartime conferences, 124–6; and United Nations, 126–7; 186, 189, 192, 204
Roosevelt, Theodore, and muckrakers, 25–6; becomes president, 26; domestic policies, 26–7; forms Progressive party, 27; foreign policies of, 30; and immigration restriction, 55–6; Far Eastern policy of, 65; and Latin America, 68–9, 98, 101, 168, 192
Roosevelt Corollary, the, 68
Root, Elihu, 64, 68
Rubber Reserve Corporation, 106
Ruby, Jack, 207
Rumania, 128
Rural Electrification Administration, 99, 169
Rusk, Dean, 197, 203
Russo–Japanese War, 30

Sabotage Act (1918), 36
Sacco and Vanzetti Case, 44, 56
Salinger, J. D., *The Catcher in the Rye*, 184
Salinger, Pierre, 189
Santo Domingo, 213
St Valentine's Day Massacre, 53
Schechter case, 95

Schultz, Dutch, 53
Scopes Trial, 54–5
Scranton, William, 212
Second World War, 114 ff.
Securities and Exchange Act (1934), 94
Securities and Exchange Commission, 94
Sedition Act (1918), 36
Selective Service Act (1917), 36
Selective Service Act (1940), 106
Servicemen's Readjustment Act (1944), 161
Seven Arts, the, 57
Seven Years' War, 10
Shantung, 65
Sherman Anti-Trust Act (1890), 26–7, 28
Shipping Board, 35
Shouse, Jowett, 90, 100
Shrine of the Little Flower, 100
Sihanouk, Norodom, 147
Silver Purchase Act (1939), 94
Simmons, William J., 42
Simon, Sir John, 71
Sinclair, Harry, 47
Sinclair, Upton, *The Jungle*, 26, 100
slavery, introduced into colonies, 4, 14; and the Civil War, 18–19, 23–4
Smith Act (1940), 171
Smith, Alfred E., 49, 85–6, 90, 100, 186
Smith, Stephen, 189
Social Darwinism, 24, 27, 33
Social Security Act (1935), 98, 99, 169
Socialist party, 49
Soil Conservation and Domestic Allotment Act (1936), 97
Soil Erosion Act (1935), 97
Sorensen, Theodore, 188–9
South-east Asia Treaty Organisation, 145, 153, 203
Southern Christian Leadership conference, 195, 206
Souvanna, Phouma, 147
Spain, empire in North America, 6–8; war with (1898), 28–30; civil war in, 80
Sparkman, John, 174
speakeasy, 53, 57
Spencer, Herbert, 24
Sputnik, 184, 219
Square Deal, 26–7, 168
Stabilization Act (1942), 108
Stalin, Joseph, 124–5, 127, 130; death, 148
Stamp Act (1765), 10–11

Standard Oil, 26
Stassen, Harold E., 165, 173
Steffens, Lincoln, *The Shame of the Cities*, 26
Stein, Gertrude, 57, 215
Steinbeck, John, *The Grapes of Wrath*, 96
Stevenson, Adlai, 173–4, 177, 186, 197, 207
Stimson, Henry L., 71, 104
Stock Exchange crash, 84–5
Stoddard, Lothrop, 55
Strategic Air Force, 142
Stuart, Douglas, 117
Student Nonviolent Co-ordinating Committee, 195, 206
Suez Canal Crisis, 151–2
Sugar Act (1764), 10
Sumner, William Graham, 24
Supply Priorities and Allocations Board, 107
Supreme Court, 92, 95, 99, 102, 110, 171, 178, 194
Surplus Marketing Administration, 97
Symington, Stuart, 185–6
Syria, 153

Taft–Hartley Labor–Management Relations Act (1947), 164, 168–9, 179
Taft, Robert, 163, 165, 173
Taft, William Howard, 27, 30
Taiwan, *see* Formosa
Tammany Hall, 200
Tanglewood, Massachusetts, 217
Tarawa, 122
Tariffs, 28, 51, 74–6, 83, 88, 201
Taylor Grazing Act (1934), 96
Teapot Dome, 47–8
Tennessee Valley Authority, 99, 162, 169, 176
Thailand, 146
Thurmond, Strom, 167–8
Tibet, 147
tidelands oilfields, 177
Townsend, Francis E., 100–1
Trade Expansion Act (1962), 201
Trading with the Enemy Act (1917), 36
Tripartite Pact (1940), 119–20, 122
Truman, Harry S., 105; foreign policies, 129 ff., 145, 147; political background, 160; domestic policies, 160 ff.; re-election 1948, 167–8, 185–6, 192; and the Negro, 194, 209
Truman doctrine, 129
Truman Memorial Library, 209

Tucker, Josiah, 13
Tugwell, Rexford G., 91
Turkey, 150, 153

U2 flights, 157–8
Underwood Tariff (1913), 28
unemployment, after First World War, 41–2, 51–2; in depression, 86, 89, 90; in New Deal, 97–8, 103; in Second World War, 106; in post-war period, 162–3; in 1950s, 176; in 1960s, 197, 201
Union of Soviet Socialist Republics, 64, 116
United Arab Republic, 153
United Mine Workers, 95, 162
United Nations, 112, 125, 126–7, 135 ff., 152, 158, 198, 203
United States Steel, 201–2
Universal Negro Improvement Association, 193
Uruguay, 156

Venezuela, 156
Versailles, Treaty of, 39, 59 ff.
Veterans Bureau, 47
Vichy France, 119
Viet Cong, 213–14
Vietnam, 144–5, 213–14
Virginia Colony, 2–4
Voice of America, 110
Volstead Act (1919), *see* prohibition

Wagner Labor Relations Act (1935), 95, 164
Wagner, Robert F., 200
Wake Island, 137–8
Wallace, George, 205
Wallace, Henry A., 92, 96, 104–5, 107, 163, 166–8
Wallace, Henry C., 47
Walsh–Healey Act, (1936), 95
Walter, Bruno, 37
War Finance Corporation, 35
War Industries Board, 35
War Manpower Commission, 106
war of 1812, 18
War Production Board, 107
War Resources Board, 106
War Shipping Administration, 107
Warner, Lloyd, 181

Warren Commission, 207
Warren, Earl, 165, 178
Warren, Robert Penn, *All The King's Men*, 100
Washington, Booker, T., 194
Washington conference (1921–2), 65–8, 72
Washington, George, 12–13, 17, 31, 103
We Shall Overcome, 206
Weeks, Sinclair, 175
West German Federal Republic, 148–9
Western European Union, 149
Westover, Virginia, 4
Westwood movement, in colonial period, 5–11, in nineteenth century, 15–19, 20
Wharton, Edith, 25
White Citizens Councils, 195
White, William Allen, 48, 118
Whitman, Walt W., 183
Whyte, William, *The Organisation Man*, 181
Willkie, Wendell, 104, 114; *One World*, 117
Wilson, Charles E., 175
Wilson, Sloan, *The Man in the Gray Flannel Suit*, 181
Wilson, William, 44
Wilson, Woodrow, election of 1912, 27; domestic policies, 27–8, 34–6, 37; foreign policies of, 30–2; and the politics of the peace, 38–41, 46, 49, 59–61, 63, 68, 92, 101, 192
Wood, Leonard, 45
Works Progress Administration, 98, 103
World Economic conference (1933), 73–6, 94
Wouk, Herman, *Marjorie Morningstar*, 182
Writs of Assistance, 11

Yalta conference (1945), 125–6, 135, 141, 172
Yalu River, 137
Yorktown, 13
Young Plan (1929), 75
Yugoslavia, 149

Zen Buddhism, 182